SWINDON WORKS

WORKS

APPRENTICE IN STEAM

SWINDON WORKS

APPRENTICE IN STEAM

KEN GIBBS

AMBERLEY

To the memory of my father Sid Gibbs (L2 & BB Shop), and father-in-law George Kane (T Shop), and to all those whose roots are deep in the works at Swindon and the Great Western Railway.

First published in 1988
This edition published 2013

Amberley Publishing
The Hill, Stroud
Gloucestershire, GL5 4EP

www.amberley-books.com

British Library Cataloguing in Publication Data.
A catalogue record for this book is available from the British Library.

ISBN 978 1 4456 0451 0

Typeset in 10pt on 13pt Sabon.
Typesetting and Origination by Amberley Publishing.
Printed in the UK.

Contents

Outline of Contents and Chapters

This book is split roughly into two sections. The first section outlines a little family background, association with the Great Western Railway, and a period spent as an 'office boy' in the Timber Stores Office with an outline of sights, sounds, etc., of the Carriage & Wagon side of the works, covered by my office boy duties (1944–46).

The major portion, about 90 per cent, covers sights, sounds, jobs, etc., as seen and experienced by an apprentice to the trade of fitting, turning and locomotive erecting through the locomotive side of the works (1946–51) and includes a record of some of the procedures and processes of the time.

Acknowledgements

I think I must first acknowledge the Swindon Works itself and all the people who worked there during the period covered in this book. Without the influence of people and works, the combination forming a whole, the impressions gained and personalities remembered would not have been retained in the memory to be recalled forty years on. It is true that one's early years are the impressionable years, but on reflection, I would not change that early 'growing up' period where the lessons learned served me well throughout a working life and left many pleasant memories.

My thanks to a schoolfriend of long ago for preparing a Foreword for the book, to The Right Honourable the Lord Marsh, one-time Minister of Transport and later Chairman of the British Railways Board – jobs far removed from 'digging for Victory' together on the school allotment – during the war years in Swindon and in the shadow of the Railway Works.

I have attempted to name as many as possible of those shown in the photographs illustrating the book, and I must express my thanks to those who have greatly assisted me with this task, to cries of 'Good heavens! There's old so-and-so'. So my thanks to Ronnie Waldron, Frank Williams, Norm Cox, Stan Rouse, Tom Wheeler, Geoff Webber, Norman Davis, Bill Spackman, and to others who, if they could not help directly, have pointed me in the right direction to those who could. Thanks also to BR/OPC Railprint for supplying a number of the photographs, and to the Great Western Railway Museum at Swindon for allowing publication of photographs taken by myself among the excellent exhibits covering 150 years of the GWR.

Finally to Monica, my wife, who put up with (but continually complained about) papers spread over the dining table, and who assisted with the checking of my handwritten scrawl against the typed draft. But mainly to Monica for just being there.

Ken Gibbs, February 1986

Illustrations

Line Drawings and Documents

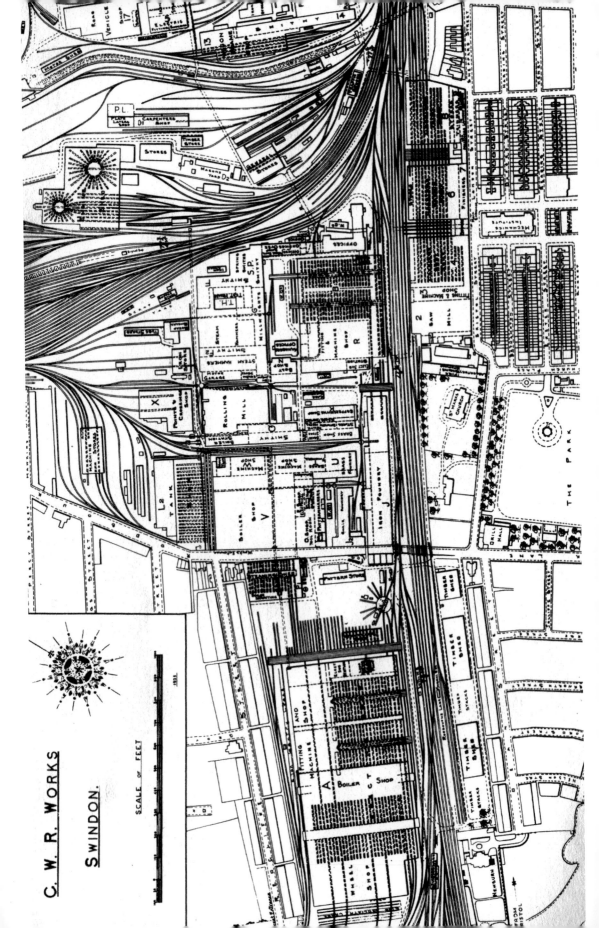

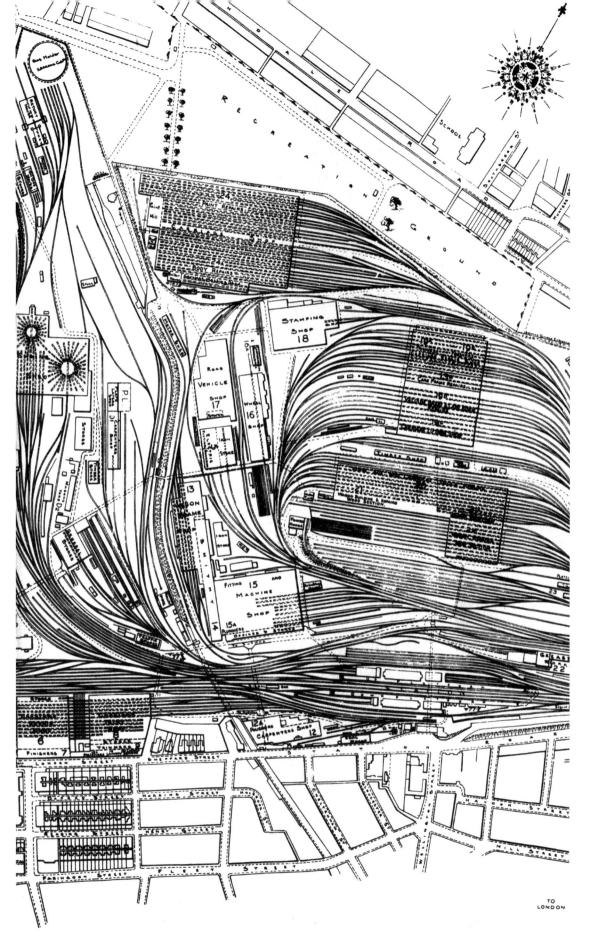

Foreword

When the Stockton & Darlington Railway was officially opened on 27 September 1825, none of those present could have realised they were watching the birth of an industry that would have a massive effect on the industrial, economic and social life of most of the civilised world.

The railway industry didn't develop; it exploded. While the railway mania was not confined to Britain, the British railway industry led the race. By 1849 Britain had three times as much railway as France, ten times as much as Belgium, and more than the rest of Europe put together.

Many of the early companies went under, but one of the greats which survived was the Great Western Railway, known generally as the GWR, or irreverently as 'God's Wonderful Railway'. Much of the success of the GWR can be traced back to its reputation from the very beginning as a centre of engineering excellence. Men like Isambard Brunel, Daniel Gooch and G. J. Churchward, were great railway engineers, famous throughout the railways of the world.

When the Great Western Railway decided to build a massive railway workshop on the edge of a Wiltshire market town called Swindon, they created a new community and a special way of life for several generations to come.

When Ken Gibbs very kindly invited me to write a foreword to this book, it brought back a host of memories. Like him, I was born in the paternalistic shadow of the Great Western Railway's Swindon factory. My father worked 'inside', as had my grandfather, and as did my uncles and virtually all the neighbours. To describe the Swindon of the early thirties as simply another company town would be to grossly underestimate the now incredible extent to which the railway, and in particular 'the works', dominated the lives of most of the population.

It was, as I have said, a paternalistic regime, providing a surprising level of what would now be called social welfare.

We lived in houses owned by the GWR, were looked after by the GWR doctors at the GWR health centre, or in the GWR hospital, and it is interesting to note that the first GWR hospital was built as far back as 1852. During 'trip week' when the works closed for the annual holiday, Swindon was like a ghost town. Unlike most industrial workers at that time, employees and the families of the Great Western Railway could afford to take their families to the seaside because rail travel, like housing, coal and medical care, was either heavily subsidised or free.

For the author and myself, as with most of our contemporaries, the future was secure and clear. We received no advice on possible career opportunities because we were well aware that there were only two. If you left school at fourteen years of age you would serve your time as an apprentice on the shop floor, and if you left at sixteen you would obtain an office job with no limit to your ultimate rank in the company.

In fact, although it would have seemed unthinkable at the time, the great days of the railway were already on the wane by the time we both left school in 1944.

The days when Britain was the richest and most powerful nation in the world were over. There was no longer an almost limitless pool of cheap labour and raw materials. The famous locomotives of the pre-war years regularly achieved speeds of well over 100 miles per hour, but at a massive cost in labour intensive track maintenance.

In the 1950s, steam was giving way to lighter, cheaper and more efficient diesel engines. By the 1960s, the growth of private car ownership and ever increasing labour and energy costs began to raise questions about the ability of the nation to finance British Rail's ever increasing demand for public money. In 1970, as chairman, I instituted a major two-year study of British Rail finances.

Yards and yards of computer print-out told the same story; the existing infrastructure designed in and for the conditions of the 1850s was not only inefficient and out of date, but a financial threat to the whole railway system.

By the mid-seventies, I had no doubt that the closure of the Swindon works, with all that would mean to the community was no longer a question of 'if', but of 'when'. Both political parties tried to delay the decision for as long as possible, in the hope that alternative industry could be attracted to the town, but the end was inevitable.

Few people who were not involved will understand the nostalgia and affection for an enormous sprawling, dirty and noisy factory. The fact is that it wasn't just a factory. It was a centre of excellence staffed by men who had a justifiable pride in their skills.

This book will bring back memories for many a grey-haired Swindonian but hopefully it will also give some of the young Swindonians an idea of what once made their town known to railway engineers throughout the world.

The Rt Hon. The Lord Marsh of Mannington, KT

Preface

This book is an attempt to recall a period of about seven years in the long history of the Swindon Workshops, a period of change from the Great Western Railway Company, through nationalisation to become British Rail (Western Region), as seen through the young eyes of an office boy and then apprentice. It records with nostalgia and affection some of the impressions gained: the sights, sounds, smells, characters and jobs of a period which, with hindsight, was the beginning of the end of steam as a motive force, although heralded at the time as the start of a new era!

The period covered is that from Easter 1944 until the beginning of 1951, terminating with departure for National Service and thus covering the end of Second World War, the end of the Great Western Railway Company and the last of the line of construction of the GWR passenger-type locomotives. A period as 'office boy' in the Stores and Carriage & Wagon departments, followed by apprenticeship in the Locomotive Works as a fitter, turner and locomotive erector, gave an impression of the complete works when everything seemed to be moving into a limitless future, the workforce at this time numbering about 14,500, and shops full of locomotives, carriages, wagons, people; in fact, possibly a works in its heyday. Lessons learned moulded the careers of thousands who passed through the shops. People, locations, products, as the period itself, has gone forever.

It is not the intention to criticise, find fault with, or poke fun at anyone or anything, but to recall a time and place, peopled by characters never to be forgotten by those who passed through one of the great, to many including myself, the greatest, of the railway workshops during the long period when steam was king.

The apprenticeship covered five years, from the age of sixteen to twenty-one, when National Service claimed us all! The sections of the apprenticeship, fitting, turning and locomotive erecting, took the form of a structured flow of lads through many of the shops on the locomotive side, and work for two or three months in those shops, which had any connection with the specific trade function, often changing 'gangs' within a shop to do a different job. Similar conditions existed with other apprenticeships such as boilermaking, blacksmithing, etc., the latter also appearing on the Carriage & Wagon side of the works, but, as with several trades, both locomotive and Carriage & Wagon, limited to one shop connected with the trade concerned. The thriving Carriage & Wagon side of the works had a similar structured pattern for apprentices, the trade usually specific to one particular shop where the function of that trade was carried out. These included such trades as coach finishing, road wagon building, etc., a number of my school friends going through the Carriage & Wagon side, were always, for some reason, being rather looked down on by those of the locomotive faction! A specialised wood trade practised in the locomotive works was that of pattern making, the pattern shop being an isolated woodworking entity among all the metal handling shops, and producing the patterns from which steam locomotive components were cast in ferrous and non-ferrous metals.

In all of this, it is essential for the reader to bear in mind that the works was not a training establishment as such. There were no craftsmen paid as 'teachers' in that sense of the word. The apprentice was, then, thrust into a manufacturing environment where, for example, he wouldn't spend the first three months making say a scribing block in a small instructional workshop, but went straight on to the shop floor to actually be involved in the process of making and repairing locomotives! The craftsmen were also, of necessity, 'slowed down' by having to teach – I almost said put up with – an attached apprentice, who, as an individual, could be quick or slow to learn, thus having a direct effect on the output of the craftsman.

There were chargehands and craftsmen who, to the apprentice, were 'good' or 'bad'. I think the latter were very few, but they were there and mostly 'bad' in the sense they may have appeared as intolerant or quick-tempered. Obviously a great deal depended on the apprentice! A learner who does not understand is vastly different from one who won't listen, and in this way the 'good' or 'bad' legends were born. Strictness, knowledge and understanding were respected, and some of the old chargehands were stinkers, but looking back they were mostly great characters and, above all, they were usually right!

Because of the nature of the training and the requirement to produce items for actual use, some of the production methods employed in the turning side of the apprenticeship were, if viewed purely from a production point of view, particularly uneconomic in present-day terms, but the use of apprentices made sense of the whole thing. If reviewed in modern terms the bleat of 'exploitation' would be heard from certain quarters in terms of pay levels, but an apprentice was receiving training, and for a period was, in practical terms, useless until he had actually learned something, and no firm can take on and train more apprentices than it actually requires to enable it to function and indeed continue, without some form of return. In the case in question, the 'return' was assistance with actual production, but the practical knowledge gained by the apprentice in an actual working environment was invaluable.

Some would make better craftsmen than others, but the experience of actually going through the Great Western Railway Works at Swindon as an 'Apprentice in Steam' will never be forgotten.

Ken Gibbs

Introduction

A RAILWAY FAMILY – 'FOUR GENERATIONS ON THE GWR'

It is a strange fact, but our lives appear to be controlled by the receipt of long buff envelopes – some sealed and some unsealed. We first become aware of this phenomenon in early life, when the sound of the postman and click of the letterbox affected, or seemed to affect, the temper of father, depending on what was contained in such envelopes, such as the size of a bill or letters from relatives, etc. We become personally involved during school days, when term end brought the long buff envelope, sealed, with our school report, a missive that again affected father's temper! Usually phrases like 'could do better if he tried harder', were not the sort of comments that brought a pat on the head in commendation!

However, the time arrived when the final report had to be collected, and the last day at school was almost over. There was a handshake from 'Pop' Phillips, the teacher, and an appointment with Mr Smith, the headmaster, this time being addressed as 'Ken' and not being in receipt of a 'rocket' for some misdemeanour. Then another handshake and wishes for all the best in the future, the handing over of a long buff envelope, unsealed this time, with my final appraisal contained therein. This small piece of paper stated that I was punctual, willing and trustworthy, and that was that! Not really much to go on!

Easter 1944, fourteen years old and school finished. Murmured thanks to the headmaster, out of the office door, down the stone stairs, down three more steps and across the playground, out of the gate, turn right, then right again, and I was in my home street, on the doorstep of the school, and starting work after the Easter holidays. Everything seemed very straightforward in those days!

We were really a railway family, in a railway street, in a railway area, an area which you couldn't leave without going under, or, with care, over a railway line, and where just about every family had at least one member who worked 'inside'.

Residents' lives had been conditioned almost from birth to recognise and be controlled by the time-honoured blasts on the factory hooter at the beginning and end of the shift periods. The blasts had been quietened during the war, which was still in progress, by being restricted to warnings of approaching enemy aircraft, but the hooter still had a controlling influence.

Looking back to the thinking of the time, I was destined to follow my father, grandfather and great-grandfather into the service of the Great Western Railway at Swindon, without any thought that there could possibly be any other acceptable form of employment. In my case this was automatically accepted, as with many other families in the Swindon of the period, as soon as I saw the light of day, or possibly the steam and smoke rising over the works. There was never a question of what did I want to do! I was destined to be a fitter, turner and locomotive erector like my grandfather.

Due to the 'rules' applying at the turn of the century with regard to the requirements for acceptance for apprenticeship in the works (or 'inside' as it was known to every Swindonian), there were various categories of trades. Fitting, on the locomotive side, was considered a premium or 'top' trade, and my grandfather, being a fitter, was allowed under the rules, to apprentice, I believe, three sons to a similar occupation. My father's three elder brothers, Ernest, Walter and Ted were therefore duly apprenticed, but when it came to father's turn, he was given the choice of blacksmithing, boilermaking or locomotive painting. By a continuation of the same rules, apparently unless one was a chargehand or foreman in these trades, a son was only entitled to the same choice of trade (free) as that given to the father, and could not be accepted for a free apprenticeship as a fitter. If a vacancy existed, payment of a premium of £100 could be made to 'purchase' such a trade apprenticeship. Father was made chargehand in 1934, so the precedent was established. Although nominally a boilermaker, all his time had been spent in the L2 Tank and Structural Steel Workshop.

All railway families have a family legend, and the story of how my grandfather became a fitter is one such legend, which I have always promised myself to research, but as with many good intentions, not yet fulfilled.

My great-great-grandfather and his immediate forebears were connected with the canals and canal traffic in the Oxford area, but his son started with the Great Western Railway as a lad on land drainage, hedging and ditching work. Many years later, the GWR Company was apparently involved in a title dispute concerning some land at Didcot – land which involved the area of the Provender Stores and the large water area or lake which stood behind it. The Provender Stores, incidentally, was a very large, brick building on the left of the line at Didcot, going towards London, which dealt with the handling and make up of all of the feed for the horses throughout the railway system of the Great Western. However, legal proceedings dragged on and enquiries were passed on down through the hierarchy searching for witnesses, proof, etc., of certain claims made by the railway company. A final measure of proof was thought to be the building, many years before, of a brick culvert or drainage shaft, leading into and now covered by the water of the lake. With special transport laid on, the court officials were transported to Didcot, where my great-grandfather had stated that, as a lad, he had helped construct such a culvert. A boat was produced and with various dignatories in attendance, the murky water was 'plumbed' by great-grandfather, and the culvert finally located, traced and measured.

The finding of the brickwork apparently proved the case for the railway company beyond doubt regarding the land title claim and, as a 'reward' for his invaluable assistance, great-grandfather was allowed to apprentice his son to the 'premium' trade of the Great Western Railway Works at Swindon, my grandfather thus becoming a fitter.

Most Swindon families of the period had some connection with the GWR. My mother's father had been a riveter/plater, her elder brother a signalman, and his son started in the C&W Stamping Shop. A younger brother had actually started in the N Bolt Shop and was later employed in the Stamping Shop. Our immediate neighbours also worked 'inside' and a listing reads as follows for the seven houses in the block: Smith's Shop labourer A Shop – boilermaker chargehand (father) and myself, apprentice – millwright chargehand G shop and son, fitter, A Shop – fitter A Shop – labourer A Shop and son, fitter's mate, A Shop – boilermaker. Ten from seven houses! The pattern repeated all along the street. The works was Swindon and Swindon was the Railway Works!

A buff envelope arrived with instructions for me to report to Park House, the centre for the works doctor, for the obligatory medical examination.

Park House, the tall building on the corner of the Railway Estate, constructed in open land in the mid-nineteenth century, but now in the town centre, was a rather gaunt place, but it faced The Park, itself once the property of the railway company. I recall a rather starkly furnished building, the doctor handing me a series of coloured patterns to check for colour blindness, then a look through each eye separately at a typical eye chart, followed by questions about diseases, most of which I had never heard of, let alone known if anyone in the family had ever suffered from! I coughed at the appropriate time and that was the end of the 'medical'. I now had to go home and wait.

1
Office Boy in the Timber Stores

The waiting seemed to be neverending, although it could only have been a few days, to include those 'sitting around in the garden days' of the Easter holiday. Something was brewing regarding the continuing war! Father mentioned the urgent armour plating of jeeps in the L2 Shop, and the rumble of heavy freight trains continued day and night, as did the rhythmic thump of the big drop hammer in the Loco Stamping Shop, clearly heard throughout the nights, marking for me, the passing time.

Following instructions received by yet another buff envelope, I duly reported to the Tunnel Entrance after the Easter holiday, the entrance being the unimposing main way into the works. Rather off-putting to the visitor, as its double doors with the single pedestrian door at the side, opened into a long, low tunnel with gas lamps at intervals along its wet girder and concrete roof, virtually unchanged since construction in 1870. We assembled at the watchman's office adjacent to the pedestrian door; quite a little crowd of youngsters all destined for somewhere in the 310 acres of the works. We were collected by an office boy, and all walked as a group along the tunnel, which smelled strongly of disinfectant, up the slope to the left, turned right and under a mass of wires (what I subsequently found out was the telephone exchange), then first left into the office block, the manager's office, and across a yard full of trucks and mounds of what appeared to be rusting scrap! We waited in a small room and our names were called, the named ones disappearing in the company of another youngster, those with a rolled-up pair of overalls departing for work in the shops. My turn came to be collected and we walked back across the yard and into an office block entered by steps from a slope, which appeared to lead back down to the tunnel from which we had recently emerged. Just inside the door was a small waiting room from which a little tubby man in a blue uniform and peaked cap peered at us as we walked past (this, I later learned, was Fred, the messenger). We turned immediately left into a small office tucked back under the large staircase which wound up to the floors above. This was the abode of Mr Lane, a thin, rather gaunt-faced man, and Mr Parkes (who in modern-day terms resembled Henry Kissinger!), and was the store's staff office, in which I was placed in a chair and given a form to fill in, with my age, birthday, parents' names, etc. Having completed the form, Mr Lane looked it over and then picked up the telephone, a tall one with the fork arm on the side for the earpiece, connected by a long, curly wire. He flicked the fork up and down a couple of times, asked for a number, had a few words, and then said I was to wait a few minutes for someone to collect me.

I was destined for the Timber Stores Office, and was to spend several weeks with the office boy, who was due to depart into the shops to start his apprenticeship at sixteen years of age. I now had almost two years to wait before my own apprenticeship would

Where the tale starts: The Timber Stores Office tucked away in a corner of No. 4 (Body) Shop.

commence. Ivor Huddy came in, a tallish lad, fair-haired and pale-faced, and off we went to my new job, through the panelled corridor of the office block, flanked by storage or filing cabinets, out of the end door by the West Time office, back down the slope into the tunnel and along towards the main entrance again. About halfway along, we turned into what I thought was a large alcove, but which had a flight of stone steps leading up from the end to the expanse of a traversing table road above, and just inside the workshop at the top of the steps (which was No. 4 Shop, Coach Body Building), was the office, approached by a couple of steps and a double door, rather narrow, marked 'Timber Stores' – one name on each door. I passed through a very small porch with doors to right and left and through the left-hand door, and there was an awareness of half a dozen faces and tall desks, one set apart in the corner, to which I was now taken and met Mr E. Day, the head clerk, a man with a pale, wrinkled face. The meeting was followed by an introduction to the other members of the office, Wilf Lambdon, Wally Bowden, Phil Brown (who, it subsequently transpired, was in my father's class at school), Stan Drewitt and Miss Nora Davis. The office was quite light and airy, rather high-ceilinged and with two long, polished sets of back-to-back three-hole desks, with a long single filing shelf along the rear of each desk. The wall at the back of the office had one large expanse of cupboard. Two very large windows on the outside wall, facing the main line, were separated by a large fireplace. By the chief's desk was a small, curtained-off tea-brewing alcove, and immediately next to the opening, a green baize-covered door leading, via a short corridor, to the office of the timber storekeeper, Mr Beasant, in overall charge of the Timber Stores organisation. I was taken in to meet Mr Beasant, seemingly a pleasant sort of chap, but in all the time I was office boy, I very rarely saw him again, and I cannot remember him ever coming out into the clerks' office.

Mr Beasant's office was rather large and wood-pannelled, with a large desk and an open fireplace with high mantle shelf, polished black. On the wall was a rather fascinating board with pockets, which contained a sample slice of all the woods available for Works' use, each with a little name tag on its polished surface. A bell-push on his desk signalled, by means of a code, each member of the clerical staff, mine being a single ring. I had the end desk backing on to the entrance door and I settled down with Ivor, who would be showing me the ropes in the few weeks before he left for the shops. I made a list of the routine jobs which had to be done, the first one every morning being to disinfect telephones. The three telephones in the office and the one in Mr Beasant's office had to be wiped over with a carbolic liquid contained in a hexagonal blue bottle, the 'phone mouthpiece being given particular attention.

An important feature stressed by Mr Day, and almost akin to signing the Official Secrets Act, was that under no circumstances was I to discuss with anyone, anything seen or overheard in the office. I took this quite literally and it was a long time before I would even tell my parents at home what I was actually doing as an office boy!

There was a little test or two for honesty when I first started. I had to regularly go into Mr Beasant's office to pull the blackout blinds and, when his fire was alight, to make sure it was well stoked. On the occasions of the blackout blinds, he was very rarely in the office, and on one occasion when I went in alone, I noticed a penknife on the windowsill; a knife I recognised as Mr Day's! I mentioned the knife to Mr Day when I came back into the other office and he feigned surprise at having 'mislaid' it, returning with me to collect it when I had pointed out its resting place. The same thing happened later with a shilling, placed on the corner of Mr Beasant's desk, but having been once accepted, the 'test' was not repeated.

A further, most important feature was the making of the tea, where I would think hundreds of youngsters start their careers! Tea was always early in the afternoon, about 2 p.m., and one strange ritual which continued throughout my office boy period was that of contacting one of the bodymakers in the shop, Wally Hext, to come and collect the cup of tea always left in the entrance porch of the office! It had the mystique of leaving an oatcake for a leprechaun before retiring to bed, and I never was able to solve the puzzle of why! With Ivor, we used to wander into the shop to the area where he worked, but later, on the departure of Ivor for the shops, I used to signal with a very piercing two-finger whistle from the office door, being usually greeted with 'Quiet, you noisy young b****r!' from the bodymakers working just outside the office. Miss Davis did the washing up, so I was spared that chore.

The coaches of that period were of the wooden frame design, with steel sheets screwed on, even the doors were wood-faced with pressed sections of soft steel plate. A coach must have contained thousands and thousands of wood screws, the large panels often having a double row of screws about two inches apart, and the thought of continually removing and replacing screws must have taken some of the gilt off the job. There was something I noticed about the body shop from that first morning. Above the shop smell of wood and iron plates was an unpleasant (to me anyway), penetrating smell which I eventually tracked down to being the smell of tallow. On every bench was a pot or tin which contained the most evil-smelling yellowish grease, like rancid cooking fat, and into which every screw was dipped before being replaced and screwed home. The grease got everywhere! On all tools, benches, overalls, aprons, and particularly the persons of the bodymakers. I used to chat to many of the men working along the main side gangway when on my way through the shop with the post for the Timber Stores Office above the Rodbourne Lane/Park Lane bridges. In particular I chatted with Roy, a little man with several teeth missing who always wore a cap with a pencil stuck under the edge, and who often let me screw in a couple of screws, but whose 'belly brace' left that foul greasy smell on my hands.

There was woodwork too, of course, in addition to the steel plate screwing, and often quite large pieces of wood were being let into the frame, a rotten area having been 'chopped out', the wood glued and screwed and then shaped to the profile of the coach frame by planing. Several craftsmen used the old wooden planes, and the procedure for removing the cutter; the blow on the button set in the front of the wooden plane, the sharpening of the cutting iron and the replacement, tried with a fine shaving being removed evenly over the width of the blade, was quite fascinating for a fourteen-year-old. For the lower frame members, some of the larger pieces of wood used were I believe of a wood called 'Gurjon', a rather oily hard redwood, which was difficult to plane to a very smooth surface and which, if you were not careful, left splinters in the hands which festered very rapidly, if not swiftly removed.

Embraced by No. 4 Shop and No. 2 Shop, the Sawmill, was a small area – No. 3 Shop a fitting section under Carriage & Wagon side control, maintaining machines and operating machines for pressing coach components and shearing plates. The pathway through the shop led past the end of No. 3 Shop and on into the Sawmill, and one of the first items to catch attention was a machine that made rail keys, those pieces of shaped wood which were then commonly used, literally in the millions, to hold the rail into its cast-iron 'chair' retaining the railway lines of the complete Great Western system, and indeed of the rest of the country. A length of rectangular, rough-sawn oak was fed into the machine and processed until it emerged as a finished key; the completed keys leaving the machine were pushed by those following onto a wooden chute or trough, which led up across the gangway to the top of an open wagon, into which fell the finished keys in a seemingly endless stream.

There were several ways out of the Sawmill. One was straight past the chair key machine along the side of the rail line and out through the big doors, passing various circular saws en route. Another way was through the mill, passing between the circular saws and band saws, and through the opening in the centre of the far stone wall into the steaming room. The coach of the period, as stated previously being of wood construction, also had wooden beams in the roof, again covered by the multi-screwed steel plates of curved form. In the corner of the steaming room stood a long steel cylinder, closed by a hinged door, and I often stopped in the room sometimes longer than I should have done, just to watch the process. A little rush of steam followed the opening of the cylinder door, and the operator, with leather apron and gloves, reached in and pulled out, say, a 5-inch by 4-inch by 10-foot length of hardwood, which had been soaking in the steam for some hours. The length of steaming wood was carried across to a machine that had a long bed or table, which hinged in the middle and on which was placed a flat steel flexible strip about 10 inches wide, the wood being placed on the metal strip. The machine was then operated to clamp the wood down in the middle while the two halves of the table lifted at each end, forcing the wood to bend around the arc of the former, attached to the centre clamp. The slowly moving table seemed to roll in a very positive way to force the wood to bend, which, because of the steaming period, 99 per cent of the pieces did without splitting. When fully bent around the roof-shaped former, a bar with a centre adjusting screw was attached to each end of the metal strip, and the screw adjusted to hold the wood very tightly into its new shape. Put aside to cool and set, when the strip was eventually removed, a perfectly shaped roof beam resulted, the grain of the wood running naturally through the complete length thus avoiding the waste and the easily split 'short grain' problem if the shape had been cut from one or more pieces, joined together to obtain the smooth curved shape.

The saws which I always felt rather squeamish about were the big band saws, the rapidly travelling blade so near to the fingers of the operators, although in fascination I often stopped to watch them in use. In a little room near the steam cylinder and wood-bending machines worked the 'saw doctors', who probably worked on more teeth in a lifetime than most dentists! In this room all sharpening and refurbishing of saw blades was undertaken, from the massive 3-foot-diameter rip saw to the narrow blades of the band saws. The use of files and setting tools ensured the edge and set of the saw blade teeth, every other tooth angled and set in the opposite direction to that of its predecessor. An interesting machine was used for the band saw blades, entailing a degree of automation. The blade was mounted on its back, teeth uppermost, around two wheels which kept it taut, and a little slide, which held a triangular or three-square file as it is known, moved back and forth at the correct angle across each alternate tooth as the blade slowly indexed its way past the moving slide, one file pass per tooth. There were also several wood turning lathes out in the mill proper, positioned against the wall in the other corner of the mill, adjacent to the entry door to the steaming room.

One of these was a semi-automatic lathe, and in a rack nearby stood a very large pile of old shunters' poles! These were of various lengths with bits broken or split, and were without the steel hook that was used to deftly remove or replace the coupling chains over the wagon or carriage drawgear hooks. These old poles must have been returned from stores all over the system, and of course showed the dirt and damage of constant use. I believe they were ideally of hickory, a very tough, resilient wood, and their usefulness was far from over! Cut to required lengths, the damaged parts discarded, the pieces were assembled in batches depending on salvageable lengths, and one by one put into the lathe. The high speed of wood turning and a shower of shavings from the rapidly moving cutter against the equally rapidly revolving wood resulted in a perfectly turned and polished hammer shaft, to go back into stores for restocking the many forms of hammer, exchanged because of a loose head or broken shaft. Nothing was wasted!

It was one of those things noticed by a fourteen-year-old, that as I chatted with various users of the machines in the mill, how many of them had a finger or part of a finger missing! You could not afford to make a mistake or let your concentration wander when using one of those frighteningly revolving big saws. One use of a circular saw (which I believe is now illegal but I'm not too sure on that point), was to cut grooves by using what were known as 'wobble washers', thus making what was also known as a 'drunken saw'.

With the washers in place, the saw, when running, wobbled from side to side, the offset of the washers determining the amount of wobble. This in its turn determined the width of the path prescribed by the periphery of the saw teeth, which could then be used to cut a simple groove in the wood at one pass through the saw, the groove being a lot wider, in a controlled way, than the actual thickness of the saw blade. On the way through the shop I often stopped to watch the operator of the 'drunken saw' cutting grooves in long lengths of wood about 5 inches by 3 inches in section, although I'm not sure what they were for. On one occasion, and it was in the first weeks of starting as an office boy, I was watching him push a piece of wood over the saw, when there was a sudden jolt in the steady movement of the wood over the blade, and he swung round shaking his hand. The blade of the saw had 'picked up' in the grain of the wood, and had thrown off an 18-inch spear of wood which had split out from the run of the grain, and had literally gone right through his hand. As he gave the first shake, the spear had broken off, leaving a 6-inch point of wood that projected through the palm and out the back of the hand! He ran to the man on the next saw, quite quietly and without fuss, and asked him to pull it out. Several other operators had now grouped round and, the request being refused, a couple helped him, or walked with him, over to the 'Red Box', the first-aid man also being called. The wood was removed at the GWR Hospital and the victim was out for a few days, returning to the same job with a bandaged hand that was now 'OK, but a bit sore', when next I stopped to watch him.

The two foremen of the Sawmill were Ben Waterhouse, a big, bluff, chatty character, and Mr Day, a small, slightly built man, brother of my own boss in the Timber Stores Office, and I often passed the time of day with them when going through the shop on my rounds. One of my regular journeys was through the Sawmill, on through the steaming room and down a flight of broad wooden steps into a lower level Timber Store Room, en route to the 'Wood Wharf', where sales of scrap wood were collected by a waiting queue of old gentlemen with trolleys. Why it was always referred to as the Wood Wharf I don't know, but it was just a name that you didn't really think about at the time. This was approached through the fire station yard, literally under the classic cast-iron water tank, the works at this time having a fully staffed, regular fire brigade solely for the works area. At the gate was a small sentry box occupied by a watchman and, previously, Ivor had taken me down there for an introduction so that I should be recognised on my way through, as I had to walk about 50 yards along the path outside the works to get into the Wood Wharf, the internal access door in the works always being kept locked. At the Wharf itself, there was a small office wherein sat Mr Woodman, the foreman, a most appropriately named man, and along the comparatively narrow entrance path, on the right were a large scales and a wooden chute and small area for the wood offcuts coming from the Sawmill above. On the left, a small cabin-like room for the two very elderly men who, in leather gloves and canvas aprons, sorted and weighed the wood into loads of 1 cwt, one for each of those who had been patiently queueing. This purchase of wood scraps by those employed by the works had, up until about this time, been the preserve of a number of retired men, who subsidised their pensions by the small sum paid for the collection of scrap wood for those neighbours and others in the area where they lived; but for a year or two a little animosity had crept into the proceedings as schoolboys had discovered a way of obtaining pocket money, so these had now poached on the considered preserves of those retired and those unemployable! I got on very well with the people at the Wharf, the two old issuers particularly, and I remember that when I mentioned I collected old and foreign coins, one of them gave me a matchbox full, including a Roman coin, still treasured to this day.

It was on a return into the works that I nearly had my career abruptly ended! I usually came through the mill to the Wood Wharf en route to the Timber Office, located by the timber storage sheds just above the Rodbourne Road bridges, and from the Wood Wharf back through the fire station yard and up a narrow slope adjacent to the mill wall, up to the top level once again. In the building to the right of the slope, on the way up, was a large incinerator/boiler for disposing of sawdust and waste from the mill. On the left of the slope stood a stationary boiler, and just by the side of the boiler was a tall, cylindrical and conical 'cyclone' plant, which sucked up and stored wood chippings and shavings that arrived from other mills, contained in sealed wagons, the contents also destined for the boiler. The wagons were on a line very close to the wall at the top of the slope, the pathway proper being on the other side of the rail line. There was always a gap left between two of the wagons in the line to allow access to the slope and, on one occasion, I ran as usual up the slope and through the gap in the wagons. I was still going forward, with my satchel of 'post' slung from my shoulder and held tight to the rear to stop it swinging as I ran, and I still had my rear foot over the second rail as I ran through, when there was an almighty bang and the wagons crashed together in a very hard shunt, trapping my satchel between the buffers! Just at the point where I had run through. Mr Day saw it all and although I wasn't touched in any way, I have never seen a man go so grey in the face. There had been no flags or any other warning that shunting was in progress, but from that time there were wooden barriers and red flags all over the place when movement of wagons was underway. He didn't say very much on that occasion but he had been very shaken.

On a more humorous note, Mr Day wore grey flannels and so did I. I found that, on occasions on my way through the mill, and down the wooden steps into the timber-storing room, I often disturbed a skiving group of timber porters, led by a tall, curly-haired man named Charlie, the group scattering in all directions. I later found I could copy Mr Day's 'walk' and that, on coming down the steps in my grey flannels, had them really worried, often being threatened by Charlie with a thick ear, but it was never administered, as the group re-appeared from hiding or from 'stacking' timber that had already been stacked, appearing to be busy and completely occupied!

The walk to the Rodbourne bridge office took me alongside the main line to Bristol on my right, and St Mark's church on my left, and against the fence which screened off the churchyard from the railway were stacked boxes and boxes of straw-packed wash basins and toilet pans for carriages, stretching virtually the whole length of the fence. I had to wait at the Rodbourne office very often for the post to arrive from the bottom Timber Stores Office by the West Sawmill, adjacent to the 'Concentration Yard'. The office boy from the mill itself passed the Timber Stores on the way up, and we very often met at Rodbourne, Peter and I walking back together as he went on to the main Carriage & Wagon office block near Swindon station, at the other end of the works. The post that I had to collect was brought by a young timber porter, who seemed to resent the whole job anyway, and there appeared to me to be some sort of feud or vendetta between the two Timber Stores Offices, but I may be wrong. There seemed an awkward atmosphere on the rare occasions that I went to that office. The office at Rodbourne was staffed by Ernie Hicks, Bob Parsons and another man, Bob Parsons being a very blunt character and a veteran of the Boer War, actually retiring at sixty-five years of age while I was still office boy. He used to delight in telling the tale when he came to the Timber Stores Office of how when he was out on

GREAT WESTERN RAILWAY - LOCOMOTIVE DEPARTMENT.

Memorandum from Manager to Mr. *J. R. Gibbs.*   *L. 2. Shop*

_____ 18 DEC 1944   194 __

                                        ~~employment~~
With reference to your application for the ~~training~~
                                        apprenticeship

of your son to *Fitting Turning & Erecting* please note that

                                        ~~employment~~
(a), his name has been registered as an applicant for this trade.

~~and you will be notified in due course when he will be~~

~~required to report for medical examination.~~
                                        apprenticeship
~~(b), there are no vacancies for this trade~~   ~~but we are~~
~~prepared to offer him employment only~~   ~~to~~
                                a training
                                ~~an apprenticeship~~

~~Please let me know if you will accept this offer.~~

~~(c), we are unable to grant your application for the~~

~~following reason :-~~

                        For K. J. Cook.

The standard application form used when the son of an employee hoped to be offered the chance of a 'trade' apprenticeship. The whole procedure depended on the employment and trade status of the father.

The Veldt, he had to bury a dead horse. He said it was very hot and dusty work and when he had finished digging, the horse didn't fit the hole so he chopped it to fit by using the spade! As soon as the story started, Nora Davis used to leave the office on some pretext or other!

Applications for apprenticeship had to be forwarded some time in advance of the birthday when such applicants could start and, unknown to me at the time, father had already started the process in motion. Receipt of the official pro-forma indicated that the application had been registered for the trade of fitting, turning and erecting. Everything was now ticking along toward apprenticeship.

About this time, a little episode took its place in the office boy legends, with stories passed on from one to the other. Apparently, two of the office boys connected with the Loco Manager's Office and known to me only by the names 'Beefy' and 'Tuck', had, rightly or wrongly, been accused of putting indelible ink in the tea urn for the office. They had then been summarily consigned to the notorious N or Bolt Shop, the works equivalent of Alcatraz or Devil's Island in the punishment stakes, and a most unpleasant place to work. I only saw the two of them very rarely anyway so didn't miss them, although the story possibly has a large measure of truth in it.

2
Timber Stores Office Boy

On some occasions if I had to go to the bottom Timber Stores Office, I wandered down on the opposite side of the line instead of going through the Sawmill. Under the tunnel and down past the B Shed, R Shop, past the long wall of the Iron Foundry to look at the steam locomotives on the table roads near the turntable opposite the Rodbourne office, then on past the 'Ash Plant' on the left and A Shop on the right, down to the weighbridge. From the Timber Stores office, I would go under the line by the tunnel at the weighbridge, and back to the Rodbourne office along the back of the timber sheds, a route always interesting and full of moving steam locomotives along the outside.

While waiting at Rodbourne, chatting to Peter, various shunting operations were under way, and on one occasion a train load of timber was being sorted and shunted to be adjacent to the correct storage sheds and yard areas of stacked timber. Several 'bogie bolster' wagons were included in the shunt, which was being done wagon by wagon 'on the fly', a method whereby the engine pushes an uncoupled wagon and then stops, the wagon travelling along by itself to be 'braked' by the shunter trotting alongside. Just outside the office were several manually operated ground point switches, which were worked by the shunters to direct the wagon down its correct rail track, and the switches were getting well used. Several small wagons were sent on their way, followed by a 'bogie bolster' which bump-bumped its first 'bogie' over the points, which then changed by themselves so that the next bogie went down a different rail track! It was quite a sight to see a large load of timber 'crabbing' along sideways on two sets of railway lines, but after about 80 yards, the whole lot derailed and tipped over. This was then a job for a large gang of men with levers, liftingjacks and a crane before the track could be used again.

At this time the war was still running its course, with D-Day memorable as being a sky full of aircraft towing gliders, all heading in one direction. We had heard the news in the office via Ernie Day, who received a 'phone call from someone to that effect, the conflict being at its possible height.

Assisting with various duties within the works were groups of Italian prisoners of war, doing all sorts of cleaning up and tidying in the yards and shops. There were two categories of prisoner, those who collaborated and those who wouldn't, and the two groups were usually kept well apart in their working areas, the former seeming to work by themselves after being given instructions, and the latter accompanied by an armed guard, a soldier who must have found the job very boring because they couldn't really go anywhere, even if they escaped. All seemed to be rather little men who waved their arms about and chattered a lot. In fact, there seemed to be more chat than work, and they all seemed to be a bit lost. Usually it was a collaborators group, which worked in the vicinity of the Rodbourne office, and I often chatted to the interpreter, one of their number nominally in charge of them and able to speak English, which he did quite well, having learned it entirely while a prisoner. They all had one wish, and that was to go home. While the collaborators wore generally a mix of khaki uniform, the other group was distinctive, with multicoloured, bright camouflage colour patches sewn on to their clothing, and they usually kept themselves to themselves.

I remember on one occasion on one of my rare visits to the other Timber Stores Office, coming back out of the subway (which ran from one side of the main line to the other in the vicinity of the locomotive weighbridge), and walking along the roadway behind the timber storage sheds, backing on to Dean Street, there was, seated very comfortably, leaning back against the timber shed wall, one of the Italian collaborator prisoners all alone and deeply absorbed in carving, with half a razor blade, a beautiful set of chess men from hardwood offcuts, probably scrounged from the mill; those completed standing in a small cardboard box, and the horse's head (knight) piece he was working on was about 3 inches high but not as a stylised version. These would be quite valuable today I would imagine. I wonder what happened to them. I wonder what happened to the carver.

I created, I think, a little problem with a gang of the non-collaborator prisoners. A number of the packing cases behind St Mark's church had, over the period of the war years while they had lain there, become damaged; one of the long 'bath' containers had broken, leaving a cross-like nailed section of wood. I wrote the word 'MUSSO' (for Mussolini, the deposed fascist leader of Italy) and 'ADOLF' for the character who had started the whole affair, in chalk on the cross piece, and stuck it into the packing case end, Italy having by then given up the struggle, which was bitterly contested by the remaining Germans. However, I understood later that a group of prisoners had refused to work until the sign was removed!

There always seemed to be an air of sadness when the long ambulance trains went through, some on occasions stopping at the signals en route through the works on the main line, and usually everyone in works and offices along the tracks waved and called to the occupants, although some trains were very quiet, being serious stretcher cases while others raced through, heavily curtained and silent. On the other side of the coin, Peter and I in our walk back from the Rodbourne office, often gave a 'thumbs up' and a call to the troop trains which rumbled through in the opposite direction, the grinning occupants leaning out of every available window. Trains of supplies were a familiar sight, a complete train of well wagons each carrying a tank. Its gun muzzle depressed and secured was quite an impressive display of what was actually being used 'over there', as was a complete train load of guns, again each secured to its wagon.

To assist with the war effort, the Americans had shipped over a number of steam locomotives of 2-8-0 wheel arrangement, the 'S160' class, which to the Great Western man, appeared to be absolutely naked, as every pipe was exposed, and they seemed to be all leaking steam, exposed rods and valve gear. I remember on one occasion watching a heavy freight train go through, pulled by one of these locomotives which had eight wheel tenders and, as it went past, noticed its rear axle box on the tender was actually on fire, flames and smoke quite clearly seen as it clanked its way slowly along! We shouted and waved but to no avail; driver and fireman still concentrated ahead. I tried my two-finger whistle, which this time they heard, and both looked over and waved. As we waved and signalled back to them, the driver looked to the rear and spotted the fire. The locomotive slowed right down and he hopped out before it had stopped and went back to view the problem. The flame subsided, but the box was still smoking as the locomotive started up again and crawled slowly forward, heading for the station about a mile ahead, and further attention or a change. With waves again, the goods wagons rattled out of sight, the tender still trailing its little column of smoke from the box, which was probably squealing its own protest, the noise completely blanketed by the general hissing and clanking of the locomotive.

A couple of other episodes noticed while waiting at Rodbourne included the sight of a pannier tank running light, but engaged on shunting work, across the tracks by the turntable, moving backwards in the direction of Bristol, clicking over points on to another line. On this line also was another locomotive, I believe a 'Hall' class, moving under steam and also running light, in the opposite direction on a collision course. The resulting probability was spotted early by the driver of the light engine who blew his whistle, slapped on his brakes hard, thus locking the wheels which just skidded and showered sparks, before leaping out with his fireman! The pannier tank seemed to slide an awful long way before being soundly belted by the 'Hall', also braking, but still travelling. There was quite a bang when the two engines met, and the smaller engine was derailed. What the skid did to the tyres of the pannier tank or what damage actually resulted on both engines, I was too far away to see, but certainly some items must have been rather bent, and I would imagine the pannier tank's wheels clicked a little when they revolved, as the skid must have worn considerable 'flats' on the tyres.

Hawkesworth, the CME, had for some time been pressing for the development of a Great Western Pacific locomotive (4-6-2 wheel arrangement) but, for various reasons outside the scope of this book, had been frustrated in his efforts. A series of experimental 'Hall' class locomotives, or at least a series of 'Halls' with individual features of an experimental nature, had been underway for a couple of years, and a design of a new locomotive incorporating such features did get the go-ahead. The resulting engine had a high boiler pressure, 280 psi, and odd size wheels; by that is meant 'non-standard' wheels of 6-foot 3-inch diameter. This batch of engines numbered from 1000 became the 'County' class, starting with County of Middlesex.

The first engine of the batch was spotted by me, again at Rodbourne, about August 1945, gently steaming away in anticipation (the engine, not yours truly!), again over by the turntable, at first glance looking something like a 'Hall', but having a most distinguishable feature in a double, copper-capped chimney. A further feature seemed to be the flat, high-placed running board along the side, making the wheels look even bigger as the tops were covered by one long 'splasher'. Not yet named, the nameplate would need to be straight as there were no splashers to curve it around. Quite a procession of viewers were moving to and fro to see the latest item from the shops and, from my viewpoint, there seemed a lot of conversation and commenting going on by those milling around.

On one of my returns from the other Timber Stores Office, and while walking up behind the Dean Street timber sheds, one of which incidentally held bays with thousands and thousands of rail keys, I found a ball in the long grass, about the size of a tennis ball, which at first I thought had been thrown by children over the fence from the backway of Dean Street. When I went over to pick it up, however, I found it was of solid cast iron, probably from an old-fashioned valve of some sort. I put it on the pathway and dribbled it with my foot round to the office by the bridge. Following the exchange of post, I walked back up the side of the track behind St Mark's church towards the Sawmill, still dribbling the ball, and on approaching the mill door saw Jack, from the big circular saw just inside the door, standing in the doorway. Slightly built, wearing his cap and with half a finger missing, he had also seen me rolling the ball, and stood in the opening like a goalie, calling out, 'Let's have a shot then!' I was now on the sleeper-constructed portion of the path, which spread around the mill door, the incinerator building and the top of the narrow slope down to the fire-station yard. 'It's a hard one!' I called back. 'Never mind,' said Jack, 'Bowl a shot at me!' and he crouched in goalie fashion. I bowled and the ball bounced over the wooden sleepers! Instead of trying to stop it under his foot as I thought he would, he made the mistake of trying to kick it back to me! There was a dull 'clunk' as the ball stopped dead, a stunned silence, and then the air turned blue. Jack did a spectacular little dance on one foot, hopping menacingly towards me, while I beat a hasty retreat round the end of the mill and along the outside of the building to return to the Timber Stores Office. I noticed he limped for some days after that episode, and his greetings were a little frosty! I never did get the ball back!

Leaving the office in the opposite direction, instead of going down to Rodbourne, the routines of postal deliveries took me regularly under the main line via the 'tunnel' to the CM&EE's, Stores and Loco Managers' office buildings, or towards the railway station to the large, brick-built offices of the Carriage & Wagon Department. There were two routes open for a trip to the latter. One was through the shops on No. 4 Shop side of the line, and then under the main line near the station via another tunnel which emerged in front of the C&W office block. If taking this route, I sometimes had a message or paperwork for the Finishers office across the wide carriage traversing table road between No. 4 and 7 Shops, and if this were the case, always stopped to chat to the craftsman whose bench was just outside the office in No. 7 Shop. This was the man who made artificial limbs for employees injured at work, and I watched in fascination as he showed me several of his products. One was a fully articulated hand, wrist and lower arm, all in wood, the fingers and wrist being jointed so that with the usual glove worn on artificial limbs in those days, they could be realistically bent (by using the other hand of course), to appear as natural as possible when the wearer went out and about.

Also in No. 7 Shop, and to the side of the office, presumably no longer a 'Military Secret', was the mock-up of the midget submarine, a wartime naval contract, for which the shop was responsible for making the wooden superstructures. I don't know what happened subsequently to the model, but I had the satisfaction of sitting on it 'in the driving seat' on one of my visits to the shop. To get to No. 7 Shop, I had to walk diagonally across the table road adjacent to No. 4 Shop, and if I walked straight across, I was in No. 6 Shop, where the products of the finishers were assembled into the coaches; the internal outfitting of compartments and corridors. On the side of No. 6 Shop, adjacent to the main line, was the long stores building for the products of the finishing shop. I remember on one occasion, watching a covered goods wagon being loaded with coach windows, the sliding version that fitted in the external doors and which was operated by a flat leather strap. These were being stacked in rows at an angle, leaning against one end of the wagon, the stacked rows progressing as more were added, and spreading along the length of the floor. Having got nearly the length of the wagon, loading stopped for a shunt. The shunt on this occasion was very hard and very bad, and the 'bang' of the line of wagons caused the windows to fall over the other way, as a row of dominoes topples, leaving the wagon full of broken glass!

Walking through the stores, with its distinctive wood and leather smell, through No. 6 Shop or No. 7 Shop, brought me out into another table road, across which was the carriage paint shop. Here, the smell was of paint and filler, the latter being a grey paste applied over the thousands of screw heads and chips in the painted panels, by a flat, flexible 'knife'. Once in the shop, the visitor was confronted by the buffer ends of lines of coaches, each row separated by a high wooden walkway approached by steps at each end of the line, steps and walkway covered in hard, dried-on paint splashes and filler smudges, and level with the running board and floor of the coaches. The place was alive with scrapers-on of filler, appliers of the X number of coats of paint, stickers-on of transfers of the Coat of Arms and designatory letters of the coach, signwriters where a transfer was not available, and, in between, the rubbers-down with 'wet and dry' papers, and finally the varnishers, the appliers of the high gloss sealer varnish. Outside the shop, removed by the rope and capstans of the traversing table, was the finished, immaculate railway carriage. The shops and product are now long gone from what remains, in 1985, of the works, having disappeared in the 1960s.

On through the shop towards the station and down the slope into the tunnel leading to the C&W offices, was a slope and tunnel similar to the works' main entrance, and known as 'Webbs Entrance' from the builders' merchants opposite. Railway offices were very much the same and the C&W followed the pattern. There were stairs with little wooden blocks, inset end grain uppermost in the cast-iron stair treads, making the tread almost everlasting, with worn, polished, mahogany handrails, cast-iron shaped ballustrading through glass-panelled swinging doors into long corridors, a smell of school, a mix of paper, pencils and floor polish, and the glass-panelled door which led into a glass-panelled office. Apart from the occupants, each office looked and smelled like any other, although I did get the impression that things looked a little older and more run-down than the offices of the CM&EE and Loco departments. Directly backing on to the offices was the C&W side main machine and Fitting Shop, designated No. 15 Shop.

Papers delivered, and back to the Stores and CM&EE's I would go with the rest of the post, but back now by a different route which took me past the end of the C&W Smith's Shop. This was where I always stopped at the open door of the long narrow shop and watched and chatted to the Smith and his 'striker' who worked on the left-hand forge looking into the double doors at the shop end. The Smith was an elderly man with grey hair and thick leather apron, pushing the ring up the handles of the tongs to secure the grip on the material as he pushed the end into the glowing coke. A move to the side of the forge and the lever pushed to open up the blast, when the fire glared back to life and the sparks danced away. During a little chat with me, he had one eye always on the 'use' in the fire, a twist of the tongs and a look at the glowing metal under the coke. There would be a nod to the striker, who withdrew his hammer from the hammer pond and stood waiting. A further twist of the tongs and the material was free of the coke and on the anvil, the other hand of the Smith gripping a set or fuller, either shafted like a hammer or wrapped with flexible wands of wood. The shaped set on to the glowing metal and a nod of the head was followed immediately by a blow on the set, struck squarely by the striker, who could use a large hammer, swinging from any angle, left- or right-handed. A few blows, and the tongs were turned, the glowing metal attaining its required shape, its brightness fading into a dull glow, obscured by rapidly forming grey scale. The finished item aside on to the floor or back into the coke, and the blast was reset for another 'heat'. Then there was a standing back and wiping of brows for the next piece of the batch – fascinating! The heat, dust, haze and darkness of the recesses of the shop were like a passageway into another world – a lifetime spent heating metal in a coke fire and hammering, stretching, bending and cutting to shape.

Overtime was worked in most shops at this time, and I remember one evening in the summer, going out of my front door at home, and walking along the street about 8 p.m., when who should I see coming in the opposite direction but the blacksmith from the C&W Works. I walked with him, back down the road for a short distance just chatting. He was on his way home he said, by a slightly different route, for a change, as it was a lovely evening. He was walking to his cottage via the fields backing the street where I lived, to a little area called Washpool, near Shaw, where he lived near the river and the village pump, his garden running alongside the winding road. This was probably a walk of 4 or 5 miles, giving possibly 9 or 10 miles a day on top of the wearing work in the Smith's Shop. I remember him long after he retired, tending his garden as I sometimes cycled past, giving and receiving a wave or short chat.

Past the Smith's Shop, the rail line curved round to No. 13 Wagon Shop. I would look left and right, cross, and proceed past the Stores Inspectors' building where samples of all the products purchased for use in the works were tested in various ways for suitability for their purpose; as someone once said, they have to strike a full box of matches to see if they actually work! In front of me, the rail lines curved away to the right, to the running shed and the Gloucester line, and to the left, and running parallel on leaving the station, was the main line to Bristol, splitting to form the Gloucester branch at the CM&EE's office building, like a river being split and diverted by a big rock, the 'lorelie' in this case to lure the traveller being the continual procession of steam locomotives. Just about here was the best part of the post journey, sometimes reversed en route to the C&W offices, but always at some stage including this area. In the triangle formed by the splitting of the rails around the CM&EE's offices stood a large group of locomotives, forever changing, but destined for the works and repairs. Often I unofficially crossed the lines here, dapping rapidly across the pathway of sleepers with extreme care to get among and around the variety of engines, which were always patiently waiting at this spot. Here I saw *Caynham Court* for the first time, the locomotive with special valve gear on an experimental basis, described later on in this book, and a number of very odd-looking locomotives, survivors of the 'Amalgamation' a number of years before, and now 'Westernised' as far as possible, but to me, all engines were of the Great Western, and therefore to be looked at and examined. Walking down towards the CM&EE office block, the nearest door was that of 'top management' entry, below the carved blocks of stone set into the building and salvaged from the 1840 engine shed, demolished only a few years before. The two blocks depicted in detailed relief carving, left and right views of a broad gauge locomotive, advocated and developed by the great 'IKB', and vanishing again before the turn of the century. Just inside the door on the left was a model of the broad gauge locomotive *Lord of the Isles*, always examined and admired, with nose pressed against its glass case, and intrigued by the 'Iron Coffin' on the back of the tender. This was an iron sentry box if you like, within which in real life sat a poor unfortunate guard, looking back over the length of the train to ensure that it arrived at its destination with the same number of trucks or coaches as it started with, and not having the embarrassment of shedding a few on the way, through broken couplings. On the wall on the right and between the three office doors were various Royal coats of arms from past Royal trains, all beautifully painted and coloured. Also mounted were the nameplates from the French locomotive *La France* and *Alliance*. On turning left down the corridor, typically lined with filing cupboards, about halfway down on the right, was Bill's sorting office where an elderly, moustached, blue-uniformed character held sway as a messenger, and also dealt with the post, a number of boxes, and labelled trays showing the various destinations of postal packets and papers. Right from the word go, I had been told not to hang about or wait in this area, so I always made a point of nipping in and out as rapidly as I could, although it was always with its complement of chattering office boys and girls. Straight ahead was the exit door and the west time office where I met Roy, another inhabitant of my own home area, and another office boy, with whom I used to visit to play billiards on his small table-top set in his front room!

Immediately before the office, the corridor turned right at 90 degrees, and in the angle was a staircase to the floor above, and tucked under the staircase, a glass-fronted room where the washing-up of tea cups and preparation of beverages was made; usually a chattering place for all the office girls of the block, girls who would eventually be absorbed into the various clerical functions in the many surrounding offices, but who at present, as with the boys, were the general dogsbodies for post deliveries and tea-making; in fact, the character building chores with which everyone starts, or at least should start, as an introduction to any job.

The main thing for success is to enjoy what you are doing; it doesn't matter at all what the job is as long as you enjoy doing it. We are all different and some will stay where they are, while some get to the top. The future is completely unknown and one of my schoolmates became my boss! In fact he became Chairman of the British Railways Board as Sir Richard (Dickie) Marsh! Quite a change from sitting in a small, worn desk and struggling with vulgar fractions under the eye and hand of 'Pop' Phillips, or acting in the plays of Frederick (Joey) Whetham at the age of thirteen. At the time of writing, some of my school colleagues are still 'inside', on the shop floor or in management, but life goes on and it's a good job there are differences or we should be very boring people.

The stairs by the washing up room, if you continued up, led to the big drawing office complex at the top of the building, not very often on my route, but I did often nip up the stairs to have a look at a range of locomotive nameplates which were attached to the arches supporting one of the corridors between offices, *The Great Bear* and *Lady of the Lake* being, I believe, among them. I also mounted the narrower flight of stairs which led directly to the Drawing Office and on the left was a rather old drawing board attached to the wall. On it was the legend, 'This board was originally owned and used by Isambard Kingdom Brunel'. What better inspiration than that could be found?

On return to the ground floor, and turning right at the stairs and tea room, the corridor led to the other door which I had entered on my first day en route to Mr Lane and the staff office, and yet another staircase leading upward. Facing the staircase at its bottom, was a cupboard, on the top of which stood a line of filing boxes, each labelled for a destination, including Timber Stores, from which I collected the contents, at the same time spreading my own contribution into the other boxes as appropriate. Back along the corridor on the left from the area of the stairs and boxes was No. 3 office, where I often called on Miss Atwood who ran a book club. Members paid a small amount per week and, from the sum, a number of magazines were purchased which were then circulated to the members, Phil Brown of the Timber Stores Office being one of them. Another of the private enterprise ventures was run by a lady in the Stores Sold Office on the second floor. One of Stan Drewitt's requests was for what he termed 'gaspers', and a visit to this lady produced the required brand of cigarette from her desk drawer; Woodbines or Goldflake, with other brands being stocked to suit the tastes of her clients. She was always quite particular that they were actually for Stan Drewitt and not for me, and occasionally would say 'Sorry, I haven't got those! I'll 'phone, shall I, and ask if some other brand will do?' I didn't smoke anyway, so when I said 'Yes, that's a good idea!' she often found the last packet, as required in the back of the drawer, which usually contained a fully varied stock. Such personal projects were strictly illegal in the terms of the company rule book, but really flourished in numerous places. Returning for a moment to No. 3 office and a little episode I remember, one afternoon I came along the corridor, as I often did, at a smart trot, and, on approaching No. 3 office, the door opened, unseen by me and screened by the filing cabinets, and the first thing I noticed was the emergence of two hands carrying a filing tray completely stacked with what I afterwards found out were about six months of sorted coal tickets, all numerically piled in neat stacks on the tray. The little man who had just finished the task was proudly delivering them to another office, but on this occasion didn't make it! I couldn't stop, and my shoulder hit the tray and spun the carrier round and down on to the floor, and when I turned round, there was the sorter, crouched with hands over his head, and a veritable snow storm of coal tickets descending and fluttering down all around him. What can you say in such circumstances? His office colleagues came out and we all assisted in picking up the small pieces of thin paper, each about 3 inch by 2 inch, but the task of resorting still remained! The coal tickets were issued, as with the wood tickets previously mentioned, at regular intervals to all householding employees. For a short while I had to collect a coal ticket for a retired member, a relative of Mr Day I believe, from the mess room' at the main tunnel entrance. The tables were set up with an alphabetical marker for surname initials in a portion of the old railway mess room, and staff from the offices manned the post at selected periods. The mess room was a relic of the very early railway days when an early shift was part of the working day, and a breakfast break was held for half an hour at 8 a.m., work having commenced at 6 a.m. At the time of writing these notes, the building is still there, stretching away to the right of the main tunnel entrance to the works, but now used by other firms and organisations. Long and low and supported by cast iron columns at close intervals, it was rather dingy with forms and plain wooden tables stretching away into the distance. I'm not certain that it had a great deal of use even during 1944/45, and it became even less used and desirable as the years progressed, being used I believe as a bicycle shed for those cycling to work.

A further visit to the tunnel entrance was quite regularly made to collect the special reduced-price rail travel ticket known as a 'PRIV' ticket (privilege ticket), a concession for railway employees, the number of tickets permissable depending on the number of years' service of the individual. A little white form was completed and taken with the appropriate cash to the window where the issue of the ticket was made, the office and the issuing windows being of a subterranean nature and actually inside the tunnel entrance to the left on entering. The concession was always a bone of contention with non-railway employees, as with the allocated number of free tickets per employee, but was always accepted as a condition of service and therefore part and parcel of any wage settlement. As an office boy, I often had to collect things from the town for various members of the office and one of the more regular trips was to the GWR Medical Fund Dispensary. There were usually two types of visit here, one being to collect, by queueing at the dispensary window, the various bottles of medicine and pills prescribed by the doctors in attendance. Visiting the doctor at this exclusive GWR medical preserve was by attending prior to his surgery hours and obtaining a metal ticket or cheque with a number on it, the position in the queue prior to the office opening for issuing such tickets governing how long you had to wait on the wooden forms outside the doctor's room, depending on the number on your ticket. Outside the door of each doctor's room was a box arrangement, like the destination board on a bus, but with numbers on the cloth roll going over the rollers. As each person entered, the roll was wound on, prior to opening the door, to the next number in the queue. It was a favourite trick by staff to send the office boy or girl to join the queue for a 'ticket' so that, on leaving work, the person wishing to see the doctor could be assured of an early entry to the room.

The days of rationing were still very much with us, and the boss, Mr Day, had many contacts in the town. One of my regular journeys was a weekly visit to one of his butcher friends, greeted by a nod of the head, recognition, then straight to the head of the queue, and a little package from under the counter with sausages or meat, and then a walk to his house to deliver in time for his lunch! En route was my grandmother's house so I used to call in for a quick cup of tea which she always seemed to have in the pot, so there were benefits all round! Wages at this time were, for me, 16*s* 4*d* per week (about 80p!), and I thought I was well off, even having a little amount to save after handing over the lot to my mother and receiving 4*s* 6*d* in return. I also made some wooden models of engines at Christmas time and sold them as presents to various people in the offices, as toys of any sort were very difficult to get in this period of shortages. I accumulated sufficient cash to buy a second-hand racing bicycle from the Western Cycles shop in Milton Road, near the GWR Medical Fund building, for £6 5*s*, a machine which I kept for about thirty years! Looked after, they never wear out and I gave it away in the end, still in excellent order! Small items were often sold off in the works, and one such occasion was the sale of old oil hand lamps! Word came into the office by 'phone and suddenly everyone was after an oil lamp, although on reflection what use they could possibly be is certainly questionable. The lamps had a chinese pagoda type air vent system on top and two swivelling handles at the back, with a knob at the base which could be moved to close a shutter behind the brass-rimmed 'bull's eye' glass front. These lamps, which had separate little paraffin reservoirs and narrow porcelain wick spouts, were surplus to requirements and had some minor dents or damage, being sold off for 6*d* each (2½p). I was instructed to go over to the General Stores to pick up several which had been put aside for members of the office, so, out of No. 4 Shop door I went, down the steps into the tunnel and walked right through to the end, the slopes going up to right and left directly in front of the General. I believe a young lady named Robins was the office girl for this establishment and was either known as 'Robbo' or 'General'! However, I went into the stores which covered several floors, with neatly kept shelves and bins of every consumable item you could think of, dozens of mops, handles, mop-heads, scrubbing brushes, dustpans, brushes and so it went on, floor after floor; you name it, they'd got it, and overall, a smell of disinfectant and tar or preservative. Through the stores to an outside loading area where a large pile of the old oil lamps stood, a little group tied with string through the handles being extracted and handed to me. Walking back through the tunnel, I felt like a cross between Florence Nightingale and old Ted Holmes, the porter/stationmaster from the classic film *The Ghost Train*, who wandered up and down his derelict platform, swinging his lamp and singing 'Rock of ages, cleft for me!', waiting patiently for a train which would never come, the bundle of lamps clanging and jangling as I walked. On arriving at that alcove in the tunnel where the steps ascended to the door of No. 4 Shop, I heard the rumbling of the traversing table overhead and knew by experience that the heavy wood and mesh ballustrade around the top of the steps would be folded down to cover the opening, not only for safety with the table in use, but also so that the table had an unobstructed passage overhead. That meant me walking on down to the tunnel entrance and back up the slope there, and I had just turned the corner to go up the slope, the queue at the priv. office watching my jingling progress, when a voice boomed 'Oi, Aladdin! Where do you think you're off to with that lot?' One of the watchmen at the gate had heard me clanking down the tunnel, which seemed to contain and project the sound, and had come out to see what was going on. A rather embarrassed explanation followed and I clanked onward, very glad to at last get inside the office and distribute my noisy burden, one lamp presented to me as a present for going.

A further, usually routine present was the Christmas Box from members of the office to the office boy. I seemed to do quite well considering the small office and I still have the little cartoon, sketched by Phil Brown, which accompanied the notes in the envelope.

Returning for a moment to the subject of the main tunnel entrance, the tunnel itself always smelled of disinfectant, and one of the regular tasks of a pair of overalled and rubber-booted characters was the routine washing down of the floor. A number of water valves stuck like gargoyles from a pipe near the low roof, and a hose connected on to these gave progressive cover as the floor was washed, disinfectant being sprayed from a separate 'bowser' or small tank towed along by the men concerned. The walls were lime-washed regularly, but the snowy-white walls were not white for very long, runs of rusty brown water running down from the main railway lines and moving ballast overhead, with the odd drip here and there through the low-arched concrete roof, also whitened and also rapidly stained. The numbers of employees at this period meant that at end of shift periods, the offices emptying five minutes before the shops, a trickle of senior staff walking through the tunnel became rapidly a flood as the other offices emptied, and a low murmur of voices became a babble as the tunnel filled with people hurrying homeward. I found it somewhat difficult on leaving the Timber Stores Office, as I was going in the opposite direction to the crowd pouring down towards the entrance, and was usually followed by Miss Davis who had even further to go along the tunnel against the flow, we stayed close to the wall and attempted to forge ahead. I often walked home with another old schoolmate, Phil Morris, who at this time had become a junior clerk, having entered the clerical profession at sixteen years of age, our paths joining as he also walked home in the same direction. Having walked through that part of the works to the Rodbourne Road/Redcliffe Street gate, past the famous 'hooter', which shed an oily rain when it blew and the steam condensed, round the corner into the L2 Shop table road, we were usually brought to a halt by the shop staff congregated round the gate. We soon timed our walk to arrive in the table road just as the hooter blew, thus avoiding the joint problem of oily rain and an impenetrable crowd round the gate, the latter clearing as we made our exit.

The routines of the office continued and appeared to be set in grooves which would last for ever; the preparation of orders for timber or receipt of timber covered literally mountains of wood of various sorts. I sometimes assisted with the checking of orders before despatch, when I completed the multi-destination design envelopes and tucked in the flap after inserting the order form. Checking consisted of reading aloud the wording of the order and checking it against the original request. Phrases such as 'Wagon Boards, Rough, 5 by 2ft.' or 'deal scantlings, planed, painted, double chamfered', 'deal boards planed, tongued and grooved', etc.; wood being sent to or received from various docks and depots, and forming huge stacks when stored, or trainloads when transported; at Swindon alone, two large Sawmills were continually employed in sawing, planing and shaping all sorts and sizes. There was even a machine in the mill which chopped wood scrap for 'kindling' wood bundles, which the machine also wrapped and tied with string, assisted in the latter case by the young operator. I believe these were for some pensioners or widows, and were usually cut from the offcut ends of long lengths of thick timber planks, the end say 8 inch, always being removed to discard initial splits or 'shakes' in the timber, and which also usually had a red-painted stencilled identification mark.

The subject of chopping kindling wood for fires, some of which found its way into the timber storekeeper's office for the cleaner of the office to light the fire in the early morning, reminds me of the quest for coal in these days of shortages, and on my way down to the Rodbourne office, I was instructed to keep an eye open for burnable items, often scrounging a large lump of coal from the fireman of the shunting engine which plied its way up and down, moving wagons in and out of the mill and around the timber sheds. Ideally, Welsh Dry Steam coal was the fuel for GWR locomotives, but although the war in Europe had ended during May 1945, very little at home seemed to have changed. Locomotive fuel was anything available and burnable, and so the lump of scrounged coal could be the hard WDS or seemingly soft, dull black house coal, which often showed great reluctance to burn at all. There was now no panic to keep everything blacked out, so Mr Beasant's blinds did not really have to be pulled down with such priority, but habits die hard and they were still pulled and checked to make sure no light showed outside.

An election came and passed, and we knew that the days of the Great Western Railway, as such, were numbered! A new era of prosperity and development was coming, at least so everyone believed, and the works could get on with its primary function, the manufacture, from readily available materials, of the railway stock for which it was world famous; full order books and full employment, not only for those already at the works, but for those returning from all parts of the world on 'demob'! So much for the dream, the reality was yet to come!

My days as office boy were also numbered, apprenticeship was approaching rapidly and very soon it was my turn to walk over to Mr Lane's office, the staff section tucked away under the stairs, and collect a new boy, a chubby-faced youngster I had known at school, and whose father I believe, had replaced Bob Parsons in the Rodbourne office on his retirement. Roy Cann was destined to become an engine driver, but for the early months, the duties of office boy to the Timber Stores would be his working life.

Mr Day and other members of the office tried to persuade me to take up a clerical post in the timber section, but by that time I had caught the whiff of oily steam and coal dust and it was apprenticeship on the steam locomotives for me. I showed Roy around for several weeks, the routes through the shops, tending Mr Beasant's fire, an introduction to the watchman at the fire-station gate and the need for caution if running up the slope between the wagons by the Sawmill! We also looked in at the C&W Blacksmiths' Shop and a 'must', the quiet engines waiting in the triangle by the CM&EE's office. There was an initiation into the mysterious cup of tea left in the porch for Wally Hext, and the need for top priority to disinfect the 'phones with carbolic!

A 'phone call to Mr Day from the Staff Office saying 'Start in the B Shed, Monday morning, 7.30', and that was that! The start of the second phase of learning, the first being the invaluable insight into people and jobs and generally 'mixing' during the period as office boy. No one knows what the future will bring, but for me at that stage it was goodbyes and handshakes all round, wishes for the best of luck, and the start of an 'Apprenticeship in Steam'.

3
Start in the B Shed
Monday Morning

The click of a light switch and a hand shaking my shoulder roused me – it was 6.15 a.m. and still dark. By the time I was fully awake, father was halfway down the stairs. Dressing quickly, I followed, to find the first small flames and smoke of the newly lit fire curling up the chimney, and father about to start his breakfast which had been the same for years; two slices of bread and marmalade!

This was the big day, the start of apprenticeship and I was both excited and apprehensive at once. A muttered 'Good morning' and then virtual silence until the time came to leave, with me going out first as I had further to go to the B Shed than father had to the L2 Shop. With a parting 'Cheerio, and all the best', I was out of the back door, down the garden path and on my way to join that almost silent crowd of men converging on the Rodbourne Lane gates, as though being sucked in through a vacuum cleaner. Those nearer the works could leave home that much later, so that as we all funnelled towards the works, the crowd was joined by others opening front doors, gripping the knockers and pulling the door shut, then joining the tramping feet. Men appeared from backways which had provided a short cut and added to the rustle of feet in that 'timed by experience' walk to work, so that arrival at the place of checking in coincided with the blowing of the last of the three hooter blasts which signalled the start of the shift. It all looked just like a typical Lowrie painting!

I had no such criteria for my walk, clad in old grey flannels worn last, and almost out, as an office boy! Gone was the light shirt and tie, to be replaced by a thick, blue, open-neck 'working' shirt, and covered by an old blue jacket of father's, cut off at the bottom so that it didn't appear to be three-quarter length, although it was still really too big, the cut off at the bottom being level with the depth of the pockets, in one of which sat my break sandwiches, wrapped in greaseproof paper and enclosed in an old paper bag. In the other pocket rested an enamel mug and spoon and inside the mug, a twist of paper with some cocoa and a very small mix of sugar, part of the weekly ration! The shortages of the war recently over, were still very much with us. Shoes were my oldest pair, the steel reinforced safety version unheard of at that time, by me anyway. A tightly rolled pair of blue overalls completed the ensemble.

On through the gates I went, down the L2/V Shop table road, I turned right at the hooter house, then left between the angle iron smiths (Q Shop) and K Shop, down between the Manager's Office and R Shop and in through the doors on the right into B Shed. I was early, the second of the three hooter blasts hadn't sounded yet, but another young lad was already waiting at the bottom of the steps leading up to the shop offices, which stretched across the end of the shop. The fitter foreman's office was at the top of the steps where we waited, then in the centre of the line was the clerical office and, finishing at the next table road door, the boilermaker foreman's office with a similar flight of steps leading down to the shop floor level. The stores, following the pattern I was to find in all the shops, was located underneath the offices, with serving hatches along the front wall facing the shop.

I chatted to Frank, the other lad, while we waited, and found he had come in straight from school as I hadn't recognised him as being an office boy in any of the areas I had covered. The foreman arrived and then an office clerk came down the steps to collect us and go through various bits of paper and formalities, explaining the 'checking in' system and allocating a check number to each of us. We were then led silently into the foreman's office where we were given a little pep talk on the dos and don'ts of shop life. As an office boy, I had already received the little red book of company rules and had read it quite thoroughly; it compared very closely to that given to my father nearly forty years previously when he had started at the works. However, all societies need rules and these just emphasised the requirements of safety and conduct necessary for such a complex organisation to run smoothly. Following the pep talk, with dutiful nods in the right places; the office boy was summoned and he proceeded to take us to our allocated gangs. Frank departed on to the locomotive bay, looking from the offices down the right-hand side of the shop, while I was to work on the tender section, roughly in the centre bays, the left-hand bay against the wall taken up by boilers in various stages of repair on a solid concrete floor, the rest of the shop trenched out with pits spreading from the traversing table roads.

A quick word from the chargehand and I was placed with Harold Stoker. At the age of sixteen, the relative ages of adults was a little vague, but Harold appeared to me to be older than my father, which seemed to be very old, but he was probably fifty-five-ish, rather stockily built, with spectacles and an Army-type fatigue cap. Harold showed me where to hang my jacket and a cupboard under a bench where I could, as he said, 'Store my tools', which as yet I didn't have, so I just looked in the cupboard, small, under the bench and with a wire grill or mesh front, typical of all those met with during the next years of apprenticeship. Next, a trip to the stores to collect a small piece of hard yellow soap and a ball of shredded cotton waste, a hammer, cold chisel and a large flat file, all second-hand and probably handed in by the last apprentice to leave the shop on the first stage of apprenticeship. The start on fitting in the B Shed was merely an introductory month or two before moving next door into R Shop for the start of lathe work.

So this was it! The start of apprenticeship in steam, probably predetermined by father on the day I was born sixteen years before; the bustle, the rattle and noise of mechanical work and movement, the shouts and conversation, the areas of smoky mist around the rivet fires and the quieter areas of the stores and the drillers in the far right-hand corner of the shop, and overall, the distinctive smell of the workshop, a mix of warm air, coke fumes, oil, metal, and a rather distinctive pungent smell which wafted across now and again, and was as yet undefined.

'We do all sorts of repairs here,' said Harold. 'New wheels and axle boxes, renew the brake gear, frame repairs, putting up the brake and the scoop gear; in fact the lot!' He took me on a conducted tour of a tender; he pointed underneath. 'There,' said Harold. 'Know what the scoop does?' I said I did and explained how it was lowered over the water troughs, set in special places along and between the lines to enable the engine to pick up water without stopping. Father had done a great deal of outstation work on the troughs, a series of metal 'U'-shaped sections joined to form a water bucket about a third of a mile long, the end sections running upward to nothing to prevent the water running out. At the side of the line would be located the water tank and balancing house, working really like a gigantic WC flush cistern, keeping the water level up to requirements, and the trough full.

When the scoop was lowered into the trough, the force of the speeding train drove the water up into the locomotive tender; the tender, looked at from the top, had a dome on the rear portion of the water tank, and it was this dome which spread the rushing intake of water and distributed it into the tank from the vertical entry pipe directly underneath, its bottom end connected to the scoop. (*See Plates 4 & 5.*)

There are a number of items when the locomotive is in service, which need to be attached firmly to the locomotive from the tender, and the first of these requirements is of course to join the tender itself to the locomotive. At each end of the tender, and indeed on the locomotive itself, is a 'drag box', an assembly of very firmly riveted plates and angle irons which contain the draw gear or drag hooks. At the rear of the tender is the large hook which connects the many tons of the carriages or wagons, and at the front, the special connection which links the tender to the locomotive. The hooks were made with a long-screwed shank which terminated in probably the largest nut used on the steam engine, being about 5–6 inches across the flats. The hook was lifted into place and slid, stem first, into the reinforced rectangular hole in the 'drag beam' or buffer beam, which carried the buffers as well as the drag hook. Nutted on from up inside the tender frame, the hook was in some measure protected from sudden snatch loading by a large metal cup, which contained rubber discs and thin steel plates, assembled as a sandwich. The nut was then screwed on tight with the biggest spanner I had seen, the whole secured by a flat key in the end of the screwed shank of the hook.

If a nut or item could not be unscrewed, or bolts could not be removed due to rust or other damage, the cry went out for 'Ernie the Burner', one of the characters of the shop, and probably of the works. No matter where the nut was, Ernie would somehow get in with his oxy-acetylene torch and cut it off. He never seemed short of work and was always around somewhere, you just had to look for him. Given the number of the tender and its general location in the shop, you would be put on his list for attention and you then returned to the tender in question. The later rumble of a trolley heralded Ernie's approach with his specially designed and constructed (by himself) trolley for his oxygen and acetylene cylinders and assorted box of torches, flexible pipes, nozzles, chipping hammers, and not forgetting his ball of cotton waste (which he always seemed to ignite sometime during the day!) and his steel plate. It appeared that at some time or other he had managed to set fire to the floor blocks and had been instructed, in future, to always use a thin steel plate on the floor to protect it from the glowing drops of molten metal from the cutting operations. No matter where he was performing, and that term is not used loosely, he set up the metal plate, often with startling results! I remember one occasion when Ernie had been called to burn off a drag hook nut, he arrived with his trolley which swayed and bounced over the floor blocks in a most disturbing way, and stopped by our tender, and peered up between the wheels under the frame, summing up the job requirements, Producing his key, he opened his gas bottle and ignited the jet, then the oxybottle to adjust the flame balance, With his large, very stiff brown canvas overalls flapping in the breeze, rather frayed around the bottoms and open all the way, or most of it, down the front where the buttons were missing, he descended down into the pit with his cutting torch and wriggled his way, clutching his metal plate, somewhere up into the rear of the 'drag box' assembly. Wedging the plate, goodness knows where, he proceeded to cut through the nut. Now, the molten drops of metal inevitably fell downwards and instead of dropping harmlessly into the bottom of the pit, were interrupted in their journey by the metal plate which they proceeded to hit and then spatter in all directions. One particularly big blob spattered and a fair amount of the glowing globules went straight down the front of Ernie's gaping overalls!

There was a loud cry of 'Arghhh, me b***s are on fire!' and Ernie dropped the torch into the pit, following it like a cormorant diving into the waves after a large fish. He literally flew along the pit under the tender, into the space at the end and cleared the pit in an Olympic-standard jump, followed by a rush over to the water tap which he turned on, and proceeded to ladle the cooling flow into the front of his smoking overalls. He later returned to the job, very non-committal about any damage he may have suffered, but just grinned at us as though it all formed an accepted hazard of a most important job.

There were hazards aplenty in a workshop, not least the inexperienced apprentice! Harold announced that we had a pair of feed clacks to put up. These were the valves which could be used to turn off the water flow from tender to engine when separation was required, the two joined normally by flexible hose and steel pipe to their respective injector on the locomotive itself. The valves could be operated by a simple L-shaped handle, which protruded at low level above the footplate of the tender, tucked back in against the front of the tanks. 'Know what a "Grummit" is?' asked Harold. I had to confess that I didn't. 'It's a little ring of special yarn you make to put under a bolt head or washer to make it watertight. Now, I have to go and see someone about something, so you go over to the stores and ask for a length of tar yarn for some grummits, and a short weight!' I dutifully trotted over to the stores and made the memorised request, indicating with my hands as Harold had done, the length of the weight required, the hands spread apart like the angler describing the size of the one which got away (incidentally, there appears to be many pronunciations and spellings, from 'Gromhead' to 'Grommets'). The storeman disappeared into the back of the stores and came back with a length of thickish brown string, which smelled very strongly of creosote or tar, hence its name. 'Here's the tar yarn,' he said, 'Hang on there a minute will you?', and with that disappeared again into the back of the stores. I leaned on the zinc top of the serving hatch counter and watched him rummaging about, apparently searching for a weight, then turned, and leaning back with my elbows on the counter, watched Ralph sorting out flexible steam and vacuum pipes. Five minutes passed and still no sign of the storeman, although several other fitters had been served by the second man. Kicking my heels and shuffling about, another five minutes passed by and eventually the storeman returned. I had by this time coiled and uncoiled the tar yarn several times in my idleness, and questioned the storeman about the short weight I had been told to ask for. 'You've been here ten minutes, you've just had it!' he said with a chuckle. The penny dropped. I'd been had – weight for wait!

My period as an office boy had primed me for all sorts of practical jokes! I knew all about the bucket of steam, the red and green oil for the signal lamps, the bubble for the little tube in the spirit level, and had resolved to always question such a request should it ever be made. But 'a length of tar yarn and a short weight' sounded so logical at the time! All in the humour of the process of growing up.

I got back to the tender as Harold arrived. 'See you've got the tar yarn!' he said. 'Yes, and I also had the 'short wait'!' I replied, and we both had a laugh.

The pits were, or at least appeared to me, to be a bit on the deep side, as it was rather a job for me to reach up to various items under the tender, the two clacks being no exception. However, stopping to make some grummits, forming a ring of tar yarn to fit over the bolt shank, and then winding the free end of the string around the ring itself, we had a series of little 'quoits' of tar yarn. Securing the clacks to the tender bottom proceeded normally and then fate played a rather nasty hand when we came to tighten the nuts. Harold was working opposite me in the pit, tightening the nuts on one clack, while I was to tighten the nuts on the one opposite. The problem was that I could not reach them properly without standing on something and the only way I could obtain a rather precarious footing was the little step, about one brick wide, built up from the bottom about 9 inches up the two sides of the pit. Standing on one side of the pit like this and reaching out across to get the spanner on the nuts was rather difficult, but at least I could now reach, but nothing is as simple as it first appears! There came a time during the tightening process, when pushing off the step to get the nuts really tight, that my direction of 'push' coincided with the jaw shape of the open-ended spanner, which slipped easily off the nut! I took off from the step with arm outstretched still clutching the spanner, hurtled across the pit and caught Harold right between the eyes with my clenched fist holding the spanner! He staggered back and sat down hard against the pit wall as though he had been poleaxed! Profuse apologies, when he had recovered sufficiently to understand what was being said to him, were accepted very nobly on his part, but he insisted on tightening the rest of the clack nuts himself, a reasonable enough request under the circumstances!

The immediate post-war period had seen a situation in which oil appeared to be easier to obtain than coal, and 1946 saw the start of a conversion programme, first on experimental lines and then a positive policy of converting steam locomotives to oil fuel, with various depots having facilities installed for replenishing oil as well as maintaining the high, drafty, dusty coal stages for the steam locomotives still requiring solid fuel. A new gang with a very new chargehand, George Mills, had been created, and the first tenders were being converted to receive liquid fuel oil! Various control valve additions were required, as well as a very large oil tank, shaped to fit into the coal space between the water tank facility. Starting very effectively, with a good steaming report from the running side of operations, the whole process was born, lived and died during the period of my apprenticeship, as all the oil-burning locomotives had been reconverted to coal-firing by 1951, and a mountain of the rectangular oil tanks to fit the tenders could be seen on the 'Con Yard' embankment, awaiting the cutting torch and recycling as scrap. Politics, and the value of oil, have been strange bedfellows ever since.

Partway through my weeks with Harold, there were a few days when he was, I believe, out sick, at least he was away for a short while, and I was moved temporarily to work with Bert Bishop, a shortish, tubby man. Following the First World War, or as it was known, 'the war before last', the Railway Companies had purchased a number of ROD (Railway Operating Department) locomotives. These were of a completely alien design to any and all GWR practice, being Great Central-type engines purchased by the Government as the standard military design. As the exception to all other odd locomotives acquired from other eventually amalgamated companies, these were never 'Great Westernised' and it was on the tender of one of these that I worked with Bert. While everything functioned in the same way as on a Great Western tender, it appeared either of different design and/or position. Bert maintained that even some of the bolts were case-hardened so that if they rusted in they were extremely difficult to drill out. Harold eventually returned and work resumed on the Great Western tenders.

I had a few weeks with Harold and a change of job, moving over with 'Ossie' on drag box assembly, which at the time appeared to be a move away from the actual tender repairs. This operation assembled a mass of angles, flats and channels of various shapes and sizes into a very elaborate reinforced box-like assembly, of necessity extremely strong to protect the ends of the tender frame and to take the blows on the buffers and the pull on the drag hook. The drag box, I suppose with the tender itself, emphasised the trade demarcation differences within the shop as two separate groups were responsible for construction, including the supervisory arrangements. Basically, the tender, the water tank, flooring and frame were assembled and maintained by the boilermakers, (the frame initially prepared and set up by the fitters), while the various mechanisms, scoop and brake handle columns, 'clack' valves, wheels and axleboxes, brake gear and draw gear, were the fitters' responsibility. The scoop itself is a good example, being installed or removed by the fitters but repaired, reshaped and riveted as required by the boilermakers. In use incidentally, the scoop only needed to dip its bottom lip about 2 inches into the trough at a very controlled speed. Travelling at about 24 mph, 2,000 gallons of water could be scooped aboard and, theoretically at least, and never attempted in practice, there was a point where, with the scoop at a lower depth and the speed too low or too high, the impact of moving scoop on static water was such that it could absorb the power of the engine like a gigantic brake, bringing the whole train to a halt. The incalculable damage resulting to trough and train precluded a practical demonstration, but the movement of water under the hydraulics heading makes interesting reading.

The drag box was another of those efforts of joint work by boilermakers and fitters, the former following the latter. I believe Ossie worked from experience, as I don't recall him ever looking at a drawing. A neatly dressed, dapper little man, he would sort through the pile of material stacked on his work area between two pits, backed by a bench at one end and the table road at the other, and position various items around a pair of very stoutly made trestles, with additional packing blocks nearby for use if required. Various small angle and channel sections would be selected and bolted loosely together, the whole taking shape, and alignment ensured by straight edge and light hammer blows, moving the items slightly to square up edges and position holes, a bolt inserted and then tightened to ensure rigidity as assembly progressed. Most of the components were pre-drilled, some possibly jig-drilled and some actually marked out prior to arrival at Ossie's work area, although there were a few items which could only be marked off actually on assembly of other items. These angles would be clamped into place, all metal faces having been painted with preservative red lead paint before delivery to site, and the mating holes scribed on to the red surfaces by the scriber, which all fitters carried, clipped over the top of the rule pocket on their overall leg. The scriber was usually smith-made from a piece of ¼-inch-diameter spring steel, with the top end flattened and bent over like the clip on a fountain pen. A sharp point ground on to the hardened opposite end and a very handy tool emerged, not only for scribing but for checking hole alignment without risking the end of your finger. The scribed items were then removed, centre-punched and taken across to the radial drill in the bottom right-hand corner of the shop, where they were drilled, usually while we waited, the driller in shirt sleeves, rolled up very tightly as far as they would go, exposing arms like Popeye of cartoon fame, the muscles rather admired at the time! Then back to the drag box and assembly of the drilled components, which now aligned perfectly, or usually so at any rate. Some of the other items, pre-drilled, often showed some of the holes as half a hole or not completely aligned as they should have been, and this called for attention on site.

Any misaligned hole had to be cleaned up, otherwise the riveter would never be able to position the rapidly cooling red hot rivet, gripped in his short tongs, and this realigning introduced me to the vagaries of using the ubiquitous air drilling machines. Using the air drills was usually a two-handed job. The machine consisted of a body containing an air turbine connected to a large chuck, one tubular handle sticking out to the left-hand side and another to the right, this one containing a twist grip like a motorcycle throttle, and carrying also the screwed connection for the length of wire-wrapped hose, which snaked off to the nearest compressed air main and valve. The nose of the drill was either complete with a chuck or a morse taper socket which held the shank of a drill or reamer, the latter cutting on its flutes and not on its point like a drill. For trueing up the holes in the drag box the latter was used, a large ⅞ inch or so diameter with a taper, allowing entry to the misaligned holes and the body of reamer opening up to the required diameter. With both of us holding very tightly, air on by the twist grip, and a bit of old sack tied over the exhaust port to stop the air blowing your hat off, the reamer was poked progressively through all the holes good and bad to make sure nothing held up the riveting process. Sometimes the reamer stuck and the machine kicked, but by pumping the handles up and down, off it went again, sounding like a gigantic dentist's drill. With all holes cleaned out, the boilermakers were notified that the box could be riveted. The reaming of the holes also cleared up the mystery of a rather pungent smell, noticed when entering the shop and starting first with Harold Stoker, although it was nothing we were working on at the time. The oil poured or squirted on to the reamer (I believe it was rapeseed oil) seemed to mix with the red lead, coating all of the pieces of angles, channels, etc., in use, and sometimes a large blob of paint would have accumulated in a drilled hole. The heat generated by the reamer caused the paint to smoke slightly and give off a distinctive aroma which I noticed subsequently in many jobs and shops throughout my apprenticeship.

There were all sorts of containers for oil, ranging from the engineer's oil can, to old tin cans, and a particular favourite, the chipped and replaced billy can, the blue enamel container which also had a blue enamel mug that served as a lid. These were often filled with 'cleaning' oil, a paraffin-like liquid which removed grime and grease from components or hands, although possibly frowned upon in the latter case. One little episode I remember involved an old blue enamel billy can, and the apprentice with whom I had started on the first morning in B Shed. One breaktime, Frank had climbed out of the pit over on the locomotive bay, wiped his hands on his inevitable ball of waste, found the dirt wouldn't come off and had looked around for some cleaning oil. Spying a battered billy can on the locomotive running board, he had, without further ado, dipped in a large chunk of his cotton waste, only to find he had dipped into someone's breaktime brew of tea. An altercation followed, the air matching the colour of the billy can!

Another occasion vividly remembered was when Ossie and I heard a furore and shouting and hammering from the locomotive bay. On one of the pits, a tank locomotive under repair had a little knot of people grouped around one side, with someone on top of the boiler looking down into the hinged flap opening through which the tank was normally filled with water. There was much arm-waving by those on the ground and proffered advice being called back and forth among those assembled. The sight of 'Ernie the Burner' haring along with his swaying trolley of oxybottles and associated items just added a further interest to the situation. Ernie stopped his trolley, unwound his pipes and stood by with his torch gently flickering a small whispy flame which could, with a split second's notice, become a roaring, cutting jet of hot gas. It appeared that a rather tall gangling apprentice, whom I believe was known as 'Granny', and who all of my contemporaries will recognise as one of the more incident prone among us, had, during the course of the job, been required to get into the side tank to secure various bolts. On trying to get out of the very restricted volume of the side tank, itself full of reinforcing angles and baffles, he had become firmly stuck! Ernie was restrained, with some difficulty, from immediately starting to demolish the locomotive with his torch, and the advice continued to flow to the unfortunate man stuck in the tank. With two fitters now on top of the tank, reaching in and also talking to the entrapped individual, a general calmness returned to the area, although Ernie still gave the occasional burst of flame with his cutting torch as a reminder that he was ready to do his stuff in the cause of freedom! Panic subsided and quiet restored, encouraging words and a quick wriggle and a rather shaken apprentice emerged through the filler hole and sat on the top of the boiler for a few minutes. The crowd dispersed, and Ernie, with reluctance and obvious disappointment, dowsed his torch, packed up his trolley and departed in search of another emergency, possibly making do with the next one on his own!

During my time as an office boy, I had many times walked through the yard at the fire station, usually a bustling area of stretched hoses drying and the old fire engine out in the yard having anything that could be polished, polished! I believe there were various practice runs into and around the works, but the mileage on the engine remained almost

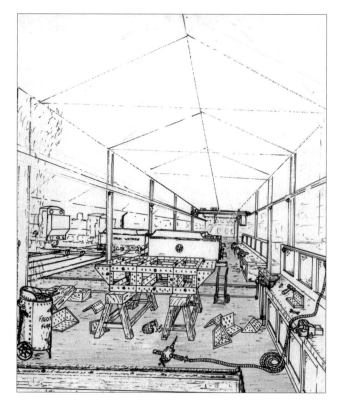

B Shed – the tender section, and a move to work with Ossie assembling drag boxes.

at showroom level. I was in B Shed when one of the rare call-out occasions occurred, the engine arriving in exceptionally quick time, oilskin and wellington boot-clad firemen rushing in, but by that time the emergency had been satisfactorily dealt with locally and so they were really not required. I was still working with Ossie on the drag boxes, and the ubiquitous Ernie and his blowtorch were required the other side of the bench line to blow some difficult bolts out of a drag beam assembly. Setting up his equipment and his steel plate, the latter directly underneath the site of operations as instructed, Ernie proceeded to blow out the bolts, a few droplets falling on to the plate in correct fashion. When the end of the cut approached with the torch held at 90 degrees to the floor, there was a sudden 'whoosh' and a 'Roman candle' effect of molten particles showered straight from the drag beam, across the gangway, and through the wire mesh fronts of several locked cupboards under the bench in the direct path of the cascade. There was then another 'whoosh' as oily waste and a can of cleaning oil ignited. Ernie looked at the conflagration, blinking his watery blue/green eyes in amazement and with a muttered 'Oh dear!', joined the group trying to open the cupboards to dowse the flames. An old ARP sand bucket, complete with its quota of cigarette butts, was produced and hurled into the cupboard with very good effect, the flames now reduced to a black pall of smoke. Seen from the office and not recognised as part of the tender repair process, the pall of smoke triggered a 'phone call. The fire brigade were summoned, arriving with bell clanging, when all the excitement was almost over. My introduction to apprenticeship and characters was certainly getting off to a good start and was very entertaining!

My stay on the drag boxes was beginning to pale a little, just running the air-driven reamer through a myriad of partly obstructed holes in very heavy metal boxes, and I was interested in getting back on to the tenders themselves, so I had a word with the chargehand to that effect. The result was a joint job, helping Ossie with the machine on the occasions when he wanted assistance, and a move down the line to the pits of the water road and Alfie Fisher. Alf was a cheerful chap with black, thin hair, Brylcreemed starkly back, and a grin which exposed a number of gaps along his front teeth. After explaining that the job was the finalising and boxing up of the tenders immediately before filling for a water test, he said 'Made yourself any tools yet?' I said that I hadn't but had brought a few odd ones with me, such as a rule and some 'inside' calipers which had been my grandfather's. 'What about "outside" calipers?' said Alf, 'You'll certainly need some next door!' 'Next door' was R Machine Shop where all apprentices started the turning section of the five years apprenticeship, this stay in B Shed being just a preliminary or introductory phase to workshop life. Alfie went to his cupboard and produced a small piece of wood about 8 inches by 3 inches by 1 inch, with a metal strip across the widest surface at one end. 'Know what this is?' he said. When I confessed ignorance he explained 'It's a caliper board! Show you how it works later! Come on, let's go and get some material!'

We put the little board aside and walked through between the pits and the benches, into the table road and on out through the open double doors into the yard facing the Manager's Office. Then across the yard, past the toilet block and into the Spring Shop. Alfie approached someone he obviously knew well, and the three of us then went to a bin full of metal pieces. Alf rummaged around and with a satisfied 'Ah, there's one!', came up with a piece of flat plate, offset in the centre. 'Spring from a regulator!' he explained, 'Ideal for what we want! Bit rusty now, but that will soon change!' Handing the piece of steel to his companion, he said we would be back for it later and we walked back to B Shed. When eventually collected, the piece of plate spring had been 'annealed' or softened, flattened and cut into several strips lengthwise. Alf produced a hacksaw, hammer and centre punch, said 'Have you got a scriber?' and, when told 'No!', gave me one of several from his cupboard, the ¼-inch-diameter steel rod variety flattened and bent on the end to clip over the pocket. The end of one of the strips was centre-punched, a circle scribed around the punch by Alf and one 'leg' of a pair of calipers marked out straight, with the explanation that the Smith would bend them later on to the correct shape. With the warning to 'Put it away if you see the Gaffer coming! , I started hacksawing and filing the legs to shape. Having got the legs shaped, the little board was produced, the legs clamped one at a time under the little metal clip, and I was introduced, via a couple of Alfie's specially kept files, to the process of draw filing to clean up the flat surface of the legs. The spring plate had cut four pieces which, over the period with Alf, were shaped and made into a pair of inside and one of outside calipers set tempered and 'blued' by the Smith to whom we paid another visit. The inside pair were lost over the years but I still have the outsiders.

A trip to the stores was made to collect joint material, tar yarn, and a couple of candles for a first foray into the depths of the tender tank! There were no low voltage hand-leads for electric light, nor any other form of portable lighting by electricity, low or high voltage, and all inside tank work was by candlelight, the yellow candles screwing into a ⅞-inch nut to form a weighted base. Some fitters had a large washer tack-welded to the nut to form a contemporary candlestick but generally a plain nut worked just as well. This time no mention had been made for the requirement of a weight, either long or short, so the stores visit was uneventful!

On the subject of tack welding incidentally, I saw a humorous but nevertheless dangerous welding episode while on the water road with Alfie. He was chatting to a couple of other fitters, one of whom had large black boots with well-studded soles and metal heel plates. It so happened that the man with the studded boot soles was standing with his heels on the rail line at the end of a pit, in which a welder was working on a tender frame. The welder nipped along the pit, held his earth clamp on the rail by jamming it under a tender wheel, and, with speed, dapped his welding rod on the heel plates of the man's boots and tack-welded them to the rail on which he was standing. Literally rooted to the spot and teetering back and forth in an attempt to keep his balance, the air got bluer than the welding flash when the arc was made on the boot tips. Trying to maintain balance, one of the welds broke, allowing the wearer to take a step and regain equilibrium, but the other boot remamed firmly secured to the rail top. Unlacing and stepping out of the secured footwear, a hammer and chisel, borrowed from Alf, soon freed the heel plate and the victim was properly shod once more, while all within sight had a good laugh.

'Air vents,' said Alfie, looking at the two weighty cast-iron mushroom-like objects on the floor. 'If you take water out of a tank, you've got to let some air in, otherwise you don't get any water out; simple! Hop up on top and I'll get the crane along.' The air vents were a lot heavier than I thought they would be, but they were eventually on the top of the tank. 'Always make sure you've got a box of matches,' said Alf. 'If you get stuck up in the front end of a tank and your candle blows out, you've got problems. He lit the candles and said, 'Right, let's go in!'

The top of the tender had a large dome over the pipe from the scoop and, just behind, a large metal lid secured with a bar and pivoting screwed handle which flicked up into place into a slot in the bar, being firmly screwed down to lock the lid. It was now open so in we climbed, through the 18-inch-diameter deep-rimmed hole. Inside it was quite dry, and a little bit of light came from underneath where the manhole drainage opening was still without its cover. This made a through draught which had allowed the tank to dry out so quickly, the draught was felt as you eased in through the filler hole. It is often a surprise when first entering a tank, to find that contrary to the space expected, the volume of the tender tank seemed to be completely taken up with integral baffle plates which divided the space into a number of small compartments, all joined or interlinked by holes of various shapes and sizes through the baffle plates themselves. The idea was that I should stay in with the bolts and grummits, which we would make from the tar yarn in the usual manner. Alf would then position an air vent, and a bolt would be fitted with a washer and grummit and poked up through the tank top and held with a spanner while the nut was put on and tightened. This was much better I thought, than poking a reamer through holes in drag boxes! However, the time was just about equalled out between the drag boxes and the tenders, the dapper figure of Ossie appearing on the water road quite regularly when my presence was required!

An opening which certainly had to be stopped up before the tender was filled was that of the drain out manhole right at the bottom of the tender well, which formed a trough-shaped section to fit between the frames. The manhole was a solidly dished disc, sealed with a rubber ring, and held in place by a heavy rectangular section bar which tapered down towards each end, and had a screwed hole in the centre into which fitted a bronze screw-in bolt. With the ends of the bar under shaped lugs, the centre bolt tightened on the cover and held it firmly in place until the next shop visit requiring its removal. The central bolt usually suffered from dirt and corrosion of the bar, which I believe was a type of cast iron. However, interaction of the materials of bar and bolt, coupled with the inevitable dust and dirt of thousands of running miles, caused the bolt to seize in the hole. One such we dealt with by setting the bar in the big leg vice on the bench and arranging a large gas jet to play on the bar and screw. When sufficiently hot, a drop of oil was poured on the screw which sputtered and smoked rather well, and I was given the task of working the screw back and forth with a view to unscrewing it. A large spanner was produced, and I started the task, but the short shank of the spanner made leverage rather difficult, so a tube was added to put over the end of the spanner shank. I know that all the books and safety regulations say 'don't use a tube which loosely fits on a spanner!' I found out, fortunately without any form of injury, just how true that warning is, but at the time it was unknown to me and the tube was general practice. The bolt was very stiff but it was beginning to unscrew, and I was really pulling on the tube when direction of pull again equalled the open end of the tube, which slipped off the spanner and I shot backwards. My next clear memory is of looking up at the roof of B Shed from flat on my back in the bottom of the nearest pit. I have no recollection of falling into the pit and I had no bruises or bumps afterwards; I just got up, under the scrutiny of several faces peering down, picked up the tube and carried on unscrewing the bolt! I must have instinctively rolled when I fell and avoided any damage to myself. I was very lucky!

Where the tender tank narrowed towards the locomotive cab and the coal chute was positioned, there were a couple of jobs which required work inside the tank right up at cab end of the narrowest sections of the tank. One was the fitting of the water level indicator float gear, and the other, the positioning of the bolts which held the toolboxes in place. The water level indicator was of bronze (*See Plate 2*), a hollow cylindrical casting about 15 inches high with a slotted flat face towards the cab, graduated with cast-on raised lines. A horizontal diamond-shaped pointer moved in the slot, pivoted off the inside of the casing, and operated by a very large ball float, similar to that in the old WC cistern. Assembling all of the items, the bolts, washers, pins, splitpins, grummits and tools, the journey into the tank began, with the smaller items in a little sack; dropping down into the darkness of the tank was like a step into the unknown. The tank echoed with a hollow boom when the sack struck one of the baffles, which had to be negotiated like a maze as the holes through each baffle were not aligned to those of the next; weaving in and out on all fours and squeezing up into the front narrow section as instructed, further instructions were called down by Alf through the slot in the indicator casting. The candlelight flickered rather eerily on the rusty brown sides and baffles, and there was always a fear, not expressed of course, that someone would start filling the tank while you were still inside! On that score, I only got into a bit of a flap once. I was doing the usual to the ball float mechanism, Alfie having finished on top and moved away, when all of a sudden there was the loud rush and splash of water pouring in. On reflection, I think I levitated through the holes in the baffles, without, as the saying goes, touching the sides, like a space craft being drawn into a black hole! On reaching the filler end of the tank I found it wasn't my tender being filled but the one behind being emptied! Phew! There was relief all round and a sit on the step formed by the well bottom for a minute or two.

A further trip into the front end of the tank was required to fit the two toolboxes, heavy design steel plate with the distinctive curved lid which overlapped the box in a continuation of the curve. These were bolted down to the tank on two strips of wood with a bolt going through the four corners of the box, the wood and the tank top. The boxes would have been delivered to the pit side and left on the ground to await lifting up by the crane, preceded by a walk along the bay to where the crane was working, and a word to 'Thunderer', the slinger to book the next lift. Thunderer was on the verge of retirement having been retained throughout the war years and was, I believe, then over seventy years old, and one of the oldest men still employed at the works. With very few teeth and a slow, rather shuffling walk, his nickname was rather a misnomer. Waiting on top of the tender for the crane allowed the preparations to be made; bolts with nuts run on, grummits made, pieces of wood positioned and a tommy bar handy for aligning the bolt holes when the boxes were lifted on. In the corner of the toolbox was a wooden block, usually very black and oily, with about six holes drilled down its length, the block was about 5 inches square and about 10 inches long. This was the storage for spare water gauge glasses, the glass tubes which fitted behind the thick protective plate glass windows of the water gauge mounted on the locomotive back head, and which, with a direct connection to the water, indicated the water level maintained in the boiler. These glasses were, I assume, usually cleared out before the tender came into the shop, but on occasions one sometimes remained. The glass was quite often seen in offices being used as a straight edge for ruling lines on paper, and was sometimes filled with strands of tightly packed coloured cotton waste, making very decorative patterns along the length of the tube. I still have one, found in a toolbox and so packed, a reminder of days long gone, of Alfie, and of days on the water road.

The rumble of the crane and the appearance of Thunderer with a rope sling meant that boxes could be positioned. When slinging or lifting by crane it is essential that only one person gives the instructions to the crane man or confusion reigns on when to lift, traverse or lower, and that situation is dangerous. 'Thunderer' attached the sling to the box, and lifted a hand, palm uppermost, while looking up at the crane driver who started the hoist, the box slowly lifting off the ground. 'Now follow him!' Thunderer called, indicating to me on the tender top, as he couldn't see properly once the box was over the top rim of the tender. The box slowly moved across as the crane traversed a yard or so and, swinging the box on its sling, I indicated, palm down, for it to be lowered onto the wood strips. Sling off, and the same process was repeated for the second box, the crane and Thunderer departing for the next lift on their list. Into the tank again on the arrival of Alfie, candle flickering off the brown, scaly baffles in the tank, through the holes and up into the narrow front end once again, the light casting odd leaping shadows as I moved. Tommy bar up through the holes, a little wiggle to align the box and up with the bolts complete with grummits, the vibration was felt as Alf screwed on and then tightened the nuts. With instructions to look around inside and to remove any and all loose items, old nuts, pins, split pins, etc., lying about on the bottom of the tank, the flickering candle and shadows moved with me to the opening and out into the blue haze of B Shed once more, the tank now ready for filling.

Another of the small jobs tackled by the apprentice, and one which assisted in teaching the use of the hammer and chisel, was that of roughing up the steps, to ensure the locomotive crews' boots did not slip on the usually wet and oily metal. The type of chisel was the diamond point, so shaped that the cutting edge was a sloping diamond, the cutting edge being of a flat point. An attempt was usually made to wedge the steps, hanging or suspended from the frame, which vibrated considerably when struck, the chisel making a 'boing-d-d-d-d' sound as the step vibrated after the blow with the hammer. This step roughing was good practice and taught the use of the hammer and chisel, in that you had to watch the cutting edge and not, as with many tyros, the top part struck by the hammer. Nevertheless, a session on step roughing, a standby job to keep the apprentice out of mischief if work slackened off, always resulted in a bruised and grazed knuckle on the chisel hand, caused by a miss with the hammer. A regular pattern of raised sharp points on the step worked quite well, but the sharpness wore off quite rapidly in use. Throughout any day there was always movement of the traversing table, in and out and along the shop, each move of a locomotive or tender was preceded by the clang of the traverser bell as a warning to all to watch out. The table driver was Frank Green, one more very close neighbour of mine, living just across the backway about five houses down. In the inevitable cap, his rather long, mournful sort of face scanned shop and road as he reached up to the bell rope for the customary clang prior to moving. Reputedly he had quite a sense of humour, but in all the years I had known him, I could not remember a smile. One afternoon the table moved in from outside the shop, returning a tender which had only gone out a day or so previously. Apparently, resplendent in new paint, it had gone out with its locomotive on a trial run and had been worked back very slowly to the shop with a hot box; the white metal bearing had started to run and the box was blackened by heat generated by a revolving dry axle! Before the foreman could get down into the shop to examine it, the man responsible for filling the boxes with oil was already waiting anxiously to find out what had caused the problem. As soon as the tender had run off the table on to the end of a pit road, he was on the spot, flap up on the axle box 'keep', and his dipstick inserted. As he had feared no oil! He had omitted to fill the keep. While all boxes were assembled on to an oiled axle journal, a supply of oil was necessary to the bearing as the box bedded itself on to the journal. Quickly filling the offending axle box with oil, he awaited the foreman, quite unable to explain how a well-lubricated journal could possibly run hot!

The foreman arrived, to be met with great concern and puzzlement on the part of the oiler on how such a thing could have happened. They looked at the box, tried the dipstick, looked at the keep, and both stood back, seemingly rather baffled. The laugh for the onlookers came when the foreman tried the dipstick in the other five boxes, his expression darkening and his brow furrowing more and more as he progressed round the tender. All were absolutely empty! The oiler had forgotten to oil up the tender completely, so they were both faced with the hilarious (to everyone else) situation that the only box which had seized was the one completely full of oil, now so obviously added after the event! The tender now had to be lifted again and all the journals checked, the hot box dealt with as a new box and remetalled and machined. With the boxes off, the journal could be examined and was found to be discoloured and scored so an axle job was also required. All in all, quite a costly mistake, but what happened to the oiler in question I don't know.

On rare occasions the tenders on which we'd been working seemed to go out together, and we had an almost empty couple of roads. There was great activity and the clanging bell of the traversing table, warning of the movement and the long snake of rope with the large hook drawing the tenders from pit to table. On occasions the rope broke with a dull pop and a shower of rope particles formed a mist, followed by invective from the hookers-on, but usually all tenders were removed without incident and run outside the shop. The waiting road outside was always full of tenders due for repair and these were soon hooked up by the rope, the slowly turning capstan drawing the tender on to the table. A clang of the bell and the table juddered into movement, rumbling in through the double doors with its load. Rope looped round the other capstan, with the hook over the frame, and the tender was on its way to the back end of the pit road. With an operator, one of the table men, on the running board, the tender bumped in the usual three places as its pairs of wheels ran over the slight gap between table road and the pit end, and rumbled along the rails, the hook releasing itself and falling on the end of the table. The tender was followed along by the other table operator carrying a wooden chock or wedge, with a long metal handle bolted on. The man on the top was to put on the brake at the appropriate spot, while the chock holder jammed the chock under one of the wheels.

During the stay in B Shed, several of us had a call to the Manager's Office where we were given a little induction chat and signed for the apprenticeship, a period of five years which at that age seemed to stretch a lifetime away into the future. Back in the shop, all sorts of cautionary tales were told of chargehands we should meet, and jobs we should be required to do, so very often there was an anticipation or a prejudice already instilled from the legends passed on to and by apprentices.

The stay in B Shed was to me, enjoyable, and a revelation of work and people and humour, the latter shown on many occasions throughout the period, some intentional, some spontaneous, but all building towards an awareness of experience. I kept in touch with the fitters I had met, both during and after apprenticeship. Harold, to whom I'd given a black eye, I believe, retired actually during the apprenticeship, so he had been older than I imagined. I still see Ossie on occasions, now getting on in years and long-since retired. Alfie, of the water road and caliper board I remember every time I use the calipers in my own home workshop, having now retired myself.

The time came when the little piece of paper arrived directing me to report to R Shop and to the Scraggery in particular, to the legendary Harry Turner and his perpetually worn cloth cap. The apprenticeship was progressing and the horizons were opening out.

4
R Shop

R Machine Shop was a nineteenth-century whitewashed building, quite tall and reasonably spacious as workshops go, and still with some of its windows blacked out, two years after the war! It was a mixed shop in terms of activities, being a fitting and machining shop, the fitting areas with very solid wooden benches with cupboards underneath, usually back-to-back with other benches, divided by the inevitable chipping screen, closely woven blacked wire mesh standing about 3 feet above the bench back.

The machinery varied from modern lathes installed at the tail end of the late war and since, and some real oldies, the most elderly I remember, although then used for lapping and not turning, was a long double lathe bed, very simple and robust cast iron with two headstocks, very plain, three-step flat pulley arrangements with no provision for backgear and with two tailstocks sharing its length. The bed was cast with 'J. Witworth 1845' in relief (now it would be a collector's item). The belt drive, of flapping flat composite belt, snaked down from the overhead shafting that ran the whole length, or virtually so, of the row of roof support columns, the Victorian cast-iron round pillars so typical of the works itself. The pillars formed a ready support for the shafting which, mounted on both sides of the pillar, made a natural division between two back-to-back rows of lathes and other belt-driven tools. The positioning of the machinery in this way thus left quite a wide space between the rows of columns, and along this area the fitting benches were positioned, along with storage racks and a few more modern self-contained machines.

In keeping with the general layout of the workshops, and in similar fashion to B Shed, which I had just left, the administration and foreman's offices were built high up at one end of the shop, like the bridge of a ship, with a balcony and handrail running the length. From this platform, indeed from the office windows, the foreman had a good view over the complete shop.

Early photographs of the shop show a seemingly tangled mass of overhead shafting and flapping belts down to the various machines but, by the time I entered its portals, it had in part been modernised. Although a great deal of the overhead shafting still existed, itself driven by very large (I believe d.c.) motors, there were numerous large pulleys still on the shafting which drove nothing, the original machine either scrapped and replaced by a more modern self-contained item, or now driven by its own separate motor, the shafting of necessity being retained to drive the remaining machines.

Interspersed among the benches and machine tools were the inevitable steel angle and plate-constructed storage racks for material and finished items, and also the inevitable black-painted, two-door cupboard which, when opened, revealed a miniature self-contained office with stool, desk and filing rack, the abode of the all-powerful controller of apprentices' destinies, the chargehand! As with the foreman's office which overlooked the shop itself, the chargehand's box was usually positioned so that a good view was obtained of his own area and labour force, and each chargehand had his own particular reputation among the succeeding generations of apprentices.

The first move of the apprentice turner, or as it was a combined trade of fitting, turning and locomotive erecting, that portion which comprised turning, was to a quite unique world known as the Scraggery, presided over in the turning side by the (to me anyway) rather awesome figure of Harry Turner! He was a tall, rather heavily built man, clad in pale, washed-out blue overalls, usually undone down the front and never seen without his cap, which he wore at all times, including, according to apprentice legend, when he had a bath and also in bed! A man of few words, his cupboard was screened partly by the back of a narrow storage rack and if at any time a glance in that direction was made, you would observe that cap, the forehead and the two eyes just showing above the top of the rack, constantly scanning, always observing the labours of the eight or so tyro turners learning the first steps of craftsmanship, i.e. to shut up, keep shut up and get on with the job!

Although part of R Shop, itself a rectangle in area, the Scraggery was a small, say 60 feet by 40 feet lower addition, tacked on to the north-east corner, R Shop proper being viewed from the Scraggery through a large doorless opening and several large window openings through the very thick Victorian stone walls, openings which had originally presumably contained glazed windows when the wall itself had been the outside of the rectangular R Shop.

Outside the end wall of the Scraggery and across the road, lay two completely distinct buildings, all (including the Scraggery and R Shop) within a radius of about 50 feet. The first of these was the Manager's Office, again a Victorian edifice, housing the Locomotive Works Manager and his administration function, two storeyed and all oak panels and triple-glazed windows, (the building, not the Locomotive Works Manager!) Parallel to the Manager's Office and covering possibly the same ground floor area, its length stretching away from the end of the Scraggery, was a building in complete and utter contrast, although only about 30 or so feet away from the top brass and white-collar employees. This building was the notorious N Shop or Bolt Shop, a place where, we were informed, miscreants and wrong-doers ended, if their alleged crimes were not sufficient to warrant dismissal.

N Shop was like no other shop in the complete works, even the major 'Hot Shops', the Smithies and Stamping Shop or even the rolling mill were, for all their heat and dust, almost rest cures compared with the Dante's Inferno-like interior of the Bolt Shop. A steam locomotive used a vast quantity of nuts and bolts and screws, from say about $\frac{1}{8}$-inch diameter up to $2\frac{1}{2}$-inch to 3-inch diameter. Depending on the component and its function, the vast array of types could be of ferrous or non-ferrous stock and, with the ferrous or steel items, could be either bright or black. A bright bolt and its associated nut would have started life as a fairly precisely rolled hexagonal bar with bright, scale-free faces, and after passing through various forms of turning process (about which more later), ended as a precise bolt and nut combination, all surfaces being machined or bright and all to again fairly precise limits, some items being required to be a push or drive fit in a specially reamed and prepared hole somewhere in the structure of the locomotive.

Again spanning the size ranges mentioned, there were other positions on the locomotive where a particularly well-finished or bright nut and bolt would not be required, some part exposed to the elements say, or a component which would very unlikely be removed until it was time for it to be replaced anyway, when nuts and bolts could be cut off and scrapped, as opposed to being undone and removed to facilitate their further reuse when they would be cleaned up and oiled to ensure, again, extraction of the component. The reader will also have probably gathered by now that the railway workshops at Swindon were virtually self-contained, manufacturing from purchased raw material all items which went to make up a steam locomotive. Even bolts and nuts were no exception, everything was made within the works and N Shop was the province of the manufacturers of the black nuts and bolts!

On entering the shop, no idea could be gained of its size because generally the working area was so filled with smoke, fumes, and haze that the far walls were indistinguishable from the closely ranked small oil-fired furnaces and associated machinery. This was far removed from modern nut and bolt production where precision machines suck in a length of bar material and proceed within themselves to form a bolt, roll the thread to precise limits, and spew forth a stream of finished items, complete with designatory letter codes on the head of each! In the case of N Shop, the bars were heated in the small furnaces, hand-fed to punch, blank, and upsetting machines, which proceeded to bang, wallop and spark out a sometimes very rough semblance of a scaled, black, smoking, unthreaded bolt or nut blank from the length of bar which had been heated. The bar was then reintroduced to the furnace related to the machine and a further length heated, and the bang, wallop and spark procedure repeated ad nauseum!

The smoke and fumes from the operation seemed to exit from the shop from every crack and cranny, broken window or open door. From the latter on occasions, a grimed figure would emerge, gaze at the sunlight or snow, depending on the season, gratefully gulp a few quick breaths of air and plunge back into murk and gloom like a fire fighter tackling a blaze in the hold of a ship. It will now be understood why the Manager's Office, 30 feet away, was triple-glazed in the windows on that side. Like the area itself, it was all part of the original 100-year-old core of the shops and administration buildings which formed the original Works of Brunel. Little had changed since.

However, having got these often rather roughly shaped nut and bolt blanks, the next process was to provide usable threads and reasonably square and bevelled flat surfaces to the faces of the nuts. This threading and facing process was the function of the inmates of the notorious Scraggery and its equally notorious chargehands.

I have mentioned chargehands in the plural, and here a further little explanation of the structure of railways shops' craft system is in order. For reasons which I have always failed to understand in the craft hierarchy of the system (and I have mentioned my trade of fitter, turner and locomotive erector), a turner was a first grade trade, and comprised use of those machines where the work revolved and the tool, apart from the sliding and surfacing motions, remained still. A machinist, on the other hand, operated a machine in which the tool or cutter revolved and the work, apart from sliding and surfacing operations, remained static. This applied to such operations as shaping, slotting, milling, and both surface and cylindrical grinding, and in these circumstances, the finishing of nuts and bolts was therefore two predetermined separate functions, the latter group being classed as second class tradesmen!

While Harry Turner kept a very beady eye on the activities of the tyro turners, the first function in presenting a finished black bolt and nut was controlled by Dave Simms who was chargehand of the group which put the threads in the nuts and on the bolts. There was an invisible barrier across the centre of the Scraggery which, apart from the chargehands, all appeared reluctant to cross, and there was generally no mixing during the short sit down for the mid-morning tea break, (itself brought in as an innovation to compensate for the long hours worked during the late war and retained afterwards), or for the hand-washing sessions prior to the end of the shift period, when the concrete wash troughs gave out the usual sprays of steam and an oily smelling water mix.

The tapping and screwing area of the Scraggery was at the outer door end, adjacent to the road and Dante's Inferno where the blanks were produced and trolleyed across either to the stores or straight to the tappers and screwers, the whole area littered, although in reasonably orderly fashion, with battered metal boxes about 15 inches by 10 inches by 6 inches with a handle attached to each of the shorter sides and a load of the blanks for the particular operation. The tapping machines were old, belt-driven bridge-like affairs with four to six vertically arranged spindles, each of which held a machine-type tap of the correct thread size for the batch going through. Each spindle was controlled by a handle and with a nut positioned by hand under the business end of the tap, and held by a shaped 'hole' block, suited to the nut size, the lever being pulled down, started the slowly moving tap through the nut blank. When it had completed its full tapping journey, the nut ran off the top of the thread on to the shank of the long tap where it was retained, of course, by the threaded portion of the tap below it. Another nut was then positioned and the cycle repeated until the tap shank contained say ten nuts. A quick movement released the tap and, gripped by the thread and upended over the metal box, the skewered nuts were removed by gravity into the container. The tap was replaced and the cycle repeated – day-in and day-out!

Bolt threading was by screwing machines, a horizontally mounted chuck arrangement gripping the bolt blank which was fed by means of a capstan bar wheel mounted in front of the small machine and controlling a slide, on to a slowly revolving die head containing the appropriate cutting dies for the bolt batch being machined. By holding the capstan wheel still at the 'stop' position, the dies opened and the bolt could be pulled straight out and then released into its tin box along with its fellows.

Any and all engineering machine shops have a distinctive smell, and R Shop was certainly no exception, the lower roof of the Scraggery seemed to hold the smell which was mainly that of the mixed cutting and cooling oils and fluids used in the processes undertaken, and which seemed to hold and get into everything, right down to your underwear, and which could, and in my case did, upset your stomach until you got used to it after a week or two. Strangely even now I can still concentrate and smell the Scraggery.

The complete process of bolt and nut production was very labour intensive and the Scraggery was peopled by the younger members of trades with the exception of, on the tapping side, a senior leading hand and on the turner side, two or three women who had been introduced for machining work during the war, and were still employed in 1946. I believe that as they then left, they were not replaced by other females. They were somewhat older than the male apprentices and it was almost an unwritten law that no conversation was held with them, apart from relating to the work in hand. Harry saw to it that there was no wasted time in chattering!

Following the activities of Dave Simms' merry men, the screwed bolts were in a completed state and were deposited in the adjacent stores to be bagged and despatched over the railway system and throughout the shops, but the nuts were still only semi-complete; the black threaded blanks now had to be faced. The trade grouping now changed from that of the revolving cutter and static work to that of revolving work and static cutters, and it was now that the turning portion of the apprenticeship commenced in a very modest and I must say very boring and sometimes painful way!

That half of the Scraggery which was Harry's domain contained several rows of small scragging machines, I believe about a dozen or so. Those in the centre of the area were comparatively new, in that they were free-standing and self-contained, but along the side wall still stood the early machines, driven by the inevitable length of line shafting and retained for being probably the only ones capable of dealing with the largest nuts, the largest machine of the group being known as 'the killer'! Along the wall separating the Scraggery from the main R Shop proper, were several 'parting off' machines, to which the tyro turners eventually graduated during their period in Scraggery incarceration.

The small machines consisted of a cast pedestal with a hollow stem and open base, roughly say 18 inches square, and the operator faced the screwed spindle nose which protruded directly at him (or her) from the enclosed headstock. A compound slide was positioned in front of the spindle, allowing motion towards and across the end of the spindle nose, controlled by two hand wheels, one to the left and one in the front of the pedestal in similar fashion to a lathe cross and top slides. Also in lathe fashion, a tool post was mounted on the top slide. To the left-hand side was a long handle which operated a fork arrangement, the two prongs of which were adjustable and which extended vertically downwards, one each side of the screwed spindle nose.

The object of the exercise was to select a screwed nut blank, introduce it to the spindle nose which ran in the correct direction for drawing the nut on to itself by, I think, pushing the lever away from you, then, by centralising the lever, the nut could be faced and chamfered by means of the cross slide tools, and finally removed by drawing the lever forward when the forks guided the nut off the spindle and allowed it to fall into the tin box placed in the base of the pedestal!

After a very short while of operating the machine, it became quickly and usually painfully obvious that, while the elements of turning were being learned by the operation of the hand wheels and control of the tools cutting into the revolving metal, the whole operation was controlled by the battle of wits between the operator and the machine in getting the nut blank 'started' on the screwed and slowly revolving spindle nose without lacerating either or both the thumb and forefinger holding the nut! A blank nut had a number of rough edges and sharp scaled corners to do extensive damage, and while the operation was to provide a nut of correct dimensions and faced top and bottom with the required bevel inside at the bottom face and outside at the top face, the stages approaching this ideal condition were fraught with hazards! It would be true, I think to say, that within the first week of a new intake of apprentices to this first stage of training, all would have a grubby piece of bandage or a tatty bit of sticking plaster over at least one of the fingers of the right hand. Often the cut was just through the top skin layers, making it very sore, but still requiring wrapping; occasionally one bled rather freely and if it was the thumb which was cut, it made things that much more difficult. A nut blank could be held with increasing difficulty, between the thumb and a descending order of fingers, depending on those remaining undamaged, and it was often that a previously cut and bandaged finger had the piece of bandage whipped off and rotated by a later nut, whirling round several times before having to be retrieved from the tin under the machine. All in all, a very trying introduction to the craft of turning and rather an off-putting start with pain added! In these days of Health and Safety at Work Acts and the like, I often wonder how it would be viewed, but at that stage it was accepted, somewhat reluctantly it must be admitted, as one of the exigencies of the job.

Apprentices could be switched around for a 'change of experience' according to Harry, which, while a good theory, meant in practice that you moved from a machine facing say the bottom of a huge batch of ⅝-inch nuts, to a machine adjacent facing and chamfering the top face of an equally huge batch of ¾-inch nuts, not really much of a change and still with a battle to avoid cutting your fingers to shreds! In fact the 'turning' became secondary to concentration on avoiding cuts! 'Good for character building, my lads!' would have been the reply to any protests, probably with a modicum of truth as one could always explain to following generations how much more difficult and hazardous it was in your day and how much easier it now is for them!

The larger nuts were faced and bevelled on the old machines against the far whitewashed but oil-stained wall, and there were about three or four retained, set up for a particular size of large nut, the largest nuts being probably those of the drag hooks (the locomotive coupling backing nuts), and those for the spring hangers, the adjusters which held and tensioned the big leaf springs of the locomotive and tender. The largest machine of the lot was known as 'the killer', everything being larger and more cumbersome than on the others. Driven by shafting with fast and loose pulleys controlled by a forked handle which moved the flat belt from a free-running pulley to that driving the machine, everything appeared to be done in slow motion and with seeming difficulty.

Quotas of output had to be maintained and Harry was continually prowling around checking product and producers alike with the same beady eye and silent approach, looking in tins before and after processing, and generally maintained edges on cutting tools and setting of stops.

After four or five weeks came the time for another intake of new apprentices and a move to the parting off machines was looked forward to very much, the thought of cut fingers now looked on as something which would soon be history.

On Monday morning, a group of new faces would appear at Harry's cupboard and several of the old faces would have departed out into R Shop to continue the next stage of the turning craft. Often, for an hour or two at the end of the preceding week, Harry would move those for the parting section on to the particular machine, to be given the general idea of the work by the operator who would be departing the following week, always, of course, with Harry himself hovering in the background to ensure talk was of lengths of material, and how the finished items were to be stacked, etc., and not of how the local football team would do at the weekend!

A steam locomotive boiler had an internal arrangement whereby the steam generated in the boiler proper was recirculated immediately before use in the cylinders through an arrangement of tubes known as 'superheaters'. These tubes returned the steam, in effect, back through the large internal boiler pipes which acted as internal chimneys or heating surfaces through which passed the heat and gaseous products of combustion on the fire grate, and en route to the smokebox and chimney at the opposite end of the boiler. This had the effect of raising the temperature of the wet steam and turning it into dry steam or an invisible gas, a more effective and efficient method of use.

As with all things required for a locomotive, the superheater elements were of course made in the workshops and the Scraggery occupants featured in a small but important way in the production of the superheater elements. The arrangement of the four tubes which comprised each element were attached at the smokebox end to a specially made 'U'-shaped rectangular section box bolted to the superheater header, the tubes themselves passing back through the heat and being, in effect, two long tubes bent double in the centre by means of a 'U'-shaped return bend joining two tubes at the fire box end. It was the piece of tube used for the return bend that the change of scene in the Scraggery now heralded.

The parting off machines were like very old-type lathes from which the tailstock had been removed and which had only possessed a cross slide, no provision for a top slide being made. The chuck was of the collet type, operated by a lever protruding horizontally at the left elbow of the operator. The cross slide had a front and rear mounted tool post, the front one holding a parting off tool and that at the rear a chamfering tool, mounted upside down (of necessity due to the rotation of the chuck). A measuring gauge consisting of a length of ¼-inch-diameter bar with set screw adjusted cross or 'T' piece completing the range of tools required, with the possible exception, although not really a tool as such, of the method of tool coolant and lubrication for the cutting operation.

Cutting fluid was supplied to the cutters by means of a tin, which was attached to a short column-mounted bracket secured to the back of the machine. The tin, about 8 inches tall

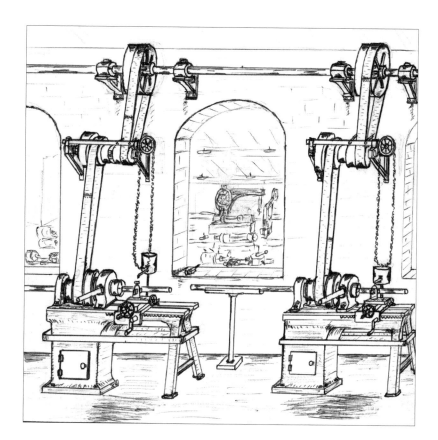

The Scraggery – Harry Turner's parting off machines, cutting tube for superheater return bends.

and 6 inches in diameter, had a long brass spout protruding from just above its bottom rim, complete with a small brass tap. The fluid, and remember this was only just after the war, was a very water-diluted soluble oil, usually known as white water or suds and which, when in use, was allowed to drip in hissing and smoking blobs on to the tool cutting edge.

It was also at this stage of training that would-be turners learned their first inevitable lesson! Using a 'parting off' tool is probably the most difficult of the whole vast range of lathe and machine tools, particularly on an ancient machine which has rather worn bearings and slides. A little bluntness of the tool, or too fast a feed, and there is an ominous lifting of the material being cut, accompanied by a simultaneous depressing of the narrow cutting blade of the parting tool, and production of a large crinkled blob of metal at the cutting edge, often deep in the groove being cut in the material, in place of the thin curly turning or shaving of metal. Accompanied by a momentary stopping of rotation and the hiss of a slipping flat drive belt, the whole episode often terminated in a loud 'crack' as the tool broke!

The hiss of a slipping belt was like a starter's gun to Harry, and in the seemingly split second it took from hissing belt to loud crack, a large shadow would fall over operator and machine as Harry hurtled out of his cupboard in a vain effort to stop the inevitable! He arrived like an avenging angel, often already clutching a pre-sharpened replacement tool, which he proceeded to install while giving a verbal tongue lashing to the very embarrassed, blushing youth who had dared to throw a spanner in the course of progress. In later years and in the light of experience, I often found it better to mount the parting tool in a rear slide as opposed to the front of tradition, but experience is gained always the hard way, and the only way to learn is by actually doing. A further lesson learned was that of setting the tool to the correct height by means of small strips of packing material placed underneath. The level of the cutting edge should be on a centre line of the revolving work; if set too high, cutting is not as effective as it should be, as greater pressure is needed to ensure a cut as the diameter of the material reduces. If set too low, the hazard of the slipping belt saga is repeated, particularly as one approaches the centre of the bar when parting off from the solid. It was a little easier with pipe or tube as there was nothing in the centre anyway. Apprentices at this stage were not allowed to use the grinding wheels for any purpose, so all sharpening of tools was done by the chargehand, and while you just got on with the job on the scragging machines, the chargehand setting the tools as well as sharpening them, the parting machines saw a little further progress when setting the tools under the watchful eye of Harry was permitted. As with the scragging machines, a change of work meant usually a change in the lengths of pipes required, and I believe tube diameters may have altered slightly as well, although the sizes could not have been greatly different as I do not recall ever changing the size of collet in the chuck. The tubes were supplied in long lengths and stored in racks adjacent to the rear supporting trough, which held the tubes horizontal and prevented them from lashing about when a complete length was inserted through the back end of the hollow mandrel and out through the front of the collet chuck. Drawn through from the front, the end of the measuring rod against the side of the parting off tool and the end of the tube gripped against the 'T' cross piece on rod, the chuck was then tightened prior to the cutting operation.

In terms of modern production methods, this was a most uneconomic way of doing things, but there is an important factor to bear in mind. The works at that time had a quite astonishing intake of apprentices and as a producing works actually making items, and not as an academic training establishment, any operator had to make a genuine contribution to the functioning of the works and all apprentices had to be given a grounding in the trades concerned. A number of the jobs which were done, particularly in the turning field, could have been undertaken more effectively by other machines and methods, but with a low-paid apprentice labour force, training had to be related to an actual usable something, produced for use in an existing system!

By starting with the repetitive, straightforward simple things, and by the system of progressive moving of apprentices from job to job, production and training were simply and adequately contained. Obviously the most simple, repetitive jobs were of necessity the most boring once the job had been grasped and the principles understood, but the apprentice himself had the satisfaction of knowing that after say four to six weeks, he would move on to somewhere else in the wide-spreading area of workshops comprising the Locomotive Works.

I had by this time developed and expanded an interest in steam locomotives, a lifelong fascinating subject, and in things mechanical, and was already on the lookout for a small, cheap lathe to install in the garden shed at home, but this item was rather a long time in presenting itself, and also being afforded.

There was within the workforce always a temptation, I suppose strictly illegal when looked at closely, to produce small items for one's own personal use. I have mentioned the dividers and calipers made while working within B Shed prior to moving into the Scraggery, and it was here that the calipers came into use for the first time. In the absence of one of the other apprentices who was away sick for a day or two, I was placed on a parting machine which dealt with a small batch of solid round bar in short lengths with one end radiused. The bar was of about 2 inches diameter, and about 1 foot long, I believe for locomotive spring hanging. However, from the remaining short offcut of bar when a batch had been completed, I cut a small piece about 1½ inches long, turned a recess in one end and a chamfer on the other and, en route through R Shop to the outside toilet, stopped at a radial drill operated by an old school friend. I requested if he could possibly drill a ¼-inch-diameter hole through the centre of the block and also through a ½-inch or ⅝-inch bolt, right through and across the threaded portion near the split pin hole which had been drilled through the turned end, so that the two holes were at 90 degrees. I collected the two drilled items a day or so later when again passing en route to the toilets. With an 8-inch length of ¼-inch-diameter steel rod, a tight fit in the hole in the block, I had my colleague on the 'solid bar' parting machine cut off the drilled bolt a short distance from the ¼-inch hole, leaving about ⁵⁄₁₆ inch of thread on either side. With a thin lock nut on each portion of the bolt end and with the drilled hole slipped over the ¼-inch rod in the block, I had the column and head of a simple scribing block. One lock nut could be tightened against the column and the other against a small steel knitting needle through the split pin hole. Set at the height of the cutting tool of the machine, it made setting to centre level an easier job. Used throughout my apprenticeship, it is still in use today for the same purpose on the small lathe I now have in my home workshop.

The lighting in the Scraggery was, as I recall, reasonably good, and I believe that the new machines were fitted with folding bracket lights. The general lighting was by large round enamel shades with quite powerful bulbs suspended from long lengths of conduit which disappeared into the gloom above the shades and were secured to the old wooden rafters supporting the roof. As with the rest of R Shop, and indeed with the rest of the shops throughout the works, the installation of electric light for general lighting had been a recent innovation, introduced at a late stage during the recent war to replace the gas mantle system. Some of the gas fittings had been bypassed by the new electric fittings, and the two forms of lighting often hung side by side, the gas still being used in the odd corners and stores, etc., in various places. The new lighting had been a contract job, and one of the supervisors of the firm which had installed it had initially lodged with my grandmother, eventually bringing his wife and son to stay when the Doodlebugs and V bombs started to arrive on London.

The widespread installation of the original gas system was powered by the railway's own gasworks, lying at the extremity of the works between the Locomotive and Carriage departments, and behind the locomotive running shed. It was quite an extensive plant, with two large gasometers and a mountain of coal for the furnaces. A by-product of the works was the coke used in the rivet fires, and which could be also purchased by employees; so much was produced. I mention the gas system for a little episode which occurred at this time. Although there were tea urns spread around the shop from which hot water could be obtained at recognised break periods, there was also a temptation to heat up food as well, particularly on the night shifts, a very much frowned on procedure, and with the widespread use of gas, a relatively simple process.

It appears that one ingenious operator had acquired an old gas ring, which he had installed in the hollow base of one of the machines, with a piece of flexible pipe which could be connected to what had been a gas bracket, attached to the nearest roof support column, and had originally held a flexible machine light of some sort. However, having connected it up and put his basin of soup over the jet, he returned later to collect his hot supper, only to find that somehow the gas had, he thought, been turned off as a joke. Actually a draught had blown out the flame and when he struck a match to relight it, the gas had collected in the hollow machine base and ignited with a very loud bang and a flash, which burnt off his eyebrows and a lot of his hair. The whole episode was hushed up at the time, but the supper was warmed with greater care on the next occasion.

Towards the end of the eight-week stay in the environs of the Scraggery, the apprehension with which we had approached the now familiar but then new challenge of starting the turning processes, returned somewhat, as we waited in anticipation of a move to the next phase, out in R Shop proper, and on to machines which looked more like lathes. During this last week, Harry became just a little more communicative and, to us at least, a little more approachable. The next move was always predictable and although we did not know the actual machine we would be working, we did know, by reputation, the chargehand under whom we would next be continuing our activities.

We would all miss the familiar 'whup', which was Harry's way of saying 'You've had a long enough tea break, now get off your backsides and get on with the job', and the little group of us dispersing to our machines carrying empty tea mugs and old floor or packing blocks, which we kept in the metal base of the machines for use as a seat. As I recall there were several tubular metal chairs around which were for the exclusive use of the women members of the group, who did not sit with us anyway. We would also miss, often making a special effort on the last day to witness the event, Harry's ritual of changing his ever-present cap at the beginning and end of a shift. He always wore a different cap in the shop at work and the change ritual had developed over the years. His coming-to-work and going-home cap was always hung on a nail at the side of his cupboard and to change, he stood as close to the cupboard as he could, simultaneously holding the peaks of both caps, then with a move like the magician's 'now you see it – now you don't', one cap was removed and replaced by the other in one sleight of hand movement, a smooth-flowing action which seemed to leave the head permanently covered at all times. Among apprentice legends was that of a previous group of apprentices who, during a shift when Harry was temporarily absent, had nailed one cap to his cupboard! Thus when the fabled move to change caps took place, his head was exposed when a cap refused to move from its hook! This had the same effect in the Scraggery as would a full row of Folies Bergeré dancers high-kicking through the centre, as his head was actually exposed! That particular group of apprentices had a rather difficult time during the rest of their stay with Harry!

We all assembled our few personal belongings, tea mug, overalls, calipers, etc., if we had them, and tucked them away in our cupboards under the machines, or if we were lucky, one of the lockable open wire mesh-fronted wooden cupboards placed in the corner of the working area like filing cabinets. The thing on arriving on Monday morning would be to collect our belongings from these cupboards, have a few shouted words of sympathy to the new knot of apprentices grouped around Harry's cupboard awaiting allocation to the machines with which we had grown so familiar over the past weeks, and to walk to the cupboard of our new chargehand and stand for the usual identification parade and job allocation ceremony, a move being repeated on this morning throughout the Locomotive Works as, like the Mad Hatter's tea party in Alice, 'everyone moved round a chair'. So the little scene being enacted in the Scraggery and with us now in the main R Shop was being repeated in fitting, turning and locomotive erecting shops. In the latter shop, some would be leaving apprenticeship and starting as journeyman or tradesmen, a nominal start only as National Service claimed all, while in B Shed, others would be waiting at the foot of the office steps on their first day.

Our move from the Scraggery was thus to the domain of yet another apprentice legend, to the control of Reggie Emmons.

5

An R Shop Move

The move into R Shop proper did not change our point of checking in or out after each shift, so my timing for getting to the shop a few seconds before the last of three hooter blasts, spaced five minutes apart, did not alter.

The checky, one of the shop labouring staff paid, I believe, a small extra amount to look after the shop check board, would be already standing with his hands on the vertically sliding glass shutter over the porcupine-like board of hooks, each with a numbered disc screwed behind it and your own removable brass numbered check suspended from the hook.

When the final blast on the factory hooter had ceased, the checky was officially supposed to bang down the window or shutter and lock it, but he usually had to wait until the queue had actually cleared before shutting. Anyone arriving when the box was closed had to report to the office and actually book-in in the time book, losing a quarter hour's pay for the lateness. The check was retained until the end of the shift when it was officially to be placed in the box built into the foot of the check board but such was usually the crowd round the box at the end of shift that checks arrived from all angles, often tossed over the heads of the crowd. All strictly against regulations but nevertheless done, as was the strictly illegal throwing in of someone else's check while he departed through the other shops to get as near to one of the gates as possible for a quick exit. In an attempt to beat this problem, particularly in a large workshop, a separate box would be placed at the opposite end of the shop for those whose direction home was best served from that end, but all checking in was done at the board. An even worse offence was that of removing someone else's check as well as your own when you checked in, but as I recall this was not a very frequent happening and, as far as I remember, I have no knowledge of such an occurrence, although the opposite, of throwing in someone else's with your own, often occurred. In the latter case, it was not that someone sneaked off early in the shift, but more that if a couple of minutes could be gained at the end, then it was possible to ensure a seat on the bus home, special buses and special bus stops arranged with the local bus company being laid on for railway workers.

While on the subject of checks and checking in and out, it had been the practice, but had finished when I started my apprenticeship, of checking in and out when visiting the WC! A large toilet block stood in the centre of the yard which actually comprised the centre of the original Swindon Railway Works; R Shop and B Shed on one side, G Shop and Spring Shop opposite, forming the other long side of the rectangle, and one short side being the Manager's Office, while the other side was bounded by a later construction of clerical offices, incorporating underneath the original building in the form of the wire rope shop.

The long double toilet block had one entrance at the end, and just inside was a small office for the attendant, complete with talk through panel in the window and a wooden sill just below a small check board. The system was that, on entering, your check was handed in and retrieved on exit, all occupants being noted in a book kept for the purpose and scrutinised regularly by someone appointed for the task, to sort those who too frequently sat and contemplated work instead of actually doing it! A stay exceeding ten minutes was also indicated in the book by the time recorded, and duly cost the thinker a related stoppage of pay. During my early apprentice years, there were those older members who could remember the original toilet block, and that which now stood on the site had separate cubicles. The wooden doors to each cubicle were about a foot short at the bottom and had a large round hole about 10-inch diameter in the centre, the door being secured by a plain wooden latch arrangement. There were no hooks on which to hang coats, etc., so, usually, you rolled up your jacket to block the hole and as somewhere to hang it. There was very little graffiti on the whitewashed walls in those days.

The original toilet, according to the old boys, consisted of a long low building with an open trough behind a low brick wall with a long slatted seat along the top. Incumbents could engage in friendly conversation with their neighbours while attending to the needs of nature, seated side by side along the wall! A trick used to be apparently to ignite a piece of oily rag and set it moving with the flow of water down the trough! This led to a number of, to use a military term, scorched earth rearguard actions and very sudden evacuation! A further tale consisted of the old lad who dropped his jacket into the moving trough of water. When questioned on its retrieval, he emphatically denied that he could wear it again, but insisted it had to be retrieved because his sandwiches were in the pocket! Such were the legends passed on to apprentices, some certainly of doubtful truth.

However, to return to the checking in. That end of R Shop which contained the board was the one nearest the yard and Manager's Office and the board was about 40 feet into the actual shop itself, approached through a rather draughty space known as the 'Grind House'. I have mentioned that the Scraggery was tacked on to a rectangular 'R Shop', and the short wall of the rectangle contained the foreman's and administrative clerical offices above a store. This construction took up probably half of the wall and was centrally placed. The space left at the Scraggery end contained an entrance door and pathway into the shop between two rows of Turret lathes, operated by some males who, I believe, were also the tool setters, and also by a number of females. The space at the other end was the same approximate area, but had an arched opening and a wall in line with the front of the offices and stores, and I believe there was a draped tarpaulin over part of the arched opening to reduce the draughts blowing in through the double doors. These doors were the entrance and exit for the motor transport, which carried and transported components on the very common flat two-wheeled trailers seen throughout the works.

The side of this small annex contained the three very large belt-driven buffing or grinding wheels. These were used to polish, clean and buff the various components which required a shiny finish before despatch. The wheels were about 15 inches or so wide and of about 3-foot diameter, revolving with their centres just above floor level. The operators sat facing the revolving wheel on a long, flat, solidly constructed narrow platform, (it couldn't really be called a seat), placed endwise to the rim of the grinding wheel and equipped with a flat board arrangement suspended from a spring-loaded bracket over the grinding wheel. The end of the board rested on the long platform and, as I recall, had a padded seat of sorts on it, the platform being cut away on the sides nearest the wheel to accommodate the operator's inner thighs as he sat astride the suspended plank. The component was picked up from the pile adjacent, placed under the plank and against the spinning wheel, and held on to the wheel by sitting on the plank and swinging to and fro, controlling the buffing process. Some of the smaller components could be just held on the wheels by hand, but the whole process looked very precarious. The area was of course rather cold and blowy with the doors open to allow the transport in and out, and in the winter months must have been a grim place to work. One or two of the wheels ran, I believe, through a water trough and while the wheel itself did not appear to run a high speed, there was certainly a water mist around the component and hands of the operator, and a wheel of that size created a draught of its own as it revolved.

It was through R Shop Grind House that one covered the last 40 feet or so to the check board. As well as your own check, there were several other checks which could be displayed, including a red one which denoted absence, and one with the ominous words 'See Foreman before starting'! When changing shops as an apprentice, the checky was the man to see to find out your new check number for the stay in the particular shop, and sometimes to which chargehand you had been allocated, although such was the general interest, and I must say apprehension, that this knowledge was usually dug out before you actually moved, by your chargehand. The move from the Scraggery to Reggie Emmons' gang was a standard second move for turner apprentices and so on this occasion, having removed the check from the board, you proceeded straight to Reggie's 'Box' or cupboard.

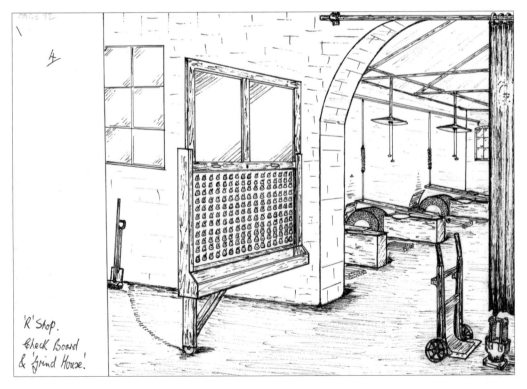

'R' Shop.
Check Board
& 'Grind House'.

The R Shop check board and beyond the Grind House. A typical check board found in every shop in the works.

R Shop was divided into roughly seven areas by the main pathways through the shop. Two pathways split the shop lengthways from the two doors in the short wall by the Manager's Office; one path across the short width, straight through from B Shed on one side to the arch of the Scraggery on the other, about a quarter of the way into the length of the shop; and the fourth pathway joined the ends of the two longer pathways about a quarter of the way in from the other end of the building. There were, of course, other ways and gangways through the maze of machinery, racks and benches, and along the row of roof columns adjacent to the wide gangway leading in from the Grind House past the check board was the row of large lathes, which dealt with locomotive piston rods and piston heads. The other side of the row of columns, and stretching almost halfway along the centre section of the divided shop, were the lathes and machines supervised by Reggie Emmons.

If one was to caricature Reggie, I think the most appropriate would be as a puffin! A short, tubby man with a large hooked nose and permanently pursed lips is how I remember him, who seemed to bounce as he walked, his feet out at the 'ten minutes to two' position, and the forefinger and thumb of his right hand always hooked in his right-hand waistcoat pocket, the other three fingers of the hand curled elegantly into the palm outside the pocket. Reggie was a great character who ruled with a rod of iron, but very fairly, taking time out to explain things if interest was shown, but standing absolutely no messing around of any kind! His eyes were everywhere and he missed nothing, the sight of his short-cut, thinning head bouncing along towards you increased your concentration in the job 50 per cent, with a feeling of relief if he continued to bounce on past you! Such characters always leave a lasting impression and the influence of their advice always remains, and certain actions can leave memories looked back on with humour. Reggie was an inveterate snuff-taker, and the waistcoat pocket into which his fingers were always hooked was the one which contained his snuff box. A fellow chargehand, I believe one of the machinists' chargehands, was also a snuff taker and at regular intervals they appeared to meet in the gangway for a snuff-taking ritual, depending on whose turn it was to proffer the snuff box. On approach, if it was Reggie's turn, he would withdraw the box from his waistcoat pocket with an olde-worlde flourish, hold it between finger and thumb in delicately curled fingers over an upturned palm, and smartly rap on the lid, twice, with the first and second fingers of the left hand, before flicking open the lid.

Following the ritual murmured thanks, the pinch of brown powder was placed on the back of the wrist and sniffed up each nostril in turn. Reggie would then take a pinch and sniff it loudly up his waiting proboscis and, with a flourish, close the box and replace it in the pocket, and after an exchange of a few courteous and traditional words, resume his patrol of labouring apprentices. There was always much speculation among the apprentices about the fairness or otherwise of the snuff-taking arrangements! Reggie's opposite number in this ritual had a unique, not to say bizarre, right hand. A big man anyway with large hands, he had two thumbs on the right hand, a second small one growing from the base of the 'main' thumb. The question which buzzed around was whether this entitled Reggie to take two pinches of snuff when it was his turn to accept the proffered box?

However, to return to the new move into Reggie's realm! This was the move to a real turning gang with real lathes and the interest quickened, along with the apprehension to the move. The first ten minutes with Reg were spent in sorting out who was who and, in retrospect, it should have been obvious to us all at the time, as our reputations had travelled before us, passed on by our previous chargehand.

There was quite a range of machines on the gang, ranging from specials, which although having the usual lathe-headstock, tailstock, saddle and cross slide, were nevertheless special lathes designed and used for one specific purpose, to the more conventional, maybe a couple of 6-inch by 3-foot centres. The cream of the lot, in my eyes anyway, were right on the end of the line nearest the gangway junction at the check box end of the shop. These three were the newest, or among the newest in the shop and had the legend 'Denham' cast in the all-geared headstock casting. Largish lathes, probably 6-inch by 3-foot centres, I had often looked very enviously at them in my desire to obtain a lathe for the garden shed at home. Here I thought, would be the ideal, but of course would have been far too big for home use, so one continued to dream.

The work which was undertaken by Reggie's gang consisted generally of plain and straightforward repetitive items which were always in constant demand with such a large works and locomotive fleet. On this occasion, I believe about four of us had moved from the Scraggery, and I was allocated a machine, one of the 'specials' which threaded the tapered plug, used in quantity in a locomotive boiler for gaining access with scraper hook and hose pipe for clearing sludge and loose scale from the inside waterways of the boiler. This was known as a mud plug and was about 2½ inches long, including a length of ¾ inches which formed a square section on the largest diameter end of the otherwise tapered steel plug.

The plugs were hot-formed by stamping and so were quite black and scaly. A colleague who moved with me was allocated to the lathe (and this was an actual lathe) which did the turning of the black plug blank down to correct length and diameter to enable me in my turn to cut the tapered thread. My machine was not in the line of lathes which formed the gang proper, but further across the shop, towards the centre, facing a small gangway at a

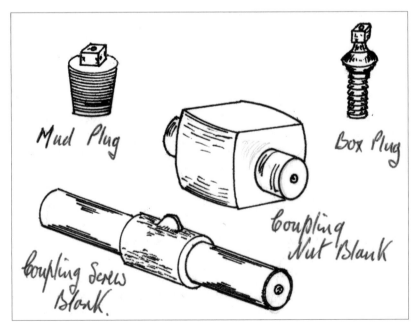

Mud Plug

Box Plug

Coupling Nut Blank

Coupling Screw Blank.

R Shop – the first turning jobs with Reggie Emmons, the charge hand.

level with the last of Reggie's line. Adjacent was the infamous centring machine which, if you were a bit stroppy with Reg, either real or imagined, or if you were 'spare' in terms of ratio of machines available to apprentices available, was where you worked!

The centring machine was used by several groups for preparing material for turning, by inserting in one or both ends of a component, a countersunk drilled hole, so that when mounted in the lathe, one end of the component was supported on the 'centre' or point of the tailstock, and the other end either by the point of the headstock 'centre' or by being gripped in a chuck. Most components machined on Reggie's gang were of the hot-formed or stamped variety and, as such, required such a centring activity. In the event that there was no surplus labour, we each had to do our own centring of the items for which we were responsible, and although I was the second operator in the pair to deal with the mud plug, I had to take my turn with the machine.

The machine consisted very simply of an adjustable clamp-cum-vice/chuck arrangement which held the component, and a spindle which contained a centre drill, being a small pilot drill containing a countersink or coned cutting area at the same taper as that of the standard lathe centre or point. It was a rather tedious and messy sort of job; just clamp, drill to the required depth, unclamp, and return to the tin box. However, it had to be done, so that was that. Leaning my weight on that centring machine lever left a lasting impression.

The job as such, the threading of the mud plug, was also quite straightforward, but was a welcome change from scragging nuts! The plug blank, previously turned to size and checked in a flat plate gauge, contained, (cut in the centre of the $\frac{3}{16}$-inch-thick plate), a truncated tapered slot. Marks on the side of the slot showed the limits within which the tapered, turned blank had to fit to be within the limits for threading on my machine. The machine itself was a rather squat affair, presumably designed to carry out the one job of either turning or threading items short enough to fit. The headstock spindle nose carried a fixture into which fitted the square on the end of the mud plug, while the opposite end was supported by the tailstock centre, entered in the pre-drilled, coned centre hole. For any item in turning which had to be supported by a tailstock solid centre, a tin of grease was kept, replenished on occasions from the stores, and before mounting a component for machining, a finger scooped a little blob of grease from the tin and pushed it into the centre hole in the component end. In the case of the mud plug, these were positioned on the machine drip tray, about a dozen at a time, and a blob of grease smeared into the upturned ends, the luxury of the revolving centre unheard of at that time. The threading was done by means of a chaser cutting tool. Generally in lathe work, not always of course, the required thread is cut by a single point tool mounted horizontally in a tool post. With the mud plug machine, the cutting tool was in the form of a metal strip about 1 inch by $\frac{3}{8}$ inch in section and about 3 inches long, its longer narrow edges forming a dovetail. One of its 1 inch wide faces contained polished ridges, specially cut to the form of the required thread, the ridges tapering when viewed from the end of the strip, from left to right. Mounted in a special holder which gripped the dovetailed edges, the strip was mounted vertically and ground to slope backwards for the required cutting clearance on the top narrow edge. The machine's internal gearing enabled the correct rate of travel to be maintained so that the ridges cut and formed a smooth, polished thread of the correct pitch. The tailstock centre was set off-centre to allow the cutter to follow the tapered shape of the plug which had, when the thread was completed, to fit into the tapered slot of the plate gauge to another final set of limit marks. This was then an introduction to the feel and sound of thread cutting or screw cutting and while after a time it became rather boring, it was another step along the turning path. The machine hand wheels all had a graduated collar round the spindle, which had a series of numbered lines in the manner of ruler, and it was the practice to note the numbers related to the tool position for first and second pass or cut and write them in chalk on the tailstock or headstock casting. We were still not allowed to grind the tools, although we were shown how to reset them in the machines when ground or exchanged by the chargehand. You would suddenly become aware, or at least have that feeling, that you were being watched and, on turning, there would be Reggie, silently watching your actions and also noting the quantity and quality of output building up in your tin under the machine. Mostly he did not say anything, or would just grunt approval before bouncing away down the gangway. Sometimes he would proffer a comment or advice on some aspect, but in all ways he knew, or seemed to know, at all times what was going on. The particular mud plug machine was positioned on one side of the row of columns down the centre of the shop, and on the other side was a row of quite, to me anyway, interesting machines which were also operated by turners and turner apprentices. These machines were the vertical lathes or borers, nicknamed 'roundabouts', and carried out a specific steam locomotive-orientated function. I would mention that steam locomotives had cylinders which ranged in diameter from about 14 inches to about 20 inches, and each piston head was grooved for two rings; I do not recall any more on Great Western locomotives, although there may have been on other companies. The rings themselves were turned from a special grade of cast iron supplied as a cast barrel or cylinder about 18 inches long with three lugs cast on to one end. The lugs were drilled to take the bolts, which were to secure the barrel to the horizontal slotted table of the vertical borers, which then from overhead descending arms, held the tools for turning the outside and boring

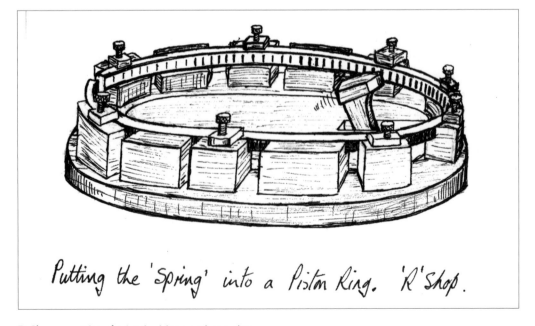

Putting the 'Spring' into a Piston Ring. 'R' Shop.

R Shop – putting the 'spring' into a piston ring.

the inside of the barrel. The turned barrel was then separated into a series of rings about ½ inch thick. The rings were then moved to the machinist function of cutting an angled slot through in one position, and moved again to a quite fascinating little machine which worked in the same way as a trip hammer, which in effect it was.

A piston ring was positioned horizontally in the machine and gripped and firmly supported in both vertical and horizontal planes. The little trip hammer was then set to work and tap-tapped its way round the inside of the ring, which was indexed and slowly revolved around it. The hammer drove a series of small vertical dents or impressions around the inside of the piston ring, being deeper and more pronounced on the side opposite to the slot, and getting shallower as the slot was approached on both sides as the ring revolved. The unusual aspect of all this is that its purpose was to instill into the ring, which was cast iron remember, a certain springiness, something certainly not associated with cast iron, which in normal circumstances is rather brittle when any attempt at bending is attempted. By a process of work hardening, the deformation of the material by the repeated blows of the small rounded V-nosed hammer allowed a small amount of flexibility in the ring, sufficient to allow it to be carefully slid over the diameter of the piston head and snap into its allotted groove, although this was another process in another shop, far removed from the environs of R Shop and turning apprentices.

Although R Shop was a very old building, with very thick walls and a wooden raftered, glazed roof, I do not recall ever feeling cold during my stay. This could, I suppose, be accounted for to a certain extent by the fact of concentration in the job in hand and the adrenalin flow of youth, but the shop itself, as with other machine shops in the works, had a steam pipe heating system both above and below ground. The centres of the main gangways were covered by metal plates, quite thick and peppered with holes with short raised ridges on the top surface between the holes. These plates covered a trough through which ran the steam heating pipes and other services for the shop, and through the holes in the plate wafted the heat into the shop, accompanied sometimes by a little haze of steam when a joint started to blow or 'weep'.

Transport within the shop was generally by means of the Shop Labouring Gang, who covered such activities as cleaning floors, emptying swarf from the machines, and fetching and carrying raw materials and finished products around to the various working and storage sites. The method of transport was by either the two-wheeled sack truck or a two-wheeled, all-metal truck of rigid construction, with a container, like half a short hollow cylinder, mounted on wheels. This latter was for transport of loose metal, items not suited to the sack truck, but both trucks had metal wheels which created quite a clatter over the gangway steel plates.

In keeping with the rest of the works, the flooring in the Machine and Fitting Shops was of wood blocks, all very tightly packed together, being slices cut from say 6-inch by 3-inch or 8-inch by 4-inch timber. Set in the floors with the end grain on the top or wearing surface, the blocks had an extremely long life, being almost everlasting. There were certain places of heavy use where they had worn down into dips, particularly in front of the various machines where the operator stood and moved continually. One of the major advantages of such a floor was that it was very easy on the feet and, although standing for most of the day, or at least moving around a very small area of the machine, I cannot remember ever suffering from aching feet. Such a floor made its repairs or replacement comparatively cheap and simple and the wood deadened the sound of the iron-wheeled trolleys as they moved around.

One of the transporters of materials and pusher of trucks was a rather craggy-faced individual named Bill, who seemed to have a strutting walk like a hen. An ex-military man I believe, or could have been ex-RN, he wore greasy trousers, black boots and a waistcoat over a usually white or off-white shirt, the sleeves of which were always rolled up past the elbow into a very tight roll. One of Bill's duties was to keep the water urns topped up. As they were always on, the water, which was continually kept hot, tended to evaporate, so Bill did a little tour after each breaktime, topping them up from the tap usually positioned on the water pipe attached to the column against which the urn and its table stood. The urn in the vicinity of the mud plug machine was across the gangway, but on the same row of columns at the far end of the shop. The first column on my side of the gangway supported a wheel-operated, stainless bowl drinking fountain and it was a noted thing, if Bill was topping up the urn and someone unsuspecting went to get a drink at the fountain, to cast an eye in the direction and watch the drinker at the fountain. The supply to the urn was on the same pipes as that of the fountain and with the victim at the fountain, Bill would control the water supply to the urn in such a way that it would also control the jet on the fountain.

The victim would approach the fountain, grasp the wheel, turn on the jet and bend forward to drink. Bill, by increasing the flow into the urn, would reduce the jet at the fountain. As the victim bent forward, the jet would get lower and lower and finally disappear altogether. As soon as the victim straightened up, with looks of amazement at fountain, up would come the jet again! Bending forward, the victim would again chase the jet down to nothing! After two or three attempts and with a very puzzled expression, he would walk away, casting an incredulous glance over his shoulder at the mysterious water fountain. Presumably pondering on the problem, he would later return for another attempt. If Bill was in the vicinity, the same chain of events would occur again and it was often hilarious to watch the renewed attempt. Some thought would have gone into the problem and often the solution appeared to be a change of position at the fountain or an approach from a different angle, and some of the contortions tried in an attempt to get a drink of water had to be seen to be believed; leaning from behind the column or working the wheel with the left hand and standing on the concrete raised rim of the drain below. All sorts of weird antics were tried. If Bill wasn't there of course for the next attempt, and if that attempt included an odd position, it would appear to the drinker that he had cracked the problem as the fountain now operated correctly. The strange contortion was then repeated the next time the victim required refreshment, much to the amusement of anyone in the vicinity, with many a cap pushed back and a head scratched.

The trick was usually played on apprentices who were new to the shop following a 'move around', and if two or three apprentices approached the fountain together, Bill often played the trick on only one of them, leading to accusations and denials with counter accusations being hurled in all directions from those who could and those who couldn't get a drink of water. Having been caught, and we all were, it all helped with a bit of character-building to see the funny side of life, even if you were the victim of a practical joke.

At this period, 1946, we still worked a 5½-day week which of course included the Saturday morning. Work usually proceeded as normal until three quarters of an hour or so towards the end of the shift when things began to visibly slow down. This developed into a time to clean machines, get tools sharpened to start fresh the following week, and also change overalls. A system had been introduced whereby an outside contract firm had been permitted to install an overall system, whereby one could be measured for a set of three boiler suits and, for 1s 6d (7½p) per week, would always have a clean suit to start the week. Quite a number of operators took advantage of this system which was spread throughout the complete works and which operated from a series of metal cabinets placed in each shop. The object was that one suit was being worn, one suit was being washed, and the other was in transit to or from the shop. Any repairs were also carried out and the suit was replaced when worn out; all in all a very good system as in some of the shops the suits got so dirty they would literally stand up by themselves, and washing at home was a tedious job; as a schoolboy I could remember my mother washing my father's overalls. However, it was through overall changing that I had the awesome occasion to displease Reggie! My compatriot who was responsible for turning the mud plugs was the same lad who had started with me on the same morning in B Shed, and such was the demand for the overall system that it was often not possible to get overalls in the shop where you worked. This applied particularly to the ubiquitous apprentice, who always seemed to be on the move. The problem was often resolved by using the system in the shop where your father worked, and I think it would be true to say that 95 per cent of apprentices had fathers or other relatives working somewhere in the shops! This latter applied to us both and, whereas in my case I had to pass L2 Shop on my way in to R Shop so that a Monday morning change on the way to work was not a problem, my colleague had his overalls from AE Shop, virtually at the other end of the Locomotive Works. At the end of the first week on Reggie's gang, came the time when our machines had been cleaned and oiled, quotas well up for the week, and we thought a little wander down to change overalls would be in order, so off we both set, with me just going for the walk to the ever-fascinating AE Shop were the steam locomotives were actually repaired and indeed constructed! We returned just before the end of the shift to find a toe-tapping Reggie waiting for us, gazing at his pocket watch and fixing us with a furrowed brow of displeasure. His opening words are engraved on my memory to this day, 'Time is not supplied for you to walk around the factory in!', as classic a rocket as you will find anywhere, and he continued to expound his rules, (really for the first time as he had not mentioned them before), and finished with the fact that he would be watching us very closely from then on! How much closer he could watch us than he already had been we could not see, but it had the desired effect relating to wandering off to change overalls. The control Reggie exercised was emphasised when one afternoon he urgently had us gather round his cupboard for a pep talk. It appeared that on this particular occasion Reggie had been crossing the yard en route to the toilet (this was itself a revelation to us that he also had the usual human requirements) when he had passed one of the number of scrap wagons, several of which were always waiting on the lines adjacent to B Shed and R Shop for rejected material. With his usual very beady eye he had found a rather chewed up component among the scrap, a component which he had immediately recognised as stemming from his gang! Someone had obviously made a machining mistake, probably broken the tool in the process and had thrown the item in the scrap wagon while he himself had been taking the same route to the toilet.

We had a long lecture on material shortages, time-wasting in turning out scrap items, and on developing the courage to admit our mistakes, in fact quite a lecture! The nature of the component was such that it was easily traceable to the lathe and hence the culprit, but it developed that due to its slightly rusty state, it was traced back to the apprentice who had since moved off the gang in the move round. It was possibly scrapped early in his period on the lathe in question, retained in the cupboard under the machine until the time came for him to move on, when he had then deposited it in the scrap wagon on possibly his last toilet visit on the last day on Reggie's gang! However, we all took note of Reggie's remarks and all dutifully nodded acceptance!

The end of 1946, beginning of 1947, and we were moving towards one of the very coldest of winters for a number of years, although we didn't know it then, of course. We were a year or so out of the war and the shortages of virtually everything were still very much with us. It was quite a common occurrence for the works to be partially blacked out by a power cut. This, apart from the obvious inconvenience, was quite hazardous to anyone working a machine because if one was in the middle of cutting, the momentum of the revolving work was suddenly reduced as the cutting tool acted as a brake and viciously dug in instead of cutting. There would be a visible slowing of the machine, then a sudden stop with a simultaneous 'click' which in the case of the mud plug machine, meant that at least one and usually more of the cutting teeth had broken off the chaser! Everyone looked aloft as the shop line shafting slowed and stopped and the lights dimmed, and on the lathes and millers, operators would be busily engaged in winding out the handles of tool slides so that the tool point could be examined, and there would be muttered cursing and shaking of heads when a small chip was found in the cutting edge of a perfectly ground and set tool, which had been good for a number of further components without resharpening.

With a lathe tool, whether for ordinary turning or screw cutting, there was a single point or cutting edge which could be hand ground back to shape again when the power came back on, but with a milling cutter, specially shaped with a number of cutting edges, one broken edge or point would literally scrap the cutter, so there were other hidden costs and problems whenever a power cut occurred.

After a couple of weeks, it was again time to swap machines and, for quite a short period, I exchanged places with the lad who had been turning the mud plugs; I have a feeling that this was probably Reggie's idea to add more experience for us both. I remember that on several occasions a turned mud plug had not been reduced to the correct diameter and although appearing to be OK, had, because it was too big, jammed the chaser and broken some of the teeth. However it was a welcome change and following Reggie's advice to 'Always get well under the skin of a forging, get under that hard layer of scale', this new experience showed us both that teamwork was the only way. The machine used for this turning was a rather large Dean Smith & Grace 6-inch lathe.

Monday morning came again after several weeks of dealing with mud plugs, and two or three new faces appeared standing round Reggie's cupboard. Time for a move round and we said goodbye to the mud plug forever, although moving on to a new set of machines, which in effect did a very similar job! We had moved now to the line of machinery adjacent to Reggie's box, on to machines which were again really specialist designed. They were both belt-driven from a countershaft, which was itself driven from the main line shafting attached to the roof support columns. The countershaft arrangement was of conventional form, comprising a pulley about 18-inch diameter driven from the line shaft and mounted on a shaft on which it was free to revolve. Immediately adjacent on the same shaft was a fixed pulley. A fork arrangement projected two metal fingers, one each side of the belt from the line shaft to the free running pulley. A lightweight endless chain hungdown from the wheel by means of which the fork could be moved across to push the belt from the free-running pulley on to the fixed pulley, thus causing the countershaft to rotate. On the countershaft, a step pulley was mounted, comprising an arrangement of three different diameters, each the width of the belt drive, and on the machine beneath, the headstock contained a matching step pulley, large diameter to small diameter of the countershaft pulley.

It was not often that speed changes were required, when the belt had to be moved from one step to another, but when it had to be done, the machine was set in motion and a special piece of wood was used to push the belt over and off on to the next pulley step, and thus alter the speed of the headstock mandrel.

These machines were quite old and were confined to turning and threading a short plug with a threaded body, parallel this time, and a combined countersunk and domed head. From the top of the head protruded the usual square for a special key or spanner. The square, as I remember, had to be reduced in diameter where it met the domed head so that it formed a permanent plug, and the square could be cut or twisted off with the wrench when screwed home.

The same process was applied as had been the case with the mud plugs; one of us turning and one threading. I remember threading these and also turning the black blank, but which of the machines I was placed on first I don't recall. Threading was by single point tool and

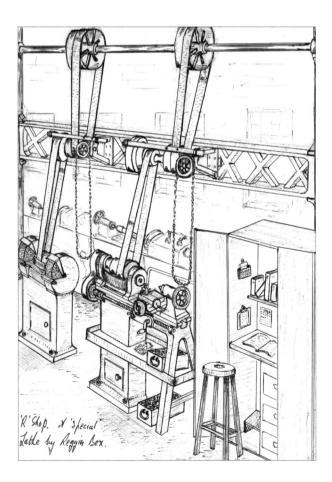

R Shop – the special lathe by Reggie's 'box', used for turning one of the many types of screwed plug.

I think finished with a chaser, the blank held with the square in a special fixture on the mandrel nose and the opposite end supported by the tailstock, of conventional design, on the very short bed of the lathe. There was a 'quick release and setting' arrangement on the cross slide, which had a lever-operated tool withdrawal mechanism which overrode the hand wheel and screw. At the end of the cut, the lever could be just lifted to withdraw the tool and disengage the feed, which carried the cut along, so avoiding the double action of winding out the tool and knocking off what was called the self act or feed.

It was on the threading lathe that I again incurred Reggie's displeasure, although this time for reasons beyond my control, which he eventually accepted. I had been operating the machine for a couple of weeks when I suddenly ran into a spate of chipped cutting points on the screwing tools. After a few days of approaching Reggie with yet another chipped tool, and facing the 'Oh, not you again!' comment, Reggie decided he would have to show me where I was going wrong. After yet another jam and chipped tool, I was told to accompany him to the grinding wheel where he explained the theory of the tool and why, if used correctly, it would cut perfectly for many components. Under a cloud and watched by the rest of the gang, he led a very red-faced me back to the machine, set the tool himself, explained once again the procedure, placed a turned blank between centres and made the first pass or cut. Withdrawing the tool with a triumphant flourish, he proceeded with the second, deeper cut. Part way along the threaded length, there was a momentary hesitation in rotation, a little click, and the tool point had broken once again! 'Ah! I know what's causing that!' said Reggie, 'You've got a slack belt from the countershaft!' With the resistance of the tool actually cutting, the belt had started to slip and the tool acting as a brake, rotation stopped momentarily until the dug-in tool point broke off.

The joint in a flat belt drive was a very simple affair, yet very effective. The belt was of a thick waxy webbing material and each end was cut off square, about 1½ inches less than the complete distance around the two related pulley wheels. By means of a special little machine, a copper wire was screwed through both flat, cut ends, in the same way as the spiral wire found in the binding of some calendars and note books. In use, the belt was placed around one pulley and off the second lower pulley and allowed to rest against its side. A copper pin was placed through both copper wire spirals when they had been pushed together. The special pin was cut from a specially formed length of copper wire, which had small projections to stop it working its way out when the belt was in use. With the belt now joined by the pin, careful operation of the countershaft and use of a piece of wood would allow the belt to be positioned over the pulleys, and the drive was complete.

In the case of the broken tools, the belt joint had worn very badly and had stretched, to the extent that several of the wires had broken in both ends of the belt. Often a belt just broke, and came snaking down from above on to the unfortunate using the lathe, an event usually triggered by the fingers of the moving fork catching in the belt joint when the chain was operated. A belt with a joint about to tear out usually gave audible notice, as well as tending to slip, a slapping noise preceding its descent.

A broken belt from countershaft to machine could usually be put back on by the chargehand, but a belt from the main line shaft to the countershaft had to be replaced by the official 'strappy'. This individual resided in a small, screened-off area in O Shop, which was the tool room of the railway Locomotive Works. His bench and screen walls were covered in pieces of belt of all sorts of size and materials from small round leather to V belts and up to the very heavy 10- to 12-inch width of belt, used to drive the line shafting itself from its large wire screened motor at the end of the line of roof columns.

If an individual belt broke, it meant a walk down to O Shop to contact the strappy and have him make up a new length of belt, or repair the broken belt. This was a little welcome change for apprentices and some of the more unscrupulous would attempt to play on a suspect belt joint by intentionally making the attempt to catch the fork in the joint whenever the chain was used to move the fork across the pulleys. For repair of a belt, the chargehand wrote out an order on an official order form and, with the coiled belt and the order, the walk took one out of R Shop, turning left along the road outside the Manager's Office, past the end of N Shop (still belching black smoke from every orifice), past the Case Hardening Plant on the left and the Rolling Mills Yard on the right, past K Shop coppersmiths and the gas producing Carbide plant, on past the end of the next two shops in line, the 'Whitemetallers', the blank wall of the Brass Shop and the open door of the Angle Iron Smiths, Q Shop, and then across another road, watching out for vehicles and shunted wagons, into and across the end of W Shop, and then waiting for a moment at the heavy wood, glass and steel plate reinforced door of the Boiler Shop. The wait here was for the ears to be closed down, at least psychologically, for what was the short 50-yard walk across a corner of the noisiest shop I have ever been into. Then sharp left through another heavy door and into a dark, wide corridor, 20 yards in on the right, the door to O Shop. Into O Shop, allowing the ears to open up again, just on the left was the little enclosure used by the strappy.

O Shop itself was the ultimate, or considered by many as the ultimate, achievement in the fitting or turning side of the apprenticeship. The various lathes and machine tools, although some of them were rather old, were not confined to the manufacture of components for the steam locomotive, but to a completely independent existence in the manufacture of machine tool items, special tools, jigs and fixtures, and the repair of any damaged machine tool. Such damage could stem from accident or natural wear and tear, and it was to O Shop that such items found their way for repair.

Finding the strappy in residence, the belt and order were left with him, with a 'Come back in fifteen minutes' suggestion from him. Just past the strappy's area was another small set-off area in which the many pneumatic hand-held drilling machines were serviced and repaired. This work was carried out by the father of a friend of mine who was also an apprentice on Reggie's job, and when I went to the area I often had a chat with him for five minutes. Standing near this repair area was a small brick-built room which housed what, I would imagine, was the machine that was the pride of the shop. Looking through the window into the room, the operator could be seen working what I believe was the only jig borer of its type in the works. It was apparently a German machine, then presumably about ten years old, and it seemed rather ironic that the room had been built around it and was really an air-raid shelter to protect it from being destroyed by the very people from whom it had been obtained!

However, time up and back for the belt, now repaired, and with the special piece of joint pin in my overall pocket, steps were retraced back to the more mundane surroundings of R Shop. Reggie was already waiting by the idle machine and, with a short length of ladder, the belt was soon over the pulleys, the joint pin inserted and production resumed. Most of the machine tools of this period had a base which formed a tray into which fell all of the machine 'swarf' or chippings. The base actually had a well section at one end covered by a grille, and just above stood a small pump for projecting a supply of cutting fluid on to the tool point, to both lubricate and cool the action of cutting metal. The fluid was the same as that used in the Scraggery on the nut-facing machines, an off-white mixture of soluble oil and water, with a rather antiseptic smell, although whether it contained any antiseptic of any sort I don't know. On the older machines, these little suds pumps were also worked by a narrow webbing belt which also broke on occasions, and the trip to O Shop strappy was repeated.

Every now and again, Bill of the strutting walk and rolled up sleeves would appear with his metal trolley and a long metal single-ended rake, and production stopped while he went around to the rear of the machine and proceeded to rake out the curled metal turnings produced by the cutting action of the tool. An apprentice learned very early and very quickly how sharp and dangerous such metal swarf could be, and often in turning, a long, spring-like coiled steel length of swarf would be produced. The length as it came off the cutting tool, seemed like a snake, coiling and slithering over the surfaces of the machine, and the temptation to take hold of it and just pull it off had to be resisted at all costs. Sometimes a snaking turning of metal would slither so far and then jam in one of the many crevices on the machine, and the unthinking action of taking hold and just pulling it out could result in very severely, deeply cut fingers.

For brushing aside such swarf, it was usual for a small brush to be provided, a brush which resembled a miniature witch's broom with very stiff bristles about 4 inches long attached to a little round handle. I believe these were also made somewhere in the works, and when the bristles wore down, as they did often, the brush could be exchanged at the stores for a new one; a little wander across the shop, even so it was advisable to let Reggie know what was going on and where you were going.

A further hazard, particularly when making an initial dry cut, (without suds splashing over and obscuring the workpiece), was a very decorative coloured turning, ranging from a dull-look polished steel, through the various shades of yellow and, at the extreme end through the various shades of blue to a deep purple. These cuttings were most certainly to be avoided because not only were they all naturally and dangerously sharp, they were also very hot as well! The apprentice learned early yet another lesson! Within the limits of safety, one was always told when using a machine with any form of rotation, to avoid any and all loose clothing and long hair, although at that period the latter applied only to females! Anything that was loose, even a thread, could catch a revolving component or spindle and draw the unfortunate victim into the machinery as the material wound itself round and round, and so shortened. A simple lesson also to learn was that of the risk of the open neck shirt, particularly one which was loose fitting. It was very painful chasing a small purple turning that had popped off the tool, bounced off your chin and disappeared down the collar of your shirt. With arched back and pulled-out shirt and overall front, a searching, grubby hand probing the waist band of your trousers often chased a hot turning along the front of your stomach before removal was achieved, several little sore places being left where the turning had burned during its wanderings.

This often led to further problems when in the quest to remove the turning, if you had been using automatic feed on the tool, you often forgot to knock off the lever, so the tool continued cutting into an area it was not supposed to go, or worse still, ran into a shoulder on the work, stopped the machine, chewed up the component, often knocking it out of the chuck, or causing it to bend itself into scrap condition, breaking the tool in the process! More problems in explaining to the chargehand!

Loose clothing was certainly a hazard. I remember seeing an apprentice on this gang, working on the Denham lathes, catch his cuff in the jaws of the chuck, which for the particular job was revolving slowly backwards or away from him, and he was slowly, although struggling, lifted off his feet and taken over towards the back of the machine before the stop lever was operated by the lad on the next lathe. He was fortunately not hurt, but certainly the experience would not be forgotten.

Back-to-back with the row of machines, one of which I now operated, stood a further row of large lathes and benches, and the area was generally taken up with the manufacture of piston rods and heads and the assembly of the rod to the 'crosshead' that large sliding arrangement which allowed the linear action of the piston to be transmitted through a large pin and associated connecting rods to the rotary motion of the locomotive wheels.

As I recall, the piston head was dealt with to the right-hand end of the line as faced by me, while at the left-hand end, two or three large lathes produced the piston rods. Although I do not recall this particular end of the line ever having apprentices attached, it could none the less be seen by the apprentices working on Reggie's gang. From my position nearer the middle of the line, I could see the area where the coned end of the piston rod (about which more later), having already been rough slotted transversely was fitted to the crosshead by means of a large flat key, driven in at an angle so that it could be easily assembled when the crosshead was being fitted on the locomotive. The two flat and recessed guide sections of the crosshead (which when white-metalled formed the bearing surfaces on the motion bars) were gripped at an angle in a special little machine so that the roughed out slot through which the flat key would be fitted was horizontal, and the complete assembly of crosshead and piston rod were very firmly supported.

The little machine used was I believe a pull broaching machine operated hydraulically, by an internal hydraulic (oil) system and not from the workshop hydraulic (water) main system. The slot was approximately say 4½ inches by 1 inches with rounded ends, and the special cutters or broaches used were shaped to suit. In essence, a broach is a tool, part of which cuts, and part is very smooth and polished. The polished portion is of very slightly larger size than the cutting portion so that it in effect forces itself past the metal and with a lubricant will impart a very smooth, hardened surface to the internal surfaces of the hole.

The round broach I found later on in the fitting section of the work was in use in a number of locations in the works where bushes had to be inserted in components and the surface internally, while it could have been reamed (using a cutter like a drill which only cuts on straight flutes and not on the point) it was better suited to broaching. The flat key broach for the piston rod/crosshead combination worked in exactly the same way as the round version, but was even more suited to key shape use, being an ideal form of cutter for the job, with the very important tight fit so essential to the safety of retaining the key in the two critical components. Most round broach machines, often seen in motor vehicle repair shops, were of the push variety in which the broaching tool is pushed through the hole in question. With a round hole the lead or plain guide section of the broach, tracks the course of the tool while it is being pushed through to form the hole. With an irregular shape of hole such as that for the crosshead key, the broach would probably have tended to wander, with the result of jamming if pushed through to form the finished shape. A much easier way in this case was to pull the broach through the material as it would then automatically try to follow the force of direction of the pull. In this case the lead on the breach was immediately behind the force of the pull and followed without wandering.

The sizes involved in these components meant that mechanical means had to be available for lifting and movement, and so from free-standing columns or from the roof principles and supports, were suspended a number of swinging jibs and fixed rails along which ran the universally used pulley block and tackle. These were all metal-geared hoists, manually operated by a lightweight endless chain over a wheel. Prevalent over all of the fitting areas of the shop, they were also mounted over all of the bigger lathes and machines, as most or many of the components of a steam locomotive are of large and heavy proportions. The components of a big lathe such as the three- and four-jaw chucks and specially adapted face plates equipped with various component holding fixtures, also required that mechanical assistance be available when a change was required as it was not possible for the operator to lift them unaided, quite apart from the components he may have had to fit into them to secure for the machining process.

The continual rattle of the chain-operated pulley blocks was a feature of work in the shop, as somewhere or other a component was always being moved aside or lifted and positioned. All the blocks were manually operated for both lifting and lowering; there was no form of quick release or other accident-prone features, and the blocks were very robust. In all my years in the works, I never heard of any accident caused by a failed pulley block, all were tested regularly in the special test shop (of which more later), and any accident which did happen to be related to lifting, was caused by incorrect slinging of the component and not due to any failure of the block.

A further aid to lifting was the monorail or walking crane as it was known. The body was about 10 feet long and 2 feet wide and about 2½ feet high, and it ran on heavy grooved wheels which fitted over a rail let into the floor. To one side of the body was a small platform on which the operator stood (I believe the operator was in this case the checky, who also had the crane duties), and the controls were quite simple, resembling those of a tram with various handles sticking up through a control panel. A column of riveted angle, curving to form a jib, had a train of large gear wheels at the top and a bearing of about 8-inch diameter and served the purpose of supporting a swinging crane jib which covered the ground and some of the machine beds to left and right of the rail, and which was itself supported by a carriage around its top which ran between two rails either side of the column and supported from the roof principles, stretching along the shop above the rail in the floor. Its distinctive ringing rattle when in use, the gears causing the 'ringing', could be heard above the general noise of the shop quite clearly.

The crane was a solidly made affair comprising a long body of say ¾-inch chequer plate, the front and rear corners forming a large radius, although front and rear is not probably the correct description as it could be said the crane was just double-ended. In appearance it could have been homemade in the workshops themselves, but I believe it had a maker's plate of some sort above one of the exposed wheel bearings on the side plates. The crane was used to lift the loosely assembled crossheads and pistons for loading into the trailers, which waited at the check board end of the shop in what had become a despatch area, along with the other shafts and items of locomotive components, including safety valves and regulator valves from adjacent fitting gangs.

After a few more weeks on the old screwing machines, came the move most looked forward to, the move on to the new, or at least seemingly new, Denham lathes. I can clearly remember two of these, and I believe the third may have turned the ends of spring buckles. The move was to the first in the line producing coupling screws or rather the blank from which the screwed portion at this stage was ommitted. The blank started as a forging or drop stamping from the Stamp Shop and was about 15 inches long by about 2½ inches in diameter with a centrally placed raised band around the middle, say 2¾-inch diameter and about 2 inches long, with a couple of flat ears about ½ inch long protruding from the raised band. All items were of course first centred in the notorious centring machine near the mud plug lathe and there was a requirement to produce a certain number per day as with all items we produced.

When mounted between centres in the lathe, the object was to face the end down to the supporting centre, turn the body down to the correct diameter for screwing (this threading was done elsewhere, I believe in the Scraggery by the machinists using a screwing machine), and clean up the face of the small raised centre band, the outside diameter and of course the ears being left strictly alone. Having cleaned one half up to the centre band, the blank was removed and replaced end for end between centres, and the turning process repeated, both ends including a radius or lead for the dies in the screwing operation. Again a very straightforward turning procedure using calipers and plate 'Go – No Go' gauges. This gauge was of simple ³⁄₁₆-inch plate construction shaped in effect like two Us back-to-back. The gap between the polished inner edges of one set of U jaws was narrower than the gap between the jaws at the other side. The difference between the jaws was the acceptable limit for the size required. Machining to such gauges was not to the limits of specific size such as a positive measurement by micrometer or vernier caliper, but was quite widely used for many applications.

Backing on to the lathes at this end of the line were the large centre lathes used to turn the ends of the piston rods, indeed to turn the complete piston rod which I believe was turned from a round bar and not from a forging of any kind. The bars were centred and turned roughly on one lathe and finished turned on the other, although I think there were occasions when all machining was completed on one machine. The piston rod in essence comprised a turned centre section which was ground to final dimensions, a screwed section at one end coned to fit into the piston head and a coned plain section at the other end to fit into the coned centre of the crosshead. It was through the latter that the flat key hole was broached, and there were right and left crossheads so that the key protruded at the correct angle from the correct side.

The rod was held by the lathe chuck and centre, supported also by a steady near the crosshead coned end. The cone had to be a virtually perfect fit into the coned hole in the crosshead and to this end, very careful preparation was made. The end was first turned by the experience of the operator to nearly the completed size, the tailstock was pushed back out of the way and the crosshead, supported by the inevitable sling and pulley block, was lowered and positioned to allow it to be pushed on to the turned cone on the rod, which had been previously oiled. The crosshead was swung, still supported, around the cone about a quarter turn backwards and forwards several times, then withdrawn and the rod examined to find the high spots. Depending on the fit, the cone was either skimmed again with the lathe tool, or filed while slowly revolving. I also recollect what appeared to be carborundum paste, or at least oil and carborundum particles, forming a grey film over the coned end of the rod as the process continued, the crosshead being pulled off and examined along with the coned end on several occasions before the rather grey-looking rod was removed from the lathe as acceptable.

The rods at this stage could have had the piston head fitted first, and I believe this to be so. The rod was screwed right through the head with the thread very closely fitting, in other words a tight fit. I recall a machine, which must have been one of the lathes, with an arrangement whereby the rod was mounted in a special clamp, an arm of which either rested on or was attached to a small item which looked a cross between a small bottle jack and a scales with a dial on the front. Presumably in the absence of the torque wrench, the dial gave an indication of the forces at work during the action of screwing the rod into the head. If the machine was a converted lathe or an adapted lathe, the stresses on the components must have been considerable.

I recall the operator at this end of the line as Tom, a tall, quiet, cheery individual who always gave a nod and a smile, but who was, or appeared to me at that stage, rather elderly, maybe in his fifties. I also believe he was rather deaf. His compatriot on the next lathe I recall as John, a much younger, smaller and rather chatty, but an equally cheerful character. With Reggie always on the prowl, however, there was never much opportunity for chatting unless one shouted across the lathes and intervening gap!

The next move along the line came after a further few weeks, and this time to yet another coupling component, the coupling nut. In use, the coupling screw had a nut on each end and a bar through its middle, the coupling links being attached to the nut by means of a 'U'-shaped link, the ends of which were shaped to fit over the two cylindrical lugs of the nut, the eventual fitting being done by the blacksmiths who formed the links of the coupling and eventually bent the U link to shape and to fit.

The coupling nut was a similar type of job to that of the coupling screw, in that a drop forging was centred and the two lugs turned down to the plate gauge requirements, the end faced down to the support centre and the face of the solid square centre section faced. Turned end for end, the process was repeated, a further larger gauge being used to ensure the width of the centre section between the two faces conformed to the required length. The nut was then taken with its batch for the centre section to be drilled and tapped to take the thread of the coupling screw.

Eventually the time came for the next move in the apprentice chain and towards the end of the last week there was great speculation on where the move would be. Reggie came around quite late on the last morning with the little slip of paper which showed I would be going to the P1 Shop; the Boiler Mounting Shop. I knew from experience that this would certainly be different in all ways from the confines of R Shop.

At this period of the apprenticeship, two events were being talked about which, while not really associated with the apprenticeship as such, certainly altered the course of events as far as the Railway Works was concerned. The first was more of an industrial progression in the neverending, or to date seemingly neverending, quest by the workforce for shorter hours for the same or more money. The working week was to be reduced by about four hours at one fell swoop by the removal of the Saturday morning from the working week, giving a forty-four-hour period and eventually introduced in June 1947.

On 6 August 1947, to become effective on 31 December 1947, occurred a further milestone in the history of the works, indeed of the whole railway network throughout the country. This was the nationalisation programme whereby after 137 years, the Great Western Railway (and the other independent systems of course), lost their individual identity in the broad, muffling blanket of British Rail Western Region, as applied to the GWR or to other regional names for the others. There was an air of expectancy and some apprehension when the day eventually dawned, with not a great deal of comment on the shop floor, although one Works Committee Union official was heard to comment 'Good! Now they will have to do as we want and not what they want!' – 'They' being presumably the management side of the operation which irrespective of who is the owner, still has to function as a management' and supervisory body. Whether nationalisation was to succeed, and it appeared that few assembled on the shop floor really had any idea of what to expect (or really cared), was at that time completely unknown, and only now with hindsight can opinions be formed. It must be left to the reader to determine the effectiveness or otherwise of the programme! I think the loss of identity, the loss of the 'Great Western Railway' label was the part most regretted by many as, apart from the undeniable difficulties relating to past prosperity and manpower of the company, there was quite a fierce sense of loyalty, a 'Great Western Railway' man being, or at least feeling, a cut above the rest!

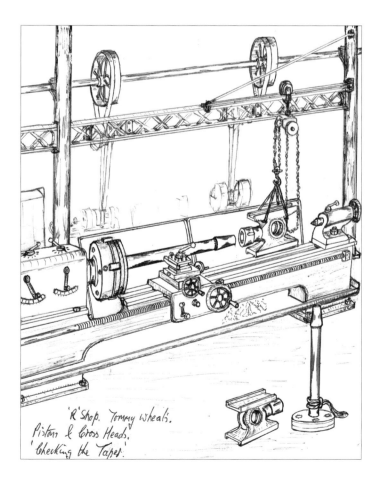

R Shop – Tommy Wheal's gang, where piston heads and rods were machined and assembled and the end of the piston rod taper-turned to fit the coned socket on the crosshead.

6
P1 Shop

P1 Shop always seemed to me to be of an odd design if it was actually used for the purpose for which it had been constructed. It seemed that a change of mind on the part of someone had switched the internal layout to such an extent that everything appeared to be in the wrong place, when looking particularly from the yard outside at the outer long wall of the rectangular shop with its series of arched openings with wooden, sealed doors.

I mentioned previously the walk from R Shop down to O Shop strappy, (incidentally 'down' in terms of the works was towards Bristol and 'up' was towards London, the direction of the main lines which ran through the works at that time). The trip to the strappy took one across the 'up' end corner of the Boiler Shop (V Shop) and if the turn off to the O Shop was passed on the left and the walk continued towards the 'down' end of the shop, the pathway suddenly sloped downwards to a tunnel. At this end of the shop, the outer end wall was actually the boundary of this part of the works, and outside was a road which completely separated one half of the works from the other, the main lines continuing over by means of two bridges. Also at this point was a bridge for foot and ordinary vehicle traffic across the works as well as the tarmac roads along the two rail bridges.

The sloping path and 'tunnel' led under the road, the tunnel showing outside or at least its course was visible, only by close scrutiny of the brick walls of the two buildings on either side of the road. The wall of V Shop and opposite, the P1 Shop, showed a tell-tale arch of blue brick just above pavement level, but many people pass without noticing. The tunnel ran from the corner of the V Shop to the corner of the rectangular P1 Shop which ran its length down the outside road parallel and to roughly the same distance as the wall of the V Shop.

The object of P1 Shop was that in the comparative quiet across the road, the boilers made in V Shop and of course boilers repaired, could have their fittings attached. In one of the various trade demarcations, while the boiler could be made by the boilermaker, all of its fittings, regulator, whistles, safety valve, water-gauge, firehole doors, in fact all of the back head fittings and the casing brackets, which supported the firebox on the locomotive frame, had to be attached by fitters, boilermakers not being allowed to touch this aspect of the work.

The boiler could not of course be trundled across the main road to get it from V Shop to P1 Shop, so adjacent to the pathway through the tunnel separating the two shops, was a very big rectangular hole which stretched the full width of the road and well into both V Shop and P1 Shop. At both ends of the hole, that is at both shops, was a hydraulically operated hoist or lift working from the (water) hydraulic main, which served most shops in the Locomotive Works. The boilers were mounted on specially designed but very simple wagons for the movements from shop to shop, the wagons consisting of an angle iron and plate platform or base, with four unsprung flanged wheels of about 2-foot diameter. At one end of the platform was a simple plate and angle saddle, just one shaped thickness of plate supported by an angle iron frame, the top angle of which, riveted to the single plate, was in the form of a radius to fit the bottom of the cylindrical section of the boiler barrel (which at this stage usually did not have a smokebox fitted, although depending on the nature of the repair could have been retained), just behind the flange to which the smokebox would be attached. The firebox end of the boiler rested usually on large baulks of timber placed across the frame of the base, (the firebox base ring on most boilers not being flat, but having a flat section which then sloped down towards the throatplate, the wood being under the flat section and the taper portion down in the well of the base). These wagons were very common and a great many, one could say all, of the requirements of the work in P1 Shop was carried out with the boiler mounted on its wagon.

The two long sides of P1 Shop were outside walls, not connecting to any other shop, the only access being under the tunnel from V Shop, or from the large open yard on the far side of which stood the massive A Shop's complex. The shop was divided roughly into two lengthways by the width of the traverser table, used to move the boiler wagons on and off the short length of rails which formed work bays or areas down the length of the shop. The wall on the main road side of the shop, that side with the hydraulic hoist platform in one corner adjacent to the access road from V Shop, usually sported a line of boilers in various stages of completion, and at the opposite end to the hoist stood the test boiler, maintained in steam usually daily, which was connected by means of flexible or semi-flexible pipes to boilers just completed and ready for steam test, although such boilers were subjected to a hydraulic test first, a hydraulic test not giving such an 'explosive' failure potential, which would be a risk with a steam test on an untried boiler.

Diagonally opposite the test boiler corner, and in front of V Shop access tunnel was the only exit from the shop into the yard. Adjacent to the access door, and next along the outer wall was a blacksmith forge with all the usual tools and accoutrements related to the blacksmith trade, used for setting the odd rods and plates associated with the boiler. Next along the arched wall with its old wooden doors, long since sealed up, was the turning gang and its lathes which would be my base for a month or two, and from the last lathe in the line to the end of the shop on that side stood the benches of K Shop welders which, with their special small hearths, dealt with the welding of the superheater elements to be fitted to the waiting boilers.

The lathes were the domain of 'Albie' Burton, a dapper little man with a white moustache, glasses, and neat collar and tie, and the seeming sole output of the gang was boiler stays. A boiler, because of the pressures involved and its strangely shaped firebox, was literally full of things other than just water! The cylindrical part of the boiler, although with the Great Western Railway pattern, the cylinder was in reality usually a long, gently sloped cone, supported its pressures relatively evenly and was therefore supported lengthways with solid steel bars screwed both ends into the smokebox header plate and at the firebox end back plate. The firebox itself was one mass of stays which supported its inner and outer shells, the shaped wrapper plate forming the sides and top, the throat plate joining the cylindrical boiler to the firebox and back head with the firehole door and all the other fittings at the cab end. There were dozens and dozens of short stays about say 9 inches long (about which more later), and several very large stays across the top of the firebox from side to side, and from the top down to the crown plate over the fire (*see Chapter 12*).

It was the threading of these large stays that formed the bulk of the work on Albie's gang; the very long stays which supported the length of the boiler and the shorter but still large stays which protected the top section of the firebox. This was quite a small gang in general terms, consisting, I believe, of only the chargehand, two turners, who were on permanent night shift, and three apprentices. The lathes consisted of three Ward 3A capstan lathes, two old and battered Ward turret lathes and one other of an indeterminate make. The lathes were positioned along the arched wall in such a way that a gangway was left between the cupboards and the capstan lathes, the cupboards including the inevitable office of the chargehand, and an old scaffold plank with some sacks on it to form a seat.

Starting at the blacksmiths' fire end, a Ward turret lathe was positioned with the operator standing in the gangway with his back to the wall, then came a long rack on a level with the lathe mandrel or headstock, or roughly so, and at the end of the rack which was about 25 feet long, the second turret lathe, positioned so that the operator faced the gangway and the wall, with his back to the shop, this being the machine on which I started. The three capstan lathes were positioned next, the operators facing the shop with backs to the chargehand's cupboard and the gangway. The turret lathes dealt with the long boiler stays, these being of about 1¼-inch diameter in the centre section with a finished size each end of about 2 inches diameter, threaded and about 4 inches long. One end was finished as a plain flat-faced end, while the other had a protruding square section which had to be undercut to a certain diameter to enable it to be cut off or twisted off when the stay had eventually been screwed home.

The object of the exercise was that my compatriot on the other turret lathe turned and threaded one end of the stay and I in my turn dealt with the other end. The long stays were quite heavy, or seemed to be to a sixteen- or seventeen-year-old, and handling could be a little tricky as the metal was black and scaled, the ends formed hot in one of the smithing shops, not I think by the smith at the end of the line in P1 Shop itself. A pair of leather industrial gloves was part of the essential equipment, as was an apron made from one of the many bolt or component sacks which were readily available from the stores, the apron was not elaborate and just tied around the middle with tar yarn, itself an essential item and available from all locomotive shop stores. The apron did not stay clean very long but at least kept most of the dirt and scaly residue from the rods from making your overalls too dirty. The gloves also did not seem to last too long and those I inherited were very worn, the pulling and positioning of the stay rods through the hollow mandrel and the collet chuck, and then withdrawing the rods to the rack, certainly giving high wear and tear rates.

To say the least, the job was a bit rough! The machines were very worn and battered and although fitted with a cross slide, which had a great deal of play in it, one soon found the quickest way of facing the rod end, by turning the diameter for screwing and turning or just cleaning up about 1½ inches of the stay centre section, was by using the tool on the turret, nominally for undercutting the square only, for all other operations as well. This tool was mounted in a small slide on one of the turret faces and was operated by a hand lever, the mechanism whereby the slide could be locked had long since given up the ghost and the tool now had to be held by the lever as the short cut progressed. It was easy to move the lever in to face the end and do the actual undercut, and also to advance it slightly to clean up the short piece of stay body where the screwed end reduced in diameter, but it took a little practice to hold it steadily while it churned off the parallel section for the screwed portion. Following Reggie's advice from the previous gang, to 'get right under the scale', the tool which we now ground and set ourselves really took some punishment, as did the complete lathe.

The thread was completed by running on a self-opening die head which had four specially shaped chasers or dies contained in a lever-operated cylindrical head on one of the turret faces. The dies were closed by pushing the short lever on top of the head, the turret fed up to the lead cut on the end of the bar and with the revs of the lathe reduced to crawling pace, pressure on the turret saddle lever centred the lead of the dies over the lead on the end of the bar and the cut commenced. The turret had to be hand fed as the cut continued and the dies drew themselves up along the turned cylindrical section of the stay end. Approaching the end of the required threaded portion of the stay, the hand feed to the turret was stopped and the feed held. The dies continued to cut for a short distance to complete the thread, then the cylindrical head moved forward about ¾ inch by itself, clicked and, moving about ¼ turn, opened, the dies ceasing to cut, and removed from contact with the metal.

Operating the turret saddle capstan wheel withdrew the whole die head back over the threaded portion of the stay, which was now ready for removal from the lathe. Two of the three capstan lathes were used in similar fashion for the shorter stays, and in this case one apprentice worked both machines set up for the short stays. The cross slides and other components were in quite good condition on these machines, so it was not a problem to move across to the other machine for tackling the other end of the shorter stays. The third of the Ward capstan lathes was the spare machine, used only very rarely and then only for any special little job which came along.

I recall with this third machine, a job came in and was scheduled for this little-used machine. When the lathe was started and the bed and slides, etc., oiled, it was now a routine thing with an all-geared head machines, as opposed to the old-style exposed three-step pulley arrangement, to check the oil level sight glass in the front of the head casting. This little window into the workings was like a little ship's porthole with a screwed-on brass surround, the little mica window with a line across the middle to denote the oil level. It appeared that the oil was exactly on the level of the line so the machine was started and turning commenced. During the next half hour, it occurred to the operator that the head gears were making rather a noise, so he called Albie to ask if it was OK. He also checked the sight glass and said it was OK as the machine always made more noise than the others. The noise got worse, so again the chargehand was called and he removed the top cover! The inside was completely and absolutely bone dry, not looking as though it had seen any oil at all for the duration of the recent war, and with a layer of fine grit under the dry gears! A good clean out and a complete fill of oil made a great deal of difference, the sight gauge window being cleaned of greasy film which had given a discoloration and appearing as a full level of oil. How much damage had been done by the drought years was not immediately apparent!

My leather gloves were beginning to fall apart so, in these days of shortages of everything, a new pair was obtained and the long stay turning recommenced. A couple of days later at the end of the day, I left the gloves inadvertently on the plank seat next to my cupboard and, of course, by the next morning they had obviously 'walked'! Albie was not very pleased at all and with some difficulty obtained a further pair of used gloves, and these sufficed until the end of my stay; although they were in a rather worn state to start with, at least there were no holes. The gloves were also very useful in the attempt to keep warm as we were now well into the dreadful winter of 1947. The wall along which we worked was the odd one of old wooden arched doorways with the odd half here and there bricked up, but mostly sealed with lengths of old sacking and cotton waste caulked into the worst of the cracks in the old and badly fitting unused doors. The shop was never too warm at the best of times as there was a right of way across the end from the V Shop hydraulic lifts and pathway through to the exit door to the yard, and the opening and shutting of the door didn't help at all. Accompanied by a draught which blew from the lift wells and blast of air which swept in from the yard when the door was opened, all contributed to the rather hard conditions in the shop.

In accordance with the carol, the snow at this period lay deep and crisp, but not very even, being rather black, churned up and frozen solid and, on one Monday morning when we eventually got to the shop, those of us who did not live far from the works, as all buses and trains were delayed, found a grim situation awaiting us. It had blown and snowed again at the weekend and the temperature had dropped seemingly to the bottom of the hydraulic lift well! Several pipes had burst when what bit of heating there was had reached the particular pipe run, but mostly the rather inadequate heating had failed anyway. The wind had whipped the snow into the shop through cracked or slipped glass panes in the roof, and there were little ridges of frozen snow across the floor and tops of the cupboards adjacent to the old, caulked doors. Whatever coats and scarves had been worn to work that morning were again put on over or under overalls as the shop attempted to get moving.

The smith had lit the fire in his forge, but there was a problem as the water coolant for the blower nozzle had frozen and the hammer pond, that rectangular metal tank near all forges in which the smith kept various hammers and swages to ensure tightness of the heads, had its contents locked in a solid block of ice about 18 inches thick, which was carefully being chipped away to assist with a hoped-for thaw when the fire burned through, but with ordinary coal to start and then coke with no blower working, it was a long job.

On the turret lathes, the coolant pumps were frozen solid, as surprisingly was the coolant itself, but in those days of shortages of everything, the soluble oil which formed the basis of the coolant was very, very diluted and the water content was solid. We had to exercise care in touching the lathes, which were very cold, as hands tended to stick when touching the stays. However, without the coolant we couldn't turn anything and so we reported to Albie in clouds of steamy breath. In reply to our complaints about the conditions, we were met with 'That's all right my lads! Work harder and you won't feel the cold!' which I suppose is correct as it was no use standing around moaning about everything, and it was certainly not the specific fault of anyone.

Under Albie's direction we sorted out three short unturned stays and took them along to the blacksmith, very pleased to be able to stand near his fire while the ends of the stays were pushed into the coke of the forge, now spitting a few sparks and showing short blue and yellow flames as it started to ignite, the blower problem now solved. After a few minutes, the bars were withdrawn and with one each, we went back to the lathes and stuck the ends of the stays into the frozen suds, then held the hot bar against the suds pump until the little pulley, with its flat belt, could move freely. Although the lathes were now operable, they were still so cold that little splashes of coolant were still freezing on the slides and parts of the casting where they fell.

In other parts of the shop, particularly with the test boiler and adjacent hydraulic pipes and ordinary water pipes and valves, problems continued for some hours. K Shop operators in the area near the three Ward capstan lathes and on towards the far end of the shop were also having problems with oxygen and acetylene bottles used for the brazing work on the superheater tubes and return bends. The little gas-assisted hearths were all alight whether operators were there or not, in the attempt to get a little warmth into the place. I saw one operator bent over in goggles and leather apron brazing a return bend, with his back close to one of the gas hearths to which he had moved. His actions fanned out the rather ragged back of his old brown smock, which dragged across the gas hearth and ignited on the torn and ragged bottom edge. While we frantically called and pointed, he pirouetted elegantly, turning this way and that while his tail end burned rather fiercely for some seconds, not knowing what all the confusion and shouting was about. A colleague eventually threw some water over the coat and fortunately he was not burned. He was probably the warmest man in the shop that day!

During the tea breaks we usually stood around stamping our feet to keep warm and with hands held closely around our cup of whatever was the brew-of-the-day, in my own case cocoa, made rather thick and with as much sugar as I could allocate from this still-rationed commodity, a long-standing relic of the late war. The weather and conditions dragged on for several weeks more and although bad enough for us during the day, conditions for those on the night shift must have been even worse. We very rarely saw the two turners from the night shift, but sometimes they waited first thing in the morning to see the chargehand about something or other, certainly not hanging around for longer than they had to. We had few visitors down the length of the lathes; sometimes a visit from the foreman, although even that was quite a rare event, and occasionally we would see the scurrying figure of Alfie from the stores, usually waving a piece of paper or stores order form which he considered had not been filled out correctly. A quietly spoken, I believe religious, man, he always seemed to us a little bit of a character, wearing an old-fashioned wing collar and tie, and his trousers always seemed to be too short and of the very narrow 'tin whistler' cut, usually showing the tops of his thin black boots, and when he hurried, a very scurrying, worried gait, his trouser bottoms pulled up so far as to show his socks. He always spoke or nodded, and his quiet tones and phrasing gave the impression that at any time he would stop by our machines and read us a short service.

After swapping ends on the long-stay lathes and moving up for a short time to the turret lathe at the blacksmith's forge end of the gang, I did a few days on the short stays, the 3A capstans a welcome change from the battered turret lathes, and the short stays much easier to handle. Again, a very straightforward, rather simple turning job but another step along the road of experience on which we all walk and which we register for future reference.

I left the shop with the ice and snow still all around, although the weather had started to ease a little. The move was certainly welcome as the conditions in the P1 Shop had certainly not been ideal for the comparative static job which comprised the 'turning' function. It was without a great deal of regret that I handed over my old leather gloves and apron of sacking, and with my compatriots, Ken Brown and Stan Harris, said farewell to Albie Burton and the P1 stay lathes.

This was not the end of the stay saga as my next move took me back to R Shop and the long double line of automatic lathes, which turned out hundreds of the short stays in steel. A further stay producing gang, but one which I did not work with, although it was on the list of possible moves for apprentices, was a rather special area attached to V Boiler Shop, although not subjected to the continuous noise of the place and always known as the 'Monkey House'!

A small workshop area on the long side of the rectangular shop, opposite the side which had the pathway leading to the hydraulic lifts to P1 Shop, and adjacent to the traversing table road between V Shop and L2 Shop, was dedicated to the production of copper boiler stays. Due to the expansion variations of the metal used in the firebox, the inner shell of which was, at that time, formed of copper about ¾-inch thick, the outside of an unlagged locomotive firebox had a definite pattern of the many stays which supported the inner shell, the ends of the stays when screwed home forming a close patterned format of riveted or hammered over ends and nutted ends on some of the stays. The small shop had several automatic lathes which dealt solely with the making of these copper stays, and the shop itself was looked after very much in the fashion of the Royal Mint, so costly at that stage was the material used and so valuable on the scrap market, whether legitimately or otherwise obtained. Very much later on, when I had started fitting, I found a spoiled copper stay, very twisted and useless, which had probably fallen from one of the factory transport trailers, and from which I made a soldering iron, but at that stage actually in the shop, the product and the raw material were very closely guarded, and although I did go in to see what the job actually was, just in case it happened to be my next move, I did not stay long as there was certainly no welcome mat, and while you were not searched on leaving, the impression gained was that even this could have been requested.

However, the last day in P1 Shop saw the little piece of paper arrive, indicating that the three of us, myself, Ken and Stan, were destined for R Shop Autos.

7
Return to R Shop

So back again to R Shop, through the misty, damp and cold Grind House, with a check once again off the board, although a different number from that previously held and on into the shop. Then past the check board, turn right up the gangway leading to the Scraggery, still ruled by Harry of-the-quick-cap-change, and now peopled by yet more fresh-faced innocents to fitting, turning and locomotive erecting. Then a left turn along the gangway before reaching the Scraggery, along the double row of five-spindle Acme-Gridley automatic lathes and, after about 50 yards, stop by the chargehand's cupboard.

The Autos were controlled by, I believe, Roy Barnes, a tallish, heavily built man with a rather square face, which always preceded him as he seemed to stick it forward rather aggressively when he walked, leading with his chin as they say. Following the preliminaries, names checked with numbers on his list, we were allocated an area or group of Autos and introduced to the setter, who looked after our particular patch. I started with Les who looked after about six of the machines at the Scraggery end of the line; he it was who had the responsibility of tool setting to ensure correct limits on the items produced, mostly at that end of the row, boiler stays in steel. These were the short stays which basically followed on a much smaller pattern, those which we had been manhandling in P1 Shop. These were about 9 inches long, say reduced to ⅝ inches in the centre portion, with about 2½ inches of thread on both ends, which were of about ⅞ inches outside diameter.

The machines themselves, which were fascinating to watch, resembled an overgrown Gatling-style machine gun, a cluster of tubes spaced around a circle about 2 feet in diameter, containing the raw material in the form of round black bars, which were fed at regular intervals on to the main cutting tools in the head, the complete tube assembly revolving at set intervals one fifth of a complete revolution, so that the next process could be performed on the length of bar which was automatically fed to the tools (*see Plate 9*).

The job of the apprentice was really to keep an eye on the machines, to ensure that the bar material was always available, and to refill the feed tubes as required, also under guidance of the setter, to on occasions, actually set a tool yourself. The process was quite fascinating to watch, although everything was continually being sprayed or jetted with a rather foul-smelling special cutting oil, not the usual white fluid used on the lathes. In action, a bar was fed automatically from say feed tube No. 1 up against a stop and the collet chuck automatically closed, as the bar revolved. A ram tool head came out of the headstock and the roller guides centred around the bar which was cut on its outside diameter by the tool which was mounted just behind the rollers for the say 9-inch length of the finished stay. The tool then withdrew, and the tube assembly turned to the next tool station. Again a ram head extended, rollers passed over a portion of the end of the turned bar, followed for a length equal to the screwed length of the end, by a special tool head withdrawn to the side and not cutting. When the designated length for threading had been passed, the withdrawn tool moved forward and started to cut the centre section of the stay, withdrawing again when the length stop was reached. The tube assembly again turned to the next section, which to me was the most fascinating of all, the threading of the stay. The next ram head to extend carried the die box which was itself revolving slightly faster than, and in the same direction as the stay material itself.

In turning, there are various optimum speeds for various materials, usually controlled nominally by the recommended cutting speed in feet per minute of the particular material being cut. With turning the stay, the speed of rotation in terms of feet per minute for the cutting of the outside of the stay shape, was much too fast for the threading process using a die box. This was overcome by enabling the die box itself to rotate, so that by travelling a little faster in the same direction, that of the material being threaded, it actually overtook the periphery of the bar at the correct cutting speed for the thread, the thin turnings from the die box slowly curling outwards as the dies progressed. In the same way as a hand-operated die head on a capstan lathe, when the ram had extended a certain distance, it stopped, the die head continued for a short distance, turned slightly, clicked and opened. The ram head then withdrew, taking the open die head with it, the head passing over the threaded bar and being closed again for the next stay when it had cleared the end of the now threaded stay. On the next turn, a preset parting tool fed itself into the stay at the correct length and the cut stay dropped into the swarf tray under the machine. This operation also slightly tapered the end of the cut bar so that when fed out for the next cycle, the rollers of the first cutting tool were led smoothly on to the bar end for the production of the next stay, and also for the smooth entry essential for the die box later in the process.

Although a tightish security area during the later part of the war, the slow move back to normal enabled a reintroduction of a set time when visitors were conducted around the works. Wednesday afternoons saw the very lengthy 'crocodiles' of literally hundreds of visitors being chaperoned through the various main Locomotive Workshops; I mention Locomotive Works as I am not too sure whether they actually went round any of the associated Carriage & Wagon Shops – I don't believe they did. It seemed that, on occasions, most Wednesday afternoons were taken up by streams of visitors, all sexes and all ages, slowly following the guides along the set routes. On special occasions I believe some apprentices were used as guides, although neither my colleagues or I were involved at this stage.

Being on the 'Auto Bank', always a must for visitors, meant that the winding columns blocked our gangways considerably on Wednesday afternoons so that any loading of machines was always attempted before they came. The bars would be brought by Bill or one of his mates, clattering over the metal plates of the gangway and along the backs of the machines to the storage racks from which we lifted the bars to load into the supporting tubes of the machines. The Autos were set at an angle to the main gangway, the long feed tubes of the first machine passing along the rear of the head of the second machine, and so on along the line. A solid cast handle protruded from the front of the head and, catching the machine just as it had turned its tube assembly over, and before any of the tools had advanced prior to cutting, pushing in the handle stopped the process and enabled the collet chuck to be opened and a bar fed in. Close the chuck and pull out the handle and the cycle recommenced with the new bar. On one occasion, not on a Wednesday, a very special party of VIPs came round, escorted through R Shop by Algy Evans, the head foreman himself, a very rare occasion indeed! The group included a number of high-ranking Army officers, the red tabs on the collars denoting a staff office post somewhere. These were also apparently engineers, so very great interest was generated among the group concerning all things mechanical, and when the Auto line was reached, enthusiasm knew no bounds. Being on the end of the line I had retreated out of the main gangway to the rear of one of the machines turning stays and, strangely enough, a tall, stately red-tabbed officer assembled some of his equally red-tabbed colleagues to explain the workings of the Auto. So far so good! I was out of the way, but with a good view.

All grouped expectantly around the machine, and he expounded at some length on its principles, then invited them to step closer and watch the cycle of events in the production of a stay. From a distance, protected by the guard over the front of the moving cutters, he indicated with his leather bound baton, the various aspects of the cutting cycle and his audience moved in closer and closer. They were all intrigued by the way the cutters withdrew and the whole tube assembly moved around to the next position, and then his explanation reached the workings of the die head, with interest growing by the second. He leaned further forward, still indicating with his stick, as the die head started its cut, and all watched in fascination as the curly, spring-like turnings emerged from the front of the die head, revolving its way around the also revolving stay. Hypnotised, they watched as a curled turning, slowly twisting and undulating, curled its way right up the business end of the coolant oil pipe! The ⅜-inch solid jet of brown coolant oil immediately diverted from the die head and redirected itself with uncanny accuracy and force at the neatly knotted tie between the red-tabbed collars of the nearest person! For a split second the leather wrapped baton remained stationary, then shot up into the air as the astonished recipient of the oil jet leapt instinctively backwards into a confused crowd of onlookers. There was now great concern with handkerchiefs produced, attempted wiping-off but just spreading the foul stuff', faces getting redder, and much concern from Railway Works officials.

As the turning got longer, the end flicked out of the oil pipe without any action on my part and the cycle continued as though nothing untoward had occurred. My recollection is of a confused murmuring and the victim being led away, presumably out of the shop to the Manager's Office for a clean up! Among those left, those who with long faces had tut-tutted the most, the grins became broader in direct proportion to the reducing amount of red on the collars and brass on the shoulders, in the latter case as someone later remarked, there was more polished brass on shoulders and buttons seen that day than we had in our foundry! I suppose the only consolation was that the oil wouldn't show as it was almost the same colour as the tie, shirt and uniform, although it did make rather a funny colour of the red tabs; a sort of shiny purple! However, it was probably a visit long remembered by the military gentlemen concerned.

The activities of Bill and his compatriots included the collection of the turnings not only from the lathes but also from the Automatics, and the metal trolleys were always on the move rumbling to and fro while long metal rakes hooked mounds of matted steel cuttings from the bases of the machines. The amount produced by the Autos as can be imagined, was considerable, as turnings in bulk, while not of great weight, certainly have considerable volume when just cut and not, of course, compressed. The surface area of such cuttings is very considerable, and when cutting oil is used, a certain amount disappears each time the tray is emptied of turnings produced.

These cuttings were not just removed from the shop and dumped into the ever-present scrap wagons; such was the quantity produced that a special little building existed outside R Shop to deal with the refuse of production machines. The 'Oil House' was a smelly, shiny building which contained an apparatus which I believe was in essence an oversize spin drier, the turnings being placed in the drums and spun so the oil was removed for further use.

One of the duties of the apprentices was to maintain the level of coolant in the Autos and for this purpose a special trolley had been prepared; the usual angle-iron frame, one mass of rivets, four iron wheels of about 8-inch diameter, the front pair mounted on a swivelling axle attached to a 'T' handle and a 2-foot by 1½-foot by 1½-foot rectangular metal riveted tank, attached to the trolley frame. The trolley tank was always collected from just outside the Oil House and was always usually full, maintained in this state by the operator whom one very rarely actually saw! I remember him, on the rare occasions he was actually seen, resembling a candidate for an early horror movie, one of the 'Mummy's Tomb' variety. Inside the Oil House, several concrete steps led up to a concrete jetty between the oil separating machinery and if you had occasion to ask for the trolley to be refilled, a tall, gaunt, grey-haired figure would slowly descend the steps, a figure in old brown overalls with a shiny sacking apron to match shiny hands and a gaunt shiny face. The slow measured tread across the concrete jetty and down the steps was emphasised by the large wooden-soled clogs with shiny, oil-soaked leather uppers, held to the wooden soles by large round-headed nails. You could well imagine him cautiously emerging into the light from some subterranean passage from the middle of a pyramid, slowly unwrapping bandages as he walked! Trolley filled, he would return to the inner sanctum, the Oil House door slowly creaking shut and the footsteps fading into the distance.

The Autos opposite the stay machines at the Scraggery end of the line comprised several differing Autos, although all working on the same principle, but with slightly differing internal arrangements. These were the machines which produced the special nuts and studs used in such profusion on a steam locomotive, nuts with special curved faces, nuts eventually to be machined into castle nuts, the plain diameter left on the hexagon of the nut to be slotted like the battlements of a castle so that when screwed home, a slot would be lined up with a hole drilled through the rod or bolt and a split pin inserted, not only retaining the nut on the screw but actually stopping it from unscrewing. These machines had the same brown look, even to the polished slides and cutters, as the stay Autos opposite. Even the distinctive smell of the warm cutting oil pervaded the area, with the same almost invisible mist of oil particles clinging to everything. The smell seemed to get everywhere, right through to socks and underwear, and even in the cupboard at home the aroma lingered. You could open your clothes cupboard on getting out of bed in the morning and it was just like stepping into R Shop without the noise. Even the moths flew smoothly as they seemed to be well lubricated!

All manner of special studs were produced in various diameters and lengths and both round and hexagon bars were continually fed into the machines in one long, continuous production run. Close attention had to be paid to the cycle when the end of the bar was reached after continually feeding out along its length. If the piece fed out was of insufficient length, any lead for the cutters would fail either to be produced or the bar would not run truly and could jam against a roller box cutter or a die head; then there would be a great noise and cloud of smoke as everything chewed up and had to be reset. The output from all the machines was monitored continuously and a very regular check was made to ensure that components conformed to the required limits, some of the dimensions having a reasonably wide higher and lower limit before being out of control.

Having got the machines running and producing, and with the continued attention to size, it was best if all were within limits, to leave well alone and maintain the strict surveillance to ensure a good production run. On the next group of the line, the setter was a character known generally as 'Squeaker'. A rather heavily built man with spectacles and a rather high voice, he was always hurrying about with shoulders hunched up and elbows held high, and never seen without a micrometer, gauge or spanner in his hand. The slightest deviation from a nominal measurement, whether within the plus or minus limits or not, and the machine was stopped and the tools ground and reset. He was friendly enough as a person but a pain to work with as you were forever stopping and starting machines and checking sizes of items produced. A trick played on him was that as he was working around his area of Automatics, someone placed a scrapped item on top of the pile already produced by the now stopped machine. He checked only the top one of the pile and panicked; all the tools were removed, ground and reset, and only then did a very worried, perspiring setter check through the others, since removed from the drip tray, to see how many could be salvaged. Of course there was nothing wrong with the rest so an extremely puzzled man checked them over several times before congratulating himself that he had saved a production run with his attention to detail!

Some of the studs produced had a collar around the middle (studs for casing brackets for example), so that the second thread could not be put on automatically, and in this case as with requirements for small special batches of items which did not form a big enough quantity to warrant a setting on the Autos, a Ward 3A capstan lathe was available. This was the other side of the gangway from the chargehand's cupboard and it was a pleasant change, in the moves around the Auto gang, to get a job on this machine, which was comparatively new and very smooth to operate, everything being well-fitting and crisply operating. I had several interesting periods on this machine, either screwing the ends of studs with collars, or with complete production of unions, entailing turning, screwing and drilling out using the sequence set up on the capstan head, which indexed automatically when wound back against its preset stop. We were shown how to set up the head and stops but as with many things the techniques tend to fade and are lost if not practised and I believe this is the last time I ever touched a capstan lathe.

The final move on the Autos was on to the very big machines at the end of the line, that end nearest to the Oil House. These were dealing with the largest items required in quantity, one of the biggest being a four-spindle example which churned out handrail knobs. These were machined from very heavy bars which took two of us to lift, and were of course shorter than the usual smaller diameter bars used on the other machines. I recall a large form tool cutting the shape of the globe portion which necked down to a tapered base with a flat bottom. The batch would be collected in the inevitable tin and taken to the machinists, where the finished sphere was then drilled either completely or part way through to suit the diameter of the handrail, a proportion being drilled along, I believe, part way to form the end of the rail. On reflection, I have the impression of a special tool head which during its cutting cycle, traversed the tool around a circular or part circular path to give the required radius to the handrail knob.

At this end of the line, large nuts were also machined, from equally large hexagon bars and, as with all the Autos in the line, the basic requirements were the same; keep them clean, watch the finished product to maintain the required limits of measurement and keep them well fed.

A little digression at this point concerning another little happening in the vicinity of the Autos, is that near the end of the line at the Scraggery end was a fitters' section marking-off table, the large flat table used for marking out castings, etc., prior to machining. I remember great activity one day with all the foremen in attendance and the maintenance chargehand there, I believe, all grouped around a large cast-iron block which had just been delivered and lifted by the overhead jib and pulley block on to the table. The block was machined all over and had a union connection screwed into one side, just above the bottom face, which had a series of holes drilled into it. The table had been cleaned off and rubbed with an oily rag, leaving a light film of oil over the surface. Each member there attempted, after a short chat by Algy Evans, the head foreman, to push the block across the table, the very large block being virtually immovable. A flexible hose from the pneumatic main was attached to the union on the block and the air turned on. It was then shown by Algy Evans that the block could be moved at will over the surface of the table with light pressure from one finger, the block gliding effortlessly across the surface in any direction! This must have been an early demonstration of the principles of the hovercraft, although I was not involved of course, and I have no idea how or what it was going to be applied, nor indeed if it was ever more than experiment. It was certainly interesting to watch, nevertheless!

I found the period on the Automatics quite interesting, and referring to the remarks regarding form and setting of machine tools, it was only later, both at work and at home on my small lathe, that the lessons learned were drawn from the memory and applied in practice, although in a different application, the same basic principles still applied.

The next move, after a few weeks on the larger machines of the Auto line, was to AM Shop, the large complex of shops across the yard from P1 Shop and back on to another turning gang.

8
AM Shop

A Shop complex was a very big area, about 11 acres under one roof and possibly the largest locomotive shop complex under such a roof in Europe. AM (M for machine) Shop formed about a quarter of the complete area and was located in the 'up' corner of the area, away from the main line. It was of a more modern appearance than R Shop, with more free-standing powered machines and less overhead line shafting. It was certainly a more airy shop with high metal roof principles and the appearance of more room between the machines, the general gangways also appearing more roomy. It was separated into areas by the same monorail or walking cranes as that in R Shop, although there were now four of them, dividing the rectangular shop, in plan, as one would prepare a paper for a noughts and crosses game, the centre being rectangular and not square, and bisected from end to end by the main through gangway.

Looking at the 'noughts and crosses' paper as a guide, and approaching from P1 yard side, a traversing table ran along the face of the end of the building serving the lines adjacent to the main line, then the end of A (Erecting) Shop, the locomotive testing plant (of which more later), and then AM Shop entrances along the two long lines of the 'noughts and crosses' format; finally the yard at the side of AM Shop, bounded by a very high brick wall backing on to the houses of Redcliffe Street, this side also covered by a crane.

A feature of the shop from a noise point of view was that of the usual hum of machine tools and occasional hammering from the fitting benches, but overall, as with R Shop, the ringing rattle of the walking cranes. The check board was just inside the door at the P1 Shop side of the shop and, contacting the checky again, the correct check removed, I walked to the first left-hand sector and on to the cupboard of chargehand Harold Sawyer, a rather elderly, blunt man who said very little but who, as with all I had met, missed absolutely nothing.

This gang seemed to be rather small in terms of manpower, as I only remember three other lathes and only two of the operators in any detail. Strangely, the two operators lived only a stone's throw from where I lived myself, and that was only about five minutes walk from AM Shop. One worked on my right along the same line of lathes. Not a very communicative man, Joe tended, to me at least, to be rather a cantankerous old fellow, seemingly older than the chargehand, stockily built, red-faced and always appearing short of breath, puffing his lips and blowing regularly. On my left and alternating on night shift, I think every two weeks, was a baby-faced, much younger man. His compatriot on the night shift or alternating day shift, was I believe named Stan, and was dark-haired and black-chinned, quite the opposite. All were engaged in the production of locomotive crank pins of varying shapes and sizes. There may have been other items produced but my memory of the job is that of crank pins.

The other apprentice whose lathe backed on to mine, had already been on the gang some weeks when I arrived and had started on the machine I was now to use, he having moved over to the machine which was used to finish the items I would now produce; in due course the procedure would be repeated, I would move across when a new apprentice arrived. On reflection, as with a number of the jobs carried out by apprentices, this was another example of a training application being used to produce a useful item as opposed to a pure training exercise. With a steam locomotive, the braking system consisted of a large suspended drop-forged hanger behind or in front of each of the driving wheels, whether four, six, eight or ten. At the bottom of each hanger and stretching across underneath the frame to the hanger on the other side of the pair of wheels, was a beam flat section in the centre about 6 inches by 2 inches with a bushed hole about a quarter of the way in from each end. The ends of the beams were turned down to suit the diameter of the bushed holes in the bottom of each hanger, and a fork ended shaft arrangement joined all the beams together longitudinally under the frame, or actually below and between the frame. The hanger behind each wheel was shaped part way up into a slot and it was into this slot that the tongue cast on the back of the very heavy cast-iron brake block fitted, and was secured by a pin through both hanger and block.

A new locomotive had a solid shaft or beam, turned down on the ends to suit the hanger bush, but this on a locomotive exposed to all the weather and dirt thrown up from the track and occasionally lubricated as required by the long-spouted oiler of the driver, often showed very great wear when eventually returned to the shops for routine servicing. There is of course not much of a problem in renewing a plain bush, which in this case was of steel pressed into the hanger, but it was a different matter with a badly worn diameter on the ends of a brake cross beam. The ends would be turned down to a set diameter, several I believe being used within a span of sizes, maintaining the strength of the item, and a sleeve would be shrunk on to the turned down end, the sleeve thus returning the beam ends to their nominal original size.

It was the production of these sleeves that formed the work of the apprentices, and although straightforward in terms of turning, gave a further range of practice to the skills which make a turner. As I mentioned, the economics would now be questioned, but then we just carried out the operations required. The first thing noticed was that it was not possible to just pop a component in the chuck and start turning! The sleeves were machined from a solid bar about 3 feet long and of 3 inches diameter, and initially were positioned in the lathe by an overhead swinging jib and pulley block, the end resting in a roller steady, while the other end was gripped in the chuck. The tailstock end was then given a nice deep centre hole using the tailstock and a centre drill, releasing the roller steady when the bar was supported by the tailstock centre. The first move was to clean up the bar down to the diameter of the collar on the end of the finished sleeve, a collar about ³⁄₁₆ inches thick and of about 2¾ inches outside diameter. The bar was then marked off, using a rule and the parting tool to make a series of grooves down the bar at the length of the finished sleeves, and what would be the outside diameter of the finished sleeve was then turned rather laboriously down, leaving a large radius per the gauge supplied where the diameter met the collar. The grooves made with the parting tool were sufficiently deep to enable the sleeve to be removed when a large drill, held in the tailstock, was applied to the centred end of the bar, now held again by the roller steady for the drilling operation and progressively fed into the bar by operation of the tailstock hand wheel. The drill, when it reached the recess made by the parting tool, automatically severing the sleeve from its fellows. Progressing up the length of the bar and moving the steady as required, produced about six sleeves, but it also meant a considerable amount of machining, and a regular visit from the cleaning out gang with their steel rakes and metal trolleys was a very regular requirement as the swarf really piled up.

The job of my colleague on the other lathe was to bore out the sleeves to a finished size, suitable for them to be heated, passed over the turned down end of the beam and allowed to shrink into position so that the beam could be returned to service. As well as being bored out, the collar or flange was faced, and a large radius machined where the sleeve would be required to fit tight against the collar on the brake beam, the shrinking done by a fitting gang in another part of the shop.

All of these turning activities were under the watchful eye of Harold, his cupboard immediately to my right rear, my colleague who worked with his back towards me having the chargehand on his left rear. It seemed that Harold, or at least that's how it appeared to me, whenever you turned around to place a finished item in the tin or prepared to lift up another large bar with the pulley blocks, was watching over the gang from his usual seated position. With shoulders drooped and head forward like a vulture surveying its next meal, his unsmiling face missed nothing, and he always seemed to sit on his stool on one cheek, his unsupported leg stretched out in front of him, his other knee bent and the heel of his boot hooked over a rung of his stool.

Harold normally walked around, when he moved off his stool, rather slowly and at a fixed pace, but on one occasion I saw him move so fast he just appeared to materialise in one spot after vanishing from his stool! I was reloading my lathe with another bar and was thus facing in the opposite direction to that normally occupied when working my lathe. My colleague had been given a special small order of sleeves to complete from a smaller diameter of bar, and had just reached the stage of trying a micrometer on the outside diameter of the turned bar. Whether he momentarily forgot, or it didn't occur to him that the practice was completely wrong, I don't know, but I saw him pick up a 0–2 inches micrometer and proceed to measure a still revolving bar! Although this practice is often (and possibly incorrectly) completed using calipers, and I have seen every turner I ever knew do it at some stage, one never uses a micrometer in this fashion as once the two anvils are closed, the mike will grip the bar and lock on.

Suddenly Harold had left his cupboard and had materialised next to the unfortunate apprentice, who was almost hurled aside and his micrometer snatched from his hands in one movement. He was then given the most tremendous dressing-down I ever heard administered! I would imagine that experience would last a lifetime and the lesson would never be forgotten.

The Works itself had always been noted for its incentive scheme, if one could call it that, of the long-established piecework system whereby a price is set for each item produced. As an incentive, the piecework system is one of the easiest to administer, but it does need to be based on fact, and something positively measurable. The piecework system was rather a pathetic shadow of what it should have been as it was a negotiated arrangement between the chargehand responsible for producing the component and the foreman responsible for the running of the shop. Without the factor of proven process and correctly established time duration, it became a haggle between the parties involved. The chargehand thought for example that the job could be done for 15s, so he would enter the negotiations claiming 17s 6d. The foreman, on the other hand, would say that the job was worth 11s. The haggle proceeded and eventually the difference would be split and a price eventually agreed. This would be a provisional price for a set period until written in the piecework book and signed for, and it could then not be altered.

It was at this period that the first moves towards dieselisation were being made and although everything was steam and would continue for a number of years, the odd diesel component was finding its way into production. Stan, on the next lathe to mine, had the job, one week, of machining another very small batch of what I believe were new pattern crank pins for a batch of diesel shunting locomotives, pins of different design to those normally encountered, and with a turned portion, I believe, 'eccentric' or offset from the centre line of the pin. The odd shape of the pin, which was eventually set in the wheel and carried the connecting rod joining the driving wheels together, meant that several rechucking operations were required to complete the machining of the pin. Stan had thus to change chucks several times as well as reset the concentricity of the pin for the next operation, and all this added to the duration of turning and hence added considerably to the eventual price allocated by the piecework system.

In all of these operations, tradition played a great part and it was left to the individual chargehands to decide how a job would be done; there seemed to be nothing in the way of a production section determining production methods before the item was due to be produced. In the case of the crank pin, it was very strongly rumoured on the gang, with the instruction 'of course don't tell anyone else', that while the process of changing chucks and continued resetting was continuing and would be used as a basis for setting the piecework price, a special jig or fixture was being surreptitiously made which could be bolted to a face plate and would eliminate all of the chuck changing and resetting. In this way, production time would be considerably reduced and the job would be known as a good payer, but the jig or fixture would not be brought out for general use until the price had been established!

As regards production methods, I had an old school chum who was apprenticed in the Carriage & Wagon Works, and he said, I believe about this time, that the newly developed pump screwdriver (in which the handle is pushed down a very quick helix or course thread to rotate a screwdriver bit), had been banned in the Carriage Repair Shops as it would give those who used it an unfair advantage over those without one! No one seemed concerned that it would improve production but the piecework price was probably based on the bellie brace for inserting screws.

However, we have digressed a little. Immediately in front of my lathe was another batch of roundabouts or vertical lathes, the chargehand being the father of yet another old school friend, Archie Brett. These machines still held a fascination as they had in R Shop and there was a further batch of them near the check board area, dealing with locomotive axleboxes, boring out the cast-on white metal bearings to suit the machined journals of the locomotive wheels. To the right of the check board, as one entered from P1 yard, and stretching for quite a distance down the right-hand wall, was the white-metalling bay where the bearings which required white-metalling (which was a solder-like bearing metal) were dealt with (more on this later).

On the left-hand wall, entering again at the check board door, was another turning gang which had several lathes in different positions in the shop, as well as the bulk of them in the left-hand area as mentioned. The apprentice, or one of the apprentices attached to this gang, was one I rather envied at the time. Just across the gangway near Stan's crankpin lathe was a fairly new machine which dealt with jobbing work. These were the odd one-off or very small batch items which would often not be likely to be repeated, and which gave a considerable variety to the whole field of turning, virtually any material to any shape and size.

I have mentioned (reference R Shop) the location of the foreman's and administrative offices, and in the case of the AM Shop, the offices were again 'up in the air', built well above the shop on the framework of steel girders which enclosed another stores area. Not only were the offices 'up in the air' however, in this case the WCs were also built on the same level, and in this respect the marble halls were again looked after by the ever-present attendant who was responsible for the cleanliness of the place which, in retrospect, could not be faulted. Something which struck me as rather incongruous at the time – the attendant, quite a young fellow, at any time when one passed by his small room, was always writing music! Whether his location gave him inspiration I don't know, but there he was, busily jotting down his notes on manuscript paper (no, in sheets, not rolls), and usually surrounded by completed music sheets. Someone suggested that he must have been composing chamber music, but I would not of course repeat that! How successful he was eventually, or even his name, I don't know.

In the huge rectangular complex of A Shop, the stores' arrangement, with offices and toilet block over, formed a natural boundary between, on the left, again from the AM check board, the AE Shop (erecting) and, at the far narrow end, the boundary was the AV Boiler Shop. Directly in front of me as I faced my lathe on Harold Sawyer's gang, an overflow from the AM Shop rectangle spread a short distance down into AE Shop, forming a small fitting and machining area dealing with locomotive connecting rods, their refurbishing, including boring out the big ends, again one of the many items which were of white-metalled bronze. The actual machining of the connecting rods was undertaken at the far end of the shop, just across the walking crane road, at the junction with the main through gangway from the check board through to the AV Shop. The smith-formed connecting rod was placed on a large, flat-surfaced, cast-iron plate mounted very solidly to form a table and, after being whitened (fitters marking blue would have been of no use on such a size of rough surface), the centres were marked off and the shape of the ends, flat section and fish-bellied centre portion were marked off as scribed lines through the whitened surface and then consolidated by a series of marks made by hammer and centre punch which could still be followed as the course of the shape, should oil, etc. obscure the line in the white surface. Machining the rod was quite fascinating to watch and was undertaken by some rather ancient but very effective machines known as plano mills. In engineering, a planer as such is a large bed that moves to and fro under a bridge, which mounts various tools, like lathe tools in shape, lowered by hand wheels as the bed moves at some speed, depending on the cutting speed in feet per minute of the material under the cutters. The plano mills, while built like a planer, had a table or bed which moved very slowly under the bridge, on which were mounted extremely large milling cutters, themselves rotating at the required speed. These very large, cylindrical cutters revolved horizontally, liberally cooled and lubricated by white suds spraying continually over both them and the workpiece, itself bolted securely down to the bed of the machine by bolts and clamps through the pilot holes in the rod ends at the centre points. The machining heads mounted on the bridge could of course be moved across the bridge as required and the bridge itself was so geared that it rose and fell to follow the shape of the fish-bellied top and bottom surfaces of the rods. A change of rod position and of the cutters, enabled a groove to be machined down the vertical faces of the rod from end to end, thus giving it H section strength, but also making for a lighter weight rod (*see Plate 26*). The walking cranes and the ever-present pulley blocks were certainly required to move these items around the shop and there seemed to be always a batch being moved or machined somewhere. I do not recall the machines ever being idle (there were two or maybe three machines), as a batch was always on order; such was the throughput of steam locomotives through the works.

Similarly, the crankpin lathes of Harold Sawyer were always busy, keeping abreast of the building programme requirements and provision of replacement items for the spares and repairs required.

I mentioned previously the acetylene gas plant in the vicinity of the Case Hardening Plant and Rolling Mill Yard up near R Shop, and there was a similar plant outside AM Shop against the very high wall which backed on to Redcliffe Street. The basis of the gas was carbide and the used, dead, white sludge resulting from the process was the whitener used when marking out. The excess was usually carted away by a snowy-white wagon, brake-locked and sitting on an adjacent siding, and occasionally taken away for dumping somewhere. It was quite usual to go out with a tin and collect a little of the lumpy sludge for use in the shop.

The turning of sleeves and then their boring to the shrink fits required, came and passed by, and while the making of crank pins continued unabated, the inevitable piece of paper arrived, returning me once again to R Shop.

9

R Shop Yet Again

The return to R Shop was to a gang very near the domain of Reggie, but this time under another elderly chargehand, rather thin, dark and craggy, Bob Jack. Some of his machines continued along the line of lathes on Reggie's patch, and stretched to the end of the line where there was one odd lathe for piston head plugs and also the very old, original machine by Whitworth, the simple double head lathe now used by the fitters for lapping, both not the responsibility of Bob. My first move on to the gang placed me on a lathe along the same row as the double head machine and the job was different but it must be said rather boring, in more senses than one, than my previous turning.

A steam locomotive has on its brake gear, a method of adjusting for wear on the brake blocks to ensure correct application to each pair of wheels. The brake rods, which connected the beams for which I had recently turned the replacement sleeves, had a linking arrangement whereby tightening a long cylindrical nut with a hexagon shape for a spanner around its centre, pulled the two halves of a rod closer together and affected an adjustment. The nut, about 14 inches long overall and of about 4 inches diameter was a drop forging, already I believe drilled out through the middle for tapping the thread for the screwed rod ends. The centre of the nut had to be relieved by boring out, allowing a right-hand thread to be tapped in one end of the adjusting nut, and a left-hand thread in the other end. In this way, screwing the nut clockwise or anti-clockwise by means of a large spanner on the centre hexagon allowed the threads to act in unison, either pushing the rod ends apart or drawing them together, depending on the direction of rotation. All that was needed for this job was the lathe, a very stoutly made, simple boring bar, and the drilled blanks! The experience to be gained from this particular job was that of working virtually completely unseen, as the sizes of diameter of the bored out centre length and its relative position from each end of the blank could only be obtained by measurement as nothing could be seen. A small lead was turned in each end for the tap (at least I believe they were tapped, as I don't remember any mention of screw cutting being made), the depth of the small lead being consistent with clearance for the outside diameter of the thread. The number on the graduated dial on the handwheel of the cross slide was noted, the tool wound out until it could be passed down the bore of the nut and then wound in again in a couple of stages, each depth of cut then being traversed along the required length. This simple job served its purpose as it gave a feel to add to the experiences of turning, and differences in the feel transmitted from the cutting tool, along the boring bar, through the cross slide to the hand wheel, gave an indication of cutting, whether smoothly or with difficulty if the tool needed sharpening.

Several things were of interest at this end of the shop and the next lathe on my right was one of a type I have not seen again anywhere. I think I was so interested in the lathe itself

R Shop – turning and inserting the piston head plugs into the tapped holes.

that I have forgotten what it actually turned, although by its size it was suited to quite large items, and on reflection it could have turned the business end of crossheads. As I recall, it was quite short and very squat and its head stock was very large due to its method of spindle speed change. In place of the usual three-step pulley arrangement of the simple lathe, and the all geared lever-controlled head of the more modern machines, this lathe had two pairs of really big V pulleys, with a very thick belt, about I suppose 8 inches wide; the steel faces of the Vs were very shiny, and the special belt as I recall had a series of thick pads on its underside, pads which seemed to be about 2 inches thick and shaped to fit the angled sides of the V pulleys. Speed changes were made by means of two hand wheels on the front of the lathe and turning these had the effect of moving the two halves of one of the pair of pulleys apart, while the other pulley of the pair had its halves moved together. Due to the thickness of the belt, the shaped pads gripped the pulley walls as they moved, becoming effectively larger or smaller in diameter and thus adjusting the speed of the machine. This was a way,

I suppose, of having an infinitely variable speed range between known limits, although it made for a very large, cumbersome headstock. A feature also of this end of the shop was the very regular periods when the ringing of hammers in a very rhythmic pattern seemed to echo around. The gang at the opposite side and opposite end of the line, that which dealt with the production of the piston rod-piston head-crosshead combination, had a further branch at this end of the shop. Two apprentices were attached to this gang for this particular aspect of the work which entailed a combined turning/partial fitting role. A locomotive piston head, say of 18½-inch diameter and 4 inches thick, was actually cast hollow. The large disc of the piston head had holes as cast where the core was removed and these holes had to be blocked up very securely.

The holes, six evenly spaced centrally on a diameter of the flat face of the disc, were carefully drilled out and tapped completely through with a comparatively fine thread. The apprentices were the turners of the plugs, which were fitted into these holes, a plug looking like a very short, fat boiler stay, with a portion of square section to enable the plug to be screwed securely home through the piston head. Once the six were screwed in and the squares cut off, the heads were secured to a very solid fixture set into the floor and the ⅛ inches or so of excess thread on either side of the head was well and truly riveted over into the countersink provided in the drilling and tapping process. The slightly domed effect was eventually turned off the plug ends when the complete head was finish-turned at the opposite end of the line and fitted to its rod, screwed very tightly and permanently and then securely plugged to make sure it stayed put.

Bob, although always around, did not seem to interfere with proceedings if no problems were apparent, so we didn't really have him hovering over us, although he was always available should we need to see him. After several weeks on the boring job, the time came for a change as one apprentice moved off the gang and a new one moved on. My next move was to a lathe at the opposite end of the row of columns where Bill of-the-rolled-up-sleeves still played his tricks with the tea urn water pressure when fresh faces went to drink at the fountain. The lathe, another 6 inches, I believe, was adjacent to the cross gangway leading to the Scraggery and on the end of the same line which contained the machine I had worked earlier to produce mud plugs under Reggie Emmons. On the other side of the gangway was the area directly in front of the stores, which itself was directly below the Foremen's and Admin offices. This area was taken up by a machinists' gang, several grinding machines being located here including the cylindrical grinders which dealt with the piston rods for the vacuum pumps and also, I believe, where the locomotive piston rods had their shanks ground for the final polished finish. A number of slotters also worked in this area, the tools operating vertically in a reciprocating motion, with the heads rising and falling and the large counterbalance weights looking at a quick glance like the oil derricks on the American oilfields. In this area also, and the first machine past the check board, was a very large surface grinder, the horizontal wheel of which had a special arrangement of abrasive segments held in a large rotating head. I often thought how one would fly if it ever became loose, and always held the machine with some suspicion, although as far as I know, nothing untoward ever occurred, and probably such an occurrence did not enter the mind of the operator who seemed to change the segments quite regularly.

The lathe I was now to work produced the spindles for locomotive safety valves and was a more interesting job than that of boring out brake adjusting nuts! The locomotive safety valve of GW pattern came in two forms of bronze casting, one which could be called vertical and the other flat for want of a better description, both of irregular shape. Selecting either type from whichever way it was viewed, one always seemed to be looking at a curved or rounded surface, apart from its flat base. The base was secured by studs to a saddle of cast steel, or forged and machined in such a way as to fit the tapered cylindrical shape of the boiler barrel or top of the firebox. With the flat version, the safety valve casting for the Great Western Railway practice for some classes of locomotive, also included two round but vertical faces on each side of the casting, where the feed water pipes introduced water to the boiler from the injectors. Injectors overcame the boiler pressure which could be as much as 280 psi in the new 1000 class 'County' locomotives.

The injector incidentally was not a pump, but by means of creating a vacuum, a suction overcame the boiler pressure to allow water to be fed into the boiler as the existing water evaporated and was used, the steam produced being exhausted through the chimney. These were cold water injectors as the injector, generally the live steam or small injector, was not suited to lifting hot water. It was thus that the exhausted steam from the cylinders which made that distinctive 'chuff-chuff-chuff' of the steam locomotive as it was blasted out of the chimney, was not condensed and used again. Some very special small tank locomotives used on the underground did have condensers, but they also required a special pump to feed the boiler, and also a condensing arrangement. In both types of safety valve casting, the centre portion had two coned holes, like the valve seats on a car engine, into which a special small valve fitted. The valve was held in place by a strong coil spring operating under and secured by a bridge plate over the top and, through the centre of the spring, with its top end through the guide plate and its opposite end on the valve, sat the spindle I was now to turn! Incidentally, the Great Western brass safety valve cover for the flat type of valve with its open top for the safe expulsion of excess steam pressure, displayed two distinctive shoulders covering the boiler feed pipes, one each side of the boiler barrel, attached to the two vertical flanges on the casting of the safety valve itself. There were some locomotives which had a variation of the flat type of valve and a separate position for the feed water pipes, and the safety valve was just that. In this case (the 2800 class being an example), a special small fitting was used on the boiler top to attach the two feed water pipes, positioned between the safety valve and the chimney.

The safety valve spindles were about 12 inches long and of about ¾-inch diameter in the spindle section, about 2 inches up from what in use would be the bottom end, was a large flange of about 4-inch diameter and about ¾ inches thick. The spindle was centred in the centring machine previously mentioned, and the long end cleaned up to about ⅝-inch diameter and for a length of about 3 inches. The flange was turned to fit the bottom of the spring and the short length below the flange was cleaned up and finished off, by using a steady on the flange, into a point. It was this point that, under pressure of the spring when assembled, held the valve in place. Thus, with the guide top end through the bridge plate which spanned the valve orifice, and the spring in preset compression between the bridge plate and the flange on the spindle, the valve itself was held firmly down into its seat until such time as boiler pressure exceeded the preset spring compression, when the spring was further compressed and the valve opened to atmosphere with the well-known hiss and cloud of condensing steam. Incidentally, a blowing safety valve was an extremely wasteful process, as for each minute, 10 gallons of water and 10–15lb of coal were needlessly expended.

It was while on this machine that I saw a rather humorous but nevertheless painful accident. My lathe at the end of the row was as usual, positioned against the row of roof support columns and the machines backing on to mine were those of a machinists' gang, the machine immediately backing on to mine being a shaper. This machine has a tool holding ram which reciprocates horizontally, the work being moved in a horizontal and vertical plane by suitably positioned slides operated by the usual hand wheel, the cut depth being applied vertically from a slide mounted on the ram head, fed in this case usually by moving the complete ram head on its slides. On a steam locomotive there are several places in which components are to be bolted which are very difficult to get to when the components have to be removed for repair, although often quite accessible when the locomotive is being built and the components are built sequentially. It is often the case that a bolt with a complete hexagon head cannot be inserted directly, as part of the head fouls a component already in place. In practice, it was the usual procedure to take a bolt to the operator of the nearest shears and ask him to half head it, when he would hold the bolt against the blade and a large piece would be removed from the head parallel to the shank of the bolt, although this process damaged the thread. Sometimes the actual design of the locomotive called for a bolt to be machined prior to fitting and such bolts would have literally half the head cut away, sloping back from the diameter of the shank to halfway across the top of the head.

The apprentice working the particular shaper had a batch of such bolts to half head, and these were gripped one at a time in a fixture which was so angled as to present the bolt head to the to and fro motion of cutting tool, which traversed also from left to right and consequently removed the excess from the bolt head. The apprentice had probably done this routine job so often that familiarity led to contempt and the process had developed into a corner cutting (no pun intended!) routine. When the cutter had traversed right across the head, the apprentice opened the fixture clamp, the bolt dropped out, and the next bolt was dropped in, the clamp being rapidly closed without stopping the machine! He did this once too often and when the bolt dropped out, he positioned the next bolt awkwardly so that it too dropped out and he banged the clamp shut on his thumb, which was duly shaped by the still moving cutter, and made a couple of cuts on the astonished victim before the thumb could be released and machine stopped. The victim, not seriously hurt but still considerably shaken, then took a trip to the red box with the little seat at the side, usually prominent at several positions around the shop, several of the operators being qualified first aid men (or women).

From where I stood to operate the spindle lathe, and between the two rows of roof support columns in the direction of the Scraggery stood the shop maintenance benches. The chargehand I believe was a short, dark-haired, bespectacled Scotsman, inevitably known only as Jock, and another fitter, who to us all resembled Peter Lorre, the actor. I just mention these characters as while working on the spindles for safety valves, the lathe suds pump stopped pumping and the gentlemen mentioned came across and had a look. It was quite a simple repair. The content of the suds or cutting oil had presumably affected the filter element, which had broken up and clogged the pump. This formed a little variation in the routine of turning and we had a little chat while the pump was stripped down and cleaned out. We were soon joined by Bob on one of his rather rare visits and he joined in the chat, showing slight irritation at this break in production, but I think he said more to me in the five minutes he was watching the pump being repaired than in my complete stay of a number of weeks under his supervision.

My stay with Bob was coming to an end, and my last move was along the same line of machinery but on the other side of the row of columns back at the end near the tea urn. This was a short-stay move as the time was fast approaching when I would finish with the lathes and start fitting. I can't remember what the component was that was produced by my latest move, but two little episodes are remembered. I was placed with a fellow apprentice on this particular machine to learn the job and was with him for probably a couple of hours while he explained, and I tackled, the requirements. Apprentices had very little contact with the shop foremen, who, while often seen in the shop, usually and probably ethically, always approached the chargehand for any information on requirements, components, etc. With the foreman around, everyone obviously got on with the job and kept their head down, as the saying goes. We had just had appointed a brand new foreman, one of I believe three in R Shop, and I noticed him as he walked up the gangway on the other side of the line of lathes; he walked around the end of the line past the tea urn and came down the gangway behind us as we were at the lathe. From the corner of an eye, I saw him walk down about 10 yards past us and then turn and come back and then stand behind us, ostensibly looking at some material on the floor. By this time I was now doing a little turning under the eye of the apprentice from whom I had taken over, and he (the other apprentice) was just watching. Suddenly a voice addressed us both in terms of getting on with the job, ignoring the presence of the foreman by continuing to talk, 'You!' (addressed to my colleague) 'Get back to your own machine, and who is your chargehand?'

We had no time to reply as a furious Bob Jack suddenly appeared from nowhere with the instruction to us 'Carry on', and the request through clenched teeth to the foreman to 'Kindly come down to my box!' where from what we could gather, the new foreman had the ethics of shop floor life explained to him in no uncertain terms. Normally with a reddish face, it was even redder when he went back to the office. We were not affected by any more visits from Arthur!

The second little episode is also to do with chattering! On occasions, particularly on the way to and from the water fountain or toilets, we would stop for a minute or two to pass a quick word with an acquaintance en route. On one occasion the apprentice who was working the boring out lathe on which I had started, came round to the fountain on the end column for a drink of water. He then walked the few yards down the gangway to my lathe and we had a natter for a few minutes. During this time and from the direction he had just come, a cloud of smoke could be seen over the top of the intervening benches and their chipping screens. The chat continued and my visitor then said, 'Looks as though someone has a real jam up!' Still chatting for a few seconds longer, he then said 'Good God! That's from my lathe!' and rushed off. The smoke had indeed come from his machine and was actually from the V belts burning where the motor pulley was still revolving inside the stationary and friction-burned faces of the belts. In a moment of absent-mindedness, he had started a boring cut and then walked off to get a drink of water. The tool had gone full travel until the tool post had locked against the end of the adjusting nut being bored; all movement had then stopped with the resulting burned belt. He was beaten in a race to the spot by first the turner on the next lathe, who turned off the machine as soon as the problem became apparent, and by Bob himself, who was also there examining this latest halt to production. I don't know what was actually said, but I'm sure my colleague wasn't actually congratulated for his achievements!

However, from the following Monday, I would start fittin.

1. The brake handle dominates this view, with the feed clack handle also visible by the left-hand corner of the typical GWR toolbox. To the rear, the top of the water tank and the angled tank face form the base of the coal space, the coal being retained by the high plate sides of the tender. Note also the fire irons and shovel to the right. (*Author*)

2. The water scoop handle and water level indicator, with the feed clack handle on the right (i.e. on the opposite side to the items shown in the view above). Connecting the indicator to its ball float and level was quite a job, in the space available inside the water tank. (*Author*)

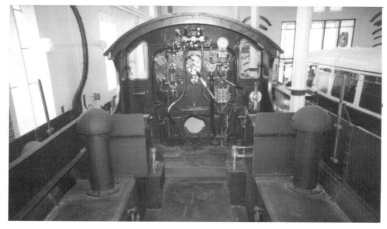

3. A view from the tender coal space toward the locomotive cab. The two cast-iron mushroom-shaped air vents allowed air into the tender to force the water out. Within the cab can be seen the boiler and firebox back head, with its various fittings. The firehole door gear is centrally placed, while the large handle to the right is the reversing screw. (*Author*)

4. At the rear, behind the coal space was the dome covering the outlet and the hinged tank access point. The dome acted as a spreader for water forced up the large pipe when picking up water from the strategically placed water troughs on the Great Western system. (*Author*)

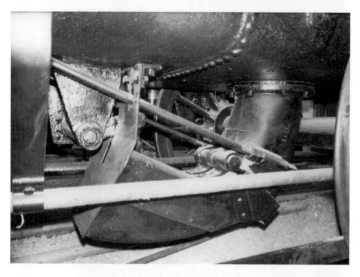

5. Secured beneath the tender, and positioned centrally between the rails, was the water scoop. The arrangement of levers allowed the scoop to be lowered into the water trough to replenish the water supply while the locomotive was on the move. When stationary, the tank was filled through the tank access point. (*Author*)

6. The Scraggery. Facing and chamfering nuts. The larger nuts were not too difficult to handle, but the smaller ones invaribaly ripped the fingers. (*OPC Railprint*)

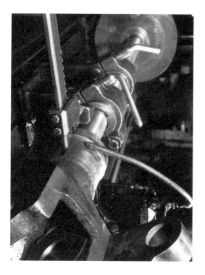

Above left: 7. Pull broaching the cotter slot through a piston rod and crosshead. Note the machined-off plugs in the piston head. (*OPC Railprint*)

Above right: 8. A general view of the central section, taken from the office balcony. Operators in the left foreground include Bill Spackman on a shaper, and Jack Titcombe and Wilf Skull operating two slotters. Note also the ever-present and versatile walking crane (centre right). (*OPC Railprint*)

Right: 9. A line of Acme-Gridley automatic lathes for boiler stay turning. The lathe at the far end of the row was the one that 'annointed' the visiting Army top brass. (*OPC Railprint*)

Below: 10. General notice from the toilet block. Literally time and motion study! Still prominently displayed although no longer relevant in the late 1940s. (*Author*)

G. W. R.
CAUTION.
NO WASTE OR SHAVINGS TO BE USED IN THESE CLOSETS, ANY PERSON DETECTED IN DISOBEYING THIS ORDER WILL BE SEVERELY DEALT WITH.
APRIL 8TH 1891.   BY ORDER.

Above: 11. The use of cotton waste possible. But wood shavings ... ouch! (*Author*)

Left: 12. A vacuum pump, repaired by Stan Major's gang, bolted in place under the running board and connected to the crosshead. The fitting would have been carried out in the Erecting Shop. (*Author*)

Below left: 13. A machining roll that squeezed and shaped the white-hot steel to ensure it was of the correct cross section for the Rolling Mill. (*OPC Railprint*)

Below right: 14. Bill Godbold oversees the machining of a large bronze valve casting for Severn Tunnel Pumping Station at Sudbrook, using the big roundabout or vertical borer. (*OPC Railprint*)

Top right: 15. A long lathe boring a 20-foot gun metal-lined dock gate cylinder. This lathe was later replaced by an even longer version, requiring a recess to be made in the end wall to accept the tailstock at full stretch. (*OPC Railprint*)

Middle right: 16. A period view, taken in the thirties, of the procedure utilised for pressing a throat plate. A finished pressing is to be seen to the right. (*OPC Railprint*)

Below left: 17. A wartime view (note the blacked-out roof) illustrating the rig for drilling a firebox prior to tapping or threading the hole to receive a stay, which screwed into both the outer and inner firebox shell. The apparent quiet and solitude belies the fact that this was one of the busiest and noisiest shops in Swindon Works. (*OPC Railprint*)

Below right: 18. One of the largest hammers forges a locomotive connecting rod. A portable shaping machine was used to square up the top surface. (*OPC Railprint*)

Above left: 19. A white-hot billet of steel about to be passed through the forming rolls. The operator on the extreme left controls the speed of the individual rolls. The iron-plated floor forms the running area beyond the roller, for the extended rolled metal. (*OPC Railprint*)

Above right: 20. An example of a bare, unlagged Great Western locomotive boiler, as captured by the author at Buckfastleigh on the Dart Valley Railway. The seats on the back head accepted the regulator, injector feed clacks, and firehole door gear. Note the casing bracket bolted to the side of the firebox. (*Author*)

21. The main steam engine that drove the bank of rolls, one bank on each side of the engine. A visit from G Shop for maintenance gave the author a unique opportunity to see this engine. (*OPC Railprint*)

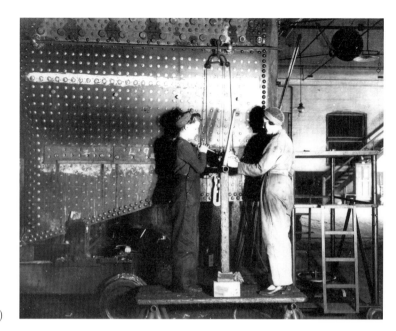

22. A wartime photograph (note the blacked-out workshop) illustrating female staff drilling out the boiler for the casing bracket studs on No. 4950 *Patshull Hall*. Male employees didn't have the luxury of the support stand, using the basic drill post and arm, and hanging on for dear life! The steps in the background led to the shop and foreman's offices. (*OPC Railprint*)

23. An example of the GWR firehole floor gear and fittings. Simple to fit and simple to operate! (*Author*)

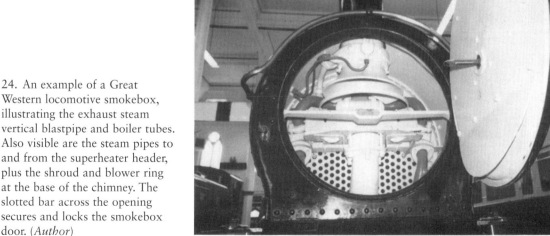

24. An example of a Great Western locomotive smokebox, illustrating the exhaust steam vertical blastpipe and boiler tubes. Also visible are the steam pipes to and from the superheater header, plus the shroud and blower ring at the base of the chimney. The slotted bar across the opening secures and locks the smokebox door. (*Author*)

Above left: 25. A view taken by the official photographer to illustrate the exhibition set of Walschaert's valve gear from the 'Castle' class locomotive (now to be seen in Swindon Railway Museum). The view was taken from the section of the shop occupied by Charley Bailey's Valve Gear Gang. Across the gangway, Charlie Bowen (chargehand) and Ray Shipway look on while minding the cylindrical grinders. Behind the left-hand bench was Harry Jarvis' Reversing Gear gang, while out of picture on the right could be found Harold Angell's choristers. (*OPC Railprint*)

Above right: 26. Denis Mills watches over a Kendal & Gent plano mill as it machines the flutes of a pair of connecting rods. To the right can be seen the old line shafting, still in the rafters. Lower right is a standard steam-and-water-mix wash trough where the grime of a shift was washed off the hands with soap and a pinch of sand. (*OPC Rialprint*)

27. Connecting rod boring machine, opening out the bearings to fit the crankpins. Facing the machine was Harold Glass' con-rod gang. (*OPC Railprint*)

Above left: 28. Chargehand Taylor supervises the lifting of No. 5091 *Cleeve Abbey*, which has had its rear coupled and bogie wheels removed. No. 5091 was originally a member of the 'Star' class, but was rebuilt as a 'Castle', and together with four companions was converted to oil-burning. In 1948 she reverted to coal-burning, but is seen here in oil-burning condition. In the background is preserved Wantage Tramway locomotive *Shannon*, with No. 4975 *Umberside Hall* and the cab of an 'Austerity' 2-8-0 to the right. (*OPC Railprint*)

Above right: 29. Harry Brown adjusts part of the Zeiss apparatus used for examining the alignment of cylinder bores with the locomotive frame. The microscope is already positioned and aligned exactly on the centre line of the cylinder bore, and is now being set on what would be the centre line of the axle in its axlebox bearing in the horn cheek opening. (*OPC Railprint*)

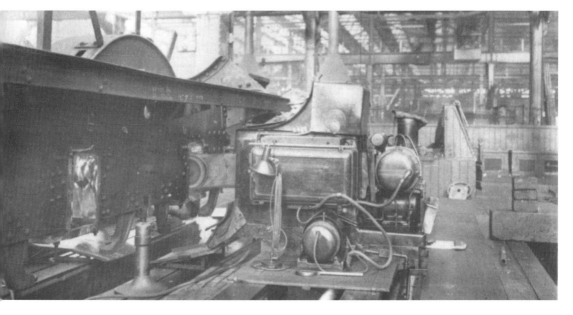

30. Horn cheek grinding machine. Utilising measurements obtained from the Zeiss apparatus, the face of the cheekblocks could be ground to a precise size and angle. This ensured absolute squareness of angle between the centreline of the cylinder bore and the centreline of the coupled axle. In the background is the AV Boiler Bay. (*OPC Railprint*)

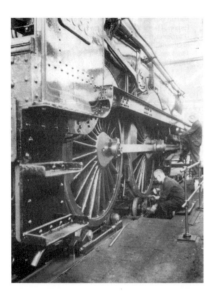

Above left: 31. The valve setting plant. This greatly assisted the work of setting, enabling the wheels to be inched around fractionally without the need to move the locomotive with 'pinch bars' along a legnth of track. 'Star' class, No. 4036 *Queen Elizabeth* is attended to by Bob Jarvis, chargehand (sitting) who is setting the wheel position at front dead centre, while Albert Walters checks the position of the valve.

Above right: 32. Reminders of the visit of HRH Princess Elizabeth. Only the nameplates remain, on the wall of Swindon Railway Museum.

Below: 33. The 'New Work' gang, photographed on 15 November 1950 immediately following the visit of HRH Princess Elizabeth to Swindon Works to perform the naming ceremony for the last Great Western 'Castle' class locomotive to be built, No. 7037 *Swindon*. Front row (from left to right): Ivor Mabberley, –?–, Bill Mills, Cecil Cox, –?–, S. Smith, Ernie Slade, Stan Millard, Percy Jarvis, Ted Oram, Hedley Mills, Peter Tampkin, Eugene Titcombe, Stan Green, Bill Rees, Gordon Williams, –?–. Front rear (left to right): Albert Cook, Wally Knight, Bill Dando, Arthur Graham, Alec Jones, Ernie Wiggins, Martin Burns, Eric Hayward, Dick Dunstan, Jack Newman, George Ashley, Frank Williams, Harry Barret, Harry Lewis, –?–, –?–, –?–. Platform front (from left to right): Stan James, Ernie Collier, Fred Dew, –?–, –?–, –?–, 'Jock' Robinson, Tom Still, John (Sam) Eylett, Ken Gibbs (author), John (Danny) White, –?–. Platform rear (from left to righr): Trevor Wheeler, Les Simms, Sam Osbourne, Arthur McGovern, Norman Sanders, Jack Dixon.

10

The Start of Fitting

Although by this time I had purchased a small treadle-operated lathe for use in the garden shed at home, my stay on the lathes had come to an end. At the time it was just another move in a five-year apprenticeship, and I was rather pleased to have started, or to be about to start, on the fitting aspect of the trade, as I had come to the conclusion that although turning had been interesting, and on reflection most of it had been quite straightforward and simple, (I mean in terms of the skills of turning, and not that apprentices found learning particularly easy and simple), I did not fancy becoming a turner, permanently.

My introduction to fitting was to start on the gang run by Stan Major, a white-haired, dapper little man who wore a grey, short jacket, almost a smoking jacket, as opposed to overalls or the ordinary waistcoat and trousers favoured by some. The gang was located again in R Shop, on a row of benches at the rear of the lathes of Reggie Emmons and adjacent to the broaching machine used for fitting keys into crossheads. The job that I would be doing was the stripping and refurbishing of the locomotive vacuum pump.

The Great Western system used the vacuum brake arrangement, considered more effective and cheaper in terms of fuel costs than the possibly more obvious steam brake worked from the motive power of the locomotive itself. The vacuum pump was about 3 feet long with a bore of about 4 inches and, in use, was suspended by integrally cast brackets at its central point of balance, bolted to the outer angle of the locomotive running board on the right-hand side. The pump rod was of about 1½ inches in diameter, and its outer end had a coned, washered and nutted end which was attached to a special bracket bolted very securely to the locomotive crosshead. The action of the crosshead as it slid between the motion bars when the engine was travelling, operated the pump and exhausted air from the braking system. The locomotive, tender and all carriages (and some trucks at this period) were fitted with suitable brake gear and the necessary vacuum cylinder and pipework to enable the full train to be connected as one continuous unit. A fitting in the locomotive cab and in the guard's van could be used to allow air to enter the system and thus apply the brakes. The control valve for this purpose looked like a small engine room telegraph as used on ships, but in place of the dial on the telegraph which showed the 'Full–Half–Stop' legend, was a brass face, perforated like a pepper pot. Moving the vertically mounted, wooden-handled lever, allowed air through the perforations and initiated the breakdown of the vacuum in the system, thus giving good control, either partial or full, to the application of the brakes.

The Great Western, or Western Region as it now was after being nationalised, had a unique system for control of the brakes, which could be instigated automatically at certain locations where, for example, many lines crossed or traffic was very heavy, such as junctions, station approaches, etc. This was the function of the ATC gear (Automatic Train Control). Attached to the right-hand side of a locomotive cab on the footplate, not outside, was a green painted box about 10 inches by 8 inches surmounted by a brass bell and carrying a reset lever. At the very front of the locomotive and attached extremely securely to the bottom of the drag beam, that assembly of plate and angle iron which took the shock of buffer contact and the stresses of pulling a load when travelling backwards, was a distinctive rectangular steel block, from the bottom of which protruded a square section ram, which had a very strong, bolted clamp arrangement at the extremity, the V section sides (the ram being about 4 inches square), stretching across the front of the locomotive. Into this clamp was fitted a very hard steel shoe, specially hardened for the purpose, about 6 inches by 3 inches by 1¼ inches and the ram itself was spring loaded by a very powerful compression spring.

At a particularly vulnerable or hazardous junction, the rail tracks criss-crossing in all directions, could be seen a special length of rail, lying between the actual railway lines themselves, about say 40 feet long and tapered down smoothly at each end. These rails were connected electrically to the signalling system (which was itself at this period mostly mechanical, with signal boxes and hand-operated levers working pull rods and wires to operate the signals themselves), and were in essence part of a simple circuit.

In operation, depending on the condition or state of the signalled length, the approaching engine would make contact with the rail by means of the suspended, hard shoe mounted under its front, the shoe making a friction contact with the top of the rail and rubbing along it, its spring loading damping out the shock of contact. Depending on the condition of the circuit in the system, the bell rang and the brakes could be applied manually as appropriate; the ringing bell indicated 'proceed normally', but always with due attention. A second audible warning or indication was from a siren enclosed in the green box, the sounding of which indicated that the driver should be prepared to stop at the next appropriate stop signal. Should the warning be disregarded, the combined brake valve and siren would apply the brakes automatically. In effect, the shoe and ram formed a simple electric switch to complete the simple circuit.

The vacuum pump was not the only method available to maintain the vacuum in the system, which included the ejector, a device utilising the rapid passage of steam through a coned orifice to draw air from the system and so create the required vacuum. Steam, obviously the motive power source of the locomotive, had to be used sparingly for ancilliary operations so the actual maintenance of the vacuum when the locomotive was running was by vacuum pump which required no steam directly as such, as it ran from the moving crosshead of the locomotive while the locomotive was in motion. To create the vacuum to start with, a large three-cone ejector was available, but maintenance of the vacuum when created was by either a vacuum pump, as indicated above, or by a single cone portion of the ejector, using less steam than the complete apparatus, incidentally known as the small ejector and large ejector respectively. A relief valve on the system ensured the regulation vacuum was not exceeded, the required level being known as 25 inches of vacuum, which referred to the calibration equipment and the height of a column of mercury supported by the vacuum.

However, Monday morning found me at Stan's cupboard, alone this time, as there was only provision for one apprentice on the gang, and after a short chat we walked round the benches to meet Reg, with whom I would be working. Reg was a tall, slightly built, very precise sort of man with collar and tie and spectacles, and what looked like ironed and pressed overalls, but they were probably new so they looked immaculate. Introductions followed and with a shake of the hand, I started on my sojourn as a fitter, while Stan disappeared back to his cupboard.

We had a little chat and a look at the various pumps in the stages of repair around the bench area, and Reg gave a general explanation of what the pump was and what it did, pointing out the various components associated with repairs. We began by selecting a pump which had been started by my immediate predecessor and left in the bench vice with the valves ready but not finished, and it was here that the first small problem became apparent! Being a little tubby lad (I haven't changed!), I couldn't reach the vice which was one of the old-fashioned leg type. By not reaching the vice it was difficult to actually get over anything secured in it, and this was particularly the case with the double valve seats at each end of the pump, the first valve seat being about 1½ inches down inside the casting anyway. Reg and I had a scrounge around the other benches and found a large wooden block about 6 inches thick which I carried back to the bench, and which proved to be the answer. Standing on that gave me the required reach to enable the bottom seat to be scraped. Using a flat scraper, to secure a sealed contact with the flat valve itself and to provide clearance, the centre portion of the valve was scraped around the central hole. A thin smear of 'red lead' or red marking paste on the valve indicated the high spots on the seat which would require attention from the scraper.

The flat valves were, I believe, steel and were of about 3-inch diameter and about ½ inch thick with a ⅝-inch hole through the middle, and a large radius round the top edge. The seat in the casting was flat with a ring of holes which coincided with the bearing surface of the valve, which itself was supplied with a surface ground face. I recall the valves being ground on the large surface grinder near the check board, a considerable number being dealt with at a time, being secured on the flat face of a large magnetic chuck, in effect a flat box affair about 2½ feet by 1 feet. Connected to the power supply, the chuck worked very simply by altering the flux of the internal electro-magnets, a small lever changing polarity internally, which either released the components or gripped them so tightly that even the friction of the rotating grinding head would not shift them.

On top of the first valve, with the necessary clearance, a second valve seat was fitted resting on the outer rim of the raised casting around the lower seat and was the same lozenge shape, its top surface carrying an identical seat to the lower valve, and requiring the same fitting and scraping procedure to ensure bedding down and central clearance for the flat valve. The holes in the valve centres were located and centred by spigots on the top seat and the cap which fitted over two studs, one each end of the lozenge shape. Fitted over the studs, nuts and washers were applied, securing the complete valve assembly. At the closed end of the pump, a brass relief valve was screwed into the top of the casting, while connections for the lubricator and train pipe were spaced between the relief valve, or snifter as it was known, and the valves at the stuffing box end. The stuffing box is a steam engineering term for a gland, which usually contained a greased ring or several rings of rope-like material, which were compressed around a reciprocating piston rod where it emerged from the cylinder, in order to preserve the seal and to stop any escape of the contents of the cylinder during movement of the piston. The flexible contents of

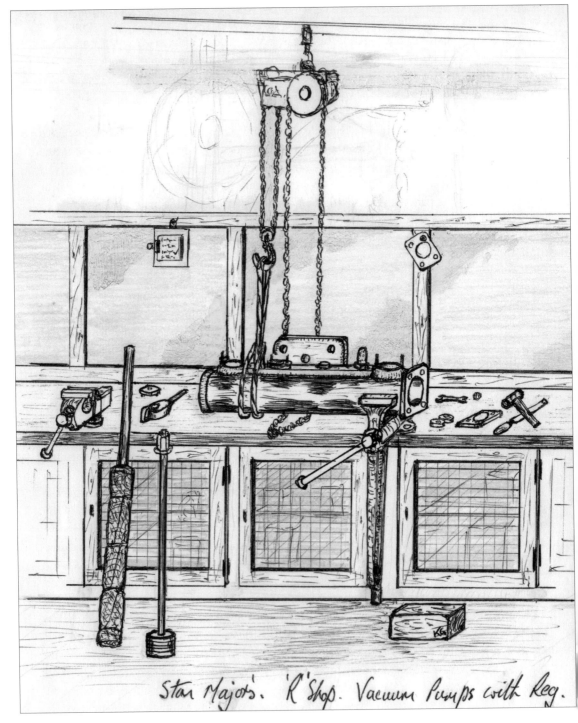

Stan Major's gang and refurbishing vacuum pumps with Reg.

the stuffing box could be compressed around the piston rod by the flanged metal short cylinder, which was located by studs and secured and adjusted by nuts, set in the face of the stuffing box and encircling the piston rod, this being known as the 'gland'.

The stuffing box packing, in the case of the vacuum pump, was not the usual flexible asbestos rope type of material, but a special metallic packing, and something which was quite new to me. The packing comprised a ring, about ⅜ inches thick and of say 2¼ inches outside diameter, made up of, I believe, three cast-iron segments which were held together by a small coil spring, formed into a sealed circle which fitted into a groove around the outer diameter of the ring, holding the segments firmly together to form a complete ring, the faces and bore of which had been finely ground to produce a polished finish, the bore being a very close fit around the piston rod. The segments were so shaped that as and when the bore of the ring wore away, the spring would slide the segments together to maintain the contact and seal around the piston rod. I believe three of these packing assemblies were used in the stuffing box, which did not need to be screwed up as tightly as was normally done in the case of the soft packing usually used.

Piston rings were fitted in the usual way, the opening in the ring being filed at the required angle and tried occasionally into the bore of the pump to ensure a good fit. To fit the rings to the piston, the usual levers positioned the ring first over the diameter of the head and then down into the two grooves. The piston was started in the bore and a piece of tar yarn knotted over one of the four cover studs, the loose end wrapped around the ring and pulled tight, thus closing the ring into the groove and enabling the piston to be pushed into the bore, which then retained the first ring, the yarn pushing off in the process, which was repeated for the second ring. Having well-oiled the bore, the piston was pushed up and down the cylinder several times to ensure that the rings were not too tight and that there was generally free movement. The recessed, rectangular head was now nutted on to the cylinder over the four studs, and the gland and packing assembled over the opposite end and secured. Screwing in the relief valve, which looked like a brass pepper pot, completed the job, and the pump was swung out of the vice by the usual swing jib and pulley block and placed on the floor. The nutted end of the piston rod was checked, its washers and castle nut in place with the flat cotter pin opened slightly to ensure it did not fall out when transported to the shop for attaching to the locomotive.

Items which came into the shop for repair had already been cleaned of the mixture of oil, grit and dirt, which had accumulated over the period when perhaps thousands of miles had been run, and so the pumps which came in for repair were generally quite clean. An old shackle and bolt were secured through one of the holes in the cast brackets on the back of the pump casting, and by operating the lifting chain of the pulley block with one hand and supporting the pump rod with the other, the pump could be lifted and swung over the open jaws of the leg vice, lowered and clamped with the jaws actually over the top of the pump and the bottom of the pump body resting on the plain section of the vice screw. Tightening the vice retained the pump which remained supported where it overhung the vice by the shackle or rope sling and pulley block. The components were then stripped out and set on the bench. One of the first activities was to clean the bore to allow Reg to examine it, although the clean and polished surface of the bore swept by the piston looked immaculate, and I don't remember any pump being rejected because the bore had worn badly. The cleaning prior to entry to the shop had included probably dunking in a large tank of cleaning fluid, which even on those items which were hand-cleaned seemed to wash dirt into various orifices, although being most effective for general cleaning externally. Cleaning of the bore was by the use of two very homemade design items! A pair of broom handles had been carefully wrapped with sacking, probably old bolt bags, to form a sacking piston on each broom handle, one being for rough cleaning and the other for the final polish! The first was oiled and the second nominally dry for the final clean up.

I should mention a couple of characters on the gang to whom I chatted briefly on occasions. One was Sid, who was into the early do-it-yourself furniture making, and who was always after pieces of wood, a rather rare commodity generally, and particularly so in an engineering workshop! Wood was still rationed at this period with a maximum purchase amount of £1 worth, I believe, per month, and on a couple of occasions I remember he made a special visit to my part of the bench to explain in detail, while I scraped a bearing for one of the pump valves, the lengths and sizes of the wood he had obtained as his 'latest poundswurf!' I kept a very wary eye on my block of wood, although I think it was too small and too oily to be of any use for Sid and his activities, and in any case I was usually standing on it! It was also on this gang that I met a distant relative for the first time. I mentioned to my father that one of the older members of the gang had our surname and father said it was his cousin, a number of years older than father himself. Bill was rather a silent chap who looked rather miserable, but when I introduced myself, found that to me at least he was quite a chatty person.

As I was still interested in turning, but not, as I mentioned, as a permanent job, I had acquired a small treadle lathe for home use. I was always interested in the small lathes that were available for the usual model engineering work which a number of my colleagues attempted, including myself, and I was quite envious of one of the apprentices whose father had a 4-inch Round Bed Drummond, a real classic of the immediate post-war scene. However, at this time I heard the tale of one of the shop characters (no names – no pack drill!) who was interested in wood-turning (no, it wasn't Sid!), and had actually made himself a large wood-turning lathe as a 'foreigner', the name given to any work, really strictly illegal, done for oneself on the company's time! This lathe had components which had been all made within the works itself. The headstock had been cast in the foundry, as had the tailstock and other castable components, and machined in R Shop, worked in with the general flow of work through the shop. Although the penalties for being caught were severe, they did not deter these things being formulated in the minds of those determined enough, and there was general admiration for the scale of this particular enterprise. The turned and machined parts were all smuggled out by the designer of the lathe when he himself would be lost in the crowds of the mass exodus of staff from the workshops. Taken out one piece at a time, the thing which intrigued everyone about the whole project was the subject of the bed of the lathe. What form would it take and how would it be got out through the gates under the noses of the 'watchmen' who manned the gates at all times, overseeing the departing workforce from the step of the small watchmen's office near each exit gate. A very simple plan was devised.

A steam locomotive boiler has a number of tubes in its construction, tubes which are removed and replaced several times during the life of the boiler and which after a long life, are scrapped. There must, in Swindon, be even to this day, many fences and clothes-drying line posts which are made from these tubes, which could be purchased very cheaply as scrap from the works. Some posts, for a very small dab in the hand in the right quarters, could even be pre-drilled and fitted with a short cross bar, around which the clothes line could be looped! For purchase, one required a 'Materials Sold' docket and a pass out. allowing such material to be taken through the gates, the dockets being handed to the watchman on duty before being allowed through. He was, of course, supposed to examine the items before final clearance was given, to ensure that what was on the paperwork was that actually being taken out.

The bed of the lathe, as shown by the patterns from which the headstock and tailstock had been produced, indicated that these two items would be bolted to, and would by their design, position and space need two round bars to form the bed, which would in total be about 6 feet long! A 'Stores Sold' material order was obtained for the purchase of two scrap boiler tubes, suitably drilled, for use as fence posts, but these would not themselves form the bed of the lathe! By various means, fair and foul (one suspects the latter!), two possibly 2½-inch-diameter solid steel bars had been obtained and suitably drilled as required to form the bed, and these bars had been then concealed, one inside each of the tubular fence posts. Armed with the relevant paperwork and having had assistance to carry the two fence posts to the bicycle rack, the tubes and their contents were then tied to the bar and carrier of the maker's cycle, which was then wheeled casually to the watchman's office, with the relevant paperwork in conspicuous display. The sight of boiler tubes, in all sorts of lengths, tied to bicycles or just carried manually, was such a common sight that the watchman just slid aside his window, gave a cursory scrutiny to ensure that the two tubes on the cycle coincided with the quantity specified on the paperwork, which was then duly taken, stamped and handed back, and the bicycle and its load passed unhindered through the open gate to the road and into legend and history. A look at the condition of the cycle tyres, and the apparent difficulty of pushing the thing, painted a different picture altogether, but it is quite possible that the lathe is still working somewhere in Swindon, possibly by now a treasured family heirloom.

As Swindon was dominated at that time by the Railway Works, which itself covered a considerable area within the town itself, it became a locally accepted phrase to describe anyone who worked within its boundary as working 'inside'. Forty years on, the works is no longer what it was, and there are so many new people in the town that the phrase had died out, and if mentioned now would give the impression that someone had been in prison if so described, but all true Swindonians would know what was meant!

I enjoyed my stay with Reg and with the work itself, as I now felt I was actually concerned with steam locomotives and their components, as opposed to the rather obscure, small components handled during the turning stage of the apprenticeship. Reg himself was a very straight-laced character with strong views on all subjects of family, religion, morals and ethics, but nevertheless a friendly, helpful sort of person, his quiet approach and quiet speech (he never shouted at anyone or anything) giving an air of calmness over the job. I was quite reluctant to move when the time came, but quite pleased with the move as it was the G Shop, the Maintenance Shop for the works and the system as a whole. I was wished the best of luck by Stan, the chargehand, and thanked for my work on the gang, this in itself being something quite new to me.

11
G Shop

G Shop, across the yard from B Shed and R Shop, was one of the original buildings dating from the founding of the works in 1846, when it had been the Boiler Shop in the days of Brunel and Gooch and their famous broad gauge concept of locomotive design. In the yard itself were rail tracks stretching from the Manager's Office to the general offices, along the longer sides of the rectangle formed by the yard, and the entrance to G Shop was in the centre of the building on the long side facing the yard. To the right of the entrance and built in cantilever fashion from the outside of the wall, stood the raised foreman's and administration offices, a wooden, rather precarious looking structure, also approached from inside the shop by the usual stairs and landing with wooden ballustrade, stairs also rising from the yard to the external door of the office.

Immediately outside the shop doorway and to the right and left were one or two hydraulically operated capstans, which were used to assist with the movement of wagons into and out of the shop, the capstans operated by a foot-operated plunger, which protruded a couple of inches above the level of the surrounding concrete. A rope around the capstan and a hook in the ironwork of the wagon soon propelled both wagon and contents in the required direction. An absolutely unique fitting, walked over by literally thousands of feet during the course of a year, and completely ignored by the hurrying staff, was the small turntable, manually operated and of about 10-foot diameter, which was in use continually to turn the wagons entering or leaving the shop through 90 degrees to suit the rail lines. This included the possibly last relic of the broad gauge in the retention of two sets of rails, the two outside being the broad gauge spacing and the two centre rails, the narrow or 4 feet 8½ inches spacing of the now standardised setting. To walk over it caused it to tip slightly and give a hollow thud as the slight blow caused when it tipped, echoed into its shallow pit around which it revolved. It was closely boarded over the top surface, including between the rails, and the two rails of broad gauge track were still in existence for a few feet leading to the turntable and up to the edge of the pit.

Through the door of G Shop, on the other side of the two broad gauge rails leading to the turntable, the main areas of the shop opened to left and right with a short spur to the rear, as in the form of a 'T' with a very heavy top bar and a short stubby stem. To the right, along the wall, was the area of Cyril Wallington's gang, and to the left, again along the wall, was that of Fred Hawksbee. The short stubby area was the one which was my immediate goal, to the gang of Fred Selby. One of the problems I found with my stay in G Shop was that of not staying on a gang really long enough to settle and have a really detailed and lasting recollection of the work undertaken, the impressions retained being what I can only think of as some of the highlights which remained in the memory.

I first worked with a rather elderly but kindly man whose name I don't recall, although as with the little chap who was the fitter's mate, I can still picture them quite clearly in my mind, but their names, no! From the turntable entrance, my cupboard under the bench was on the right of the area, near a door which led into a stores, and one of the smaller episodes I do recall is going into the stores and among the items which we had to collect, I was shown a very large piece of leather about 2½ inches thick and about 4 feet by 3 feet, which I was told was rhinoceros hide, used for making machine buffs, cut and mounted like a small grinding wheel, and using oil and carborundum powder as the buffing medium, or used in the form of a strip-wrapped flat around a central core to form a wider wheel face. The material now, I would imagine, is strictly prohibited in use as it comes from a protected species.

It came about by the luck of the draw that my short period with this gang included a routine visit to the works' water pump station at Kemble. As the works had expanded around the turn of the century, the need for a good supply of water had become a very great priority. While a possible source nearer the works had been considered, various difficulties had precluded its development and the Kemble supply potential was considered the best proposition. Along the rail line from Swindon to Gloucester is a branch line, or was a branch line, to Tetbury, and at this small junction was developed a low-level pump station, in effect at the bottom of the embankment, possibly about 14 feet below the level of the railway lines. The station was steam-driven and the low level enabled the tipping of coal very simply from the supply wagons regularly shunted for the purpose.

The pumps were driven by beams at low level through a special link motion, the power source being two horizontal double expansion engines with a stroke of 3 feet and the two cylinder being of 18-inch diameter for the high pressure cylinder and 32-inch diameter for the lower. These engines had been superseded by electric pumps a number of years before and by my time at the works, the boilers had long since been removed, but the engines and associated pumps were maintained and retained at this period for use in emergencies. For the periodic servicing to maintain the capabilities for pumping should the electric power fail for any reason, particularly emergencies related to the war only just over, provision had been made to run the engines from a small pannier tank locomotive run on to the line adjacent to the wall of the pump/engine house. Having been asked by Fred the previous day if I would like to go with the fitters who were to carry out the routine maintenance, and having jumped at the chance, a rail ticket was obtained from the office, and quite early the following morning we assembled at Swindon station for the short journey on the local 'stopper' round to the nearest station and then took the short walk to the pumphouse, loaded with a few tools, large packets of sandwiches and the makings of a good brew of tea!

I remember experiencing a slight disappointment on entering the pumphouse as having been told we were going to service the beam-engine-driven pumps, I had somehow expected to see a Watt type beam engine with the massive beam swinging away above our heads, but of course the beams, as such, were virtually at ground level. However, the locomotive was on station outside and an interesting day was spent really just watching operations as apart from handing up tools as requested and then of course cleaning them after use, there was little on this occasion that I could actually do.

G Shop, being a maintenance shop, had on any occasion various individuals who would be away working somewhere on the Western system, and one of the checks often seen on the check board hook was the white check with letters 'OS' in red, signifying the holder of the particular number backing the check board hook was one of those out of the shop on duty, in fact 'Out Station'. A further check which could be said to be the most popular, appeared on the board every Thursday afternoon, replacing the pear-shaped brass check used on all other days or periods of the week. The Thursday afternoon check was of copper, oval in shape, about 1½ inches long and signified that it was indeed pay day once again.

The pay system was really quite unique and really a period piece which I would imagine could never occur again! To start the ball rolling, at a specific time on Thursday morning as regular as clockwork, one of the factory transport runabout vehicles, suitably displaying its registered numberplate enabling it to travel on public roads, would hare off in the direction of the famous tunnel entrance to the works. Before actually passing through the main double doors, a brief stop by the watchman's office was made so that a trailer with pneumatic tyres and consisting of a large black box, rectangular in shape and about 6 feet by 4 feet by 3 feet could be attached to the towing hook. Complete then with driver and two officials from the pay office, sitting completely exposed to the elements with no external cover whatsoever, the assembly passed out through the gates on to the public road outside. It only needed Wyatt Earp riding shotgun and horses in place of the factory runabout vehicle, and it could have been reminiscent of a Wild West scene of seventy years before!

This rather naive cavalcade headed straight for the bank, its route unchanged for many years, to collect the wages for the possible 12,500 employees of the Swindon Railway

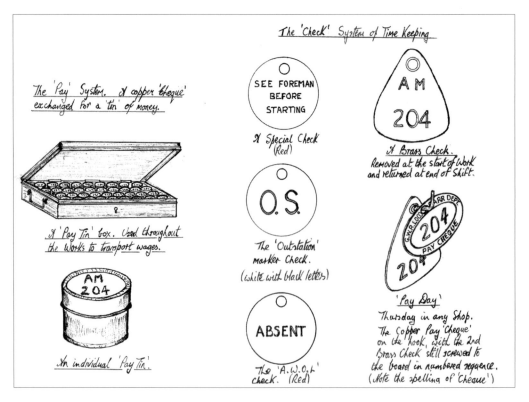

Used through out the works, the checking-in system of time keeping. Some of the checks or tallys used.

Works! Wages collected in cash and transported back to the works with absolute timing and precision by the route again followed for years! While the 'iron coffin', as it was called, was making this completely routine and uneventful journey, the Pay Office personnel had been assembling, augmented by others so delegated from other 'white collar' workers, at the metal-topped desks where the massive bulk of notes and cash would be split down, shop by shop and office by office, and further split into the individual amounts governed by the rates of pay and hours worked by the individuals. To my knowledge, there was rarely a mistake in the amount received and as indicated on the pay slip which accompanied each amount.

The earnings of each individual worker were placed in a round 'pay tin', each tin of about 1½-inch diameter and 1¼ inches high, made from substantial metal (not just thin 'cocoa tin' material) with a closely and well-fitting push fit lid, stamped with the individual's check number. About forty such tins were then placed in numerical order in a flat, lockable tin plate box about 18 inches by 12 inches and about 2 inches deep. There was a routine way of placing the money in the small round tin, with the change wrapped in the notes with the pay slip on top. The procedure of allocating the pay and placing it in the tins, to coincide with the amounts specified on the shop paybills would have progressed throughout the remainder of Thursday morning and on well into the afternoon. At about 5 p.m., emerging from the various shops and due to converge on the pay office, could be seen one of the shop labourers pushing his 'bogie' or sack truck and, on arrival at the pay office, joining the queue from other shops to commence the transport of the cash tins back to the workshop. At homebase in the workshop, G Shop taken as an example of what was happening all over the works, the ubiquitous checky would walk to the store, or often under the stairs leading to the foreman's office, and emerge with components of the prefabricated pay table. This was an assembly comprising a very narrow counter front about 5 feet long and 10 inches wide by about 4 feet high, supported by two 'wing' pieces which hooked on to the sides and extended to form a three-sided box, the back left open. On the centre of the counter section was a brass inlay tapering to the rear, both down and dovetail in shape, below which was a narrow shelf.

The labourer who transported the cash back to the shop would now be on his way back, escorted by a nominated representative from the payment section who would himself be accompanied by a junior clerk, male or female (usually the latter), carrying the paybill documents to undertake the actual payment. Arriving at the shop, the tins of tins would be unloaded on to the rear shelf of the pay table, behind the counter of which, unrolling the various paybill documents, would stand the pay clerk and assistant. The time would now be approaching about 5.25 p.m. and in front of the pay table, the members of the shop workforce would be almost completely assembled in check number order. An air of expectancy would now prevail in the final wait for the key person to arrive before payment could actually commence. The whole pay ritual had to be supervised by the shop foreman, and eyes would be continually flickering up to the office to detect the slightest movement which would signify the appearance of the man on the landing outside the office door. An opening door, rattle of feet slowly descending from the office and the arrival of the foreman at the table, a look at his pocket watch, a slight nod to the pay clerk and the thump of the first pay tin on the top of the table, the first number called from the paybill simultaneously, and in one move the first man in the queue had placed his check with a click on top of the brass insert, from which it had been, with equal rapidity, scooped into the hand of the pay clerk (who in a swift movement, placed it over the metal spike in front of himself), taken his wages tin and stepped across in front of the foreman to open the tin and check the contents. Wages extracted and checked, and tin discarded into the adjacent box, the recipient was already on his way home! So through to the end of the queue which usually featured the apprentices, but all was done so rapidly once started that the complete shop was usually on its way home before the hooter signified that it was 5.30 p.m., and end of shift.

I remember on one occasion, the shop foreman had been delayed in coming from his office to start the paying out (not in G Shop). Probably he had been caught by a late telephone call, but on his appearance a ragged cheer had gone up from those assembled at the pay table. The foreman had then stopped, leaned on the rail and looked over at the crowd expectantly waiting, turned around very smartly on his heel and disappeared back into his office for a further two or three minutes. When he eventually appeared there was silence this time and a delayed procedure commenced. Any discrepancy in wages had to be reported at once to the foreman and the complainant had to wait till the end to consult the clerical staff. In my experience this was quite a rare occurrence, the organisation, for all its apparent faults, working generally quite well and with extreme smoothness.

Throughout the works, across darkened yards, between stacks of timber and down dark passages between shops, the wages trios, the man with the trolley and the two accompanying wages clerks, could be regularly found on Thursdays transporting literally thousands of pounds around the vast area of the Railway Works. As far as I am aware, there was never a recorded incident of any attempted theft or snatch of the cash as it was trundled around in the familiar black flat rectangular tins, along routes which never varied and times which never changed. There was somehow a feeling of security about, which has long since regrettably evaporated!

My stay on Fred Selby's gang coincided with the works annual holiday when with the exception of a few maintenance staff who had pre-arranged attendance, the whole Works closed down for two weeks. This was quite a strange, empty period in Swindon as with such a working population actually at the Railway Works, the town seemed to empty out, certainly for the first of the two weeks. This period was always known locally as 'Trip'; an odd word which when mentioned quite naturally among the local population, with questions such as 'Where are you going Trip?', caused raised eyebrows and furrowed brows among 'foreigners' who did not understand the question. There was certainly a mass exodus from Swindon of railway employees and their families who crowded round in the local railway sidings on Trip morning to board the special trains laid on to transport thousands to the West Country for a week's holiday.

With regard to the Trip holiday, there was always great speculation on the gangs with regard to what was called the Trip Balance. The piecework system, still prevalent as the type of incentive scheme as I mentioned before, entailed a price for any job completed. It was the custom for all, or at least all the chargehands I ever knew, to maintain a piecework book in which the total weekly receipts under the piecework system were booked to maintain a reasonably regular amount of financial return for each of the members of the gang. There was also a fear, with some justification probably based on experience, that any regular over-booking or booking suddenly and consistently above the usual average or norm, would result in getting the prices cut or reduced. It was therefore the practice to keep a little 'in the back of the book'; these were jobs which had been completed in a particularly smoothly running week which had produced more than the usual output. To book the work in for that particular week would probably have caused questions from the office, so it was put into the back of the book and retained for a rainy day when production had been problematical and would have caused a drop in the piecework payments for that particular week. Certain times of the year were accepted as reasonable for booking a higher amount of work than usual. Christmas and Trip were two of the accepted periods.

I have mentioned the Trip holiday as it ties in with a job remembered from the Friday preceding the Trip holiday Saturday, 1948. One of the shops for which the fitter with whom I now worked was responsible for certain repair aspects, was the stamping shop, a long, rather dull and dusty building adjacent to the Smith's Shop, and while containing a few steam hammers, comprised the drop hammer section. The difference between the two forms of hammer is very distinctive. The steam hammer (invented by Nasmith in 1839) comprises a steam cylinder with the usual piston and piston rod, and attached to the rod is a very solid crosshead, which runs as in a locomotive, between two guides, but differing from the usual locomotive arrangement by being vertical instead of horizontal. The crosshead formed the hammer, and the blow was controlled by operation of a side lever, which altered the valve travel controlling the piston and could also thus alter the force of the blow. I have actually seen a hammer driver, a skilled job in terms of hammer work, crack a walnut under the head of one of the largest hammers, such was his control and experience in the use of the hammer!

The drop hammer, on the other hand, delivered one very heavy blow at a time and usually was not used for repeated, controlled series of blows. The drop hammer or stamp was usually taller than a steam hammer and did not have the characteristic bow legs of the latter, which allowed clearance and movement around the anvil, the block on which the work was held while the controlled hammering took place. The hammer head, in the case of the drop hammer, (the head also known as a 'tupp' or 'monkey'), was a very heavy metal block running between two guides and hauled to the top by a very substantial strap or belt wound around a drum at the top of the support columns. In the manner of the French Revolution guillotine, when the tupp reached the top portion of its travel, it tripped a release and then fell freely down on to the piece of red hot metal on the anvil underneath. Both the tupp and the anvil block would have been machined and hand-finished to include an inset impression of the particular item to be produced, a half section in each block. A batch of small chunks of metal, each in volume approximating to the volume of the finished product, would be heated in an adjacent furnace to a bright, soft condition red heat. Selecting one piece with long tongs, the hammer man would swing the piece on to the bottom block while the driver raised the tupp to the top of its travel. On release, the tupp dropped and the metal was driven into the shape cut into the two blocks, tupp and anvil. Sometimes the tupp was raised part way again and allowed to fall, depending on the complexity of the finished product, which of course was not of too complicated a shape anyway.

Among the largest and most complicated drop forgings produced was the locomotive brake hanger bracket, possibly 2½ feet long and 5 inches wide at its widest part. With every blow on to the red hot billet of steel, a shower of red hot, sparkling slag particles spread out and covered a radius of about 15 feet around the biggest of the drop hammers. It was also the practice, when the red hot billet was in position and when the tupp was descending, for the hammerman to throw a handful of sawdust on to the billet to assist, so I understood, the formation of the surface slag or scale caused by the oxidisation of the metal surface exposed to the air.

When the tupp had dropped on to the steel billet, the recesses of the shapes cut in the top and bottom blocks would be filled with metal to form the component, but in so doing, an excess of thin metal was squeezed out between the blocks to form a small skirt or band around the still red hot component. With the dulling red heat still showing between the cracking blue/black scale layer on the component's surface, the hammer man would rapidly remove the component with his long tongs and in one smooth movement transfer it to a scragging press working away within reach of the drop hammer. The component would be quickly and easily positioned and the descending powered ram of the press would push it through a flat plate type cutter, which would be shaped like the overall silhouette of the component. On being forced through, the component would lose its skirt and its dulling red heat would fade into the blue/black of the scale, which covered its contemporaries in the pile under the press and the irregular ring of rag from the skirt would be consigned to the adjacent pile with its scrap fellows.

The shape of the component governed the way the dies were formed in the tupp and bottom blocks. For example, say a component had a larger mass at one end than at the other and the dies were cut centrally in the mating block faces, when the hammer dropped with the potential of many tons, the thickness of the metal at one side of the centre line would cause a very great tilting force every time a blow was struck, and this would eventually cause severe damage to the hammer structure. As it was, there was often a spectacular bounce when the hammer came down on a large component which often jumped out of its shape in the bottom block and was pushed hastily back should another blow be required. With such continual hammering, particularly throughout the recent war years and afterwards in the recent 'shortage of everything' period, a number of machines throughout the works, not only in the Stamping Shop, were in need of attention.

The drop stamps, as with the steam hammers, had virtually permanent bases as such, on to which the various anvil blocks with their many types of die could be keyed or secured. With the very heavy and continuous hammer blows to which they were continually subjected, a certain amount of looseness would creep in, and while such looseness, when detected and apparent, would be rectified at once by re-securing the keys, any movement, however slight, would begin the process of abrasive wear. When an anvil block was moved or changed, the base to which it was secured would show worn patches, some with a high polish where continual slight movement, and the continual blows work-hardened parts of the surface. This surface had to be returned to its original state or at least to a state approaching as near as possible a truly square, flat surface at 90 degrees to the vertical force of the descending hammer block.

The block which required re-facing could not be easily removed from the almost ground level position of its top face, being part and parcel of the base and foundations of the hammer, so a way had to be found of refacing *in situ*. Probably in the 'old days', such refacing would have been done with the usual hammer and cold chisel, and it is surprising the quality of surface which could be obtained by someone skilled and experienced in the use of such seemingly crude tools.

However, to return to me and G Shop! On the Thursday afternoon prior to the Saturday start of the Trip holiday, the fitter with whom I worked said we had a job in the Stamp Shop 'for tomorrow', to face a hammer base, and we would go to the stores to fetch the machine which would then be prepared for use the following day. With the fitter's mate pushing one trolley and me with another, borrowed for the occasion, and the fitter, himself, carrying a small bag of spanners, we proceeded to the stores, the same stores in which I had been shown the piece of rhinoceros hide. Up to now I had no idea what sort of machine we were looking for but, with a cry of triumph, the fitter unwrapped some old sacking from a bundle standing in a corner, half buried in other odds and ends, and exposed a small portable shaper! This little machine was about 3 feet long with a separate framework which could be clamped to the base block of the hammer, being set square with a spirit level. The components were transported back to the bench in the two trolleys and there generally cleaned up and oiled. The geared motor, which was to be mounted on the rear of the shaper, was tested separately on the bench to make sure it was still in working order; being plugged in and run on and off for a few minutes.

First thing next morning, the three of us set off with the trolleys and the shaper, along with a small tool bag, and arrived at the hammer which required attention. The clamping and levelling completed, the next thing was the search for an electric outlet socket for the plug, located with some difficulty and a very long extension wire lead snaking off into the distance. The machine was controlled from the rear of the hammer base and it seemed that from this position it was only a matter of a few feet away from the vertically opening, counterbalanced door of a large furnace. Little tongues of blue/yellow flame were already licking around the edges of the metal frame of the fire brick door when we arrived and it proceeded to get hotter and hotter, as outside the sun rose to make a very warm, sunny summer day, and inside as the furnace temperature rose and the content of steel billets attained the glowing red heat essential for the stamping process, the perspiration trickled well!

The furnace was actually further away than it at first appeared, but the use of the adjacent hammer and the opening of the furnace door to extract the billets, or to top up the numbers by inserting cold chunks of metal, caused a hot blast of air to envelop the three overall-clad individuals attempting to operate the little shaper. Having set everything up, the motor switched on and the ram working smoothly, the only thing missing was the cutting tool, so we all looked expectantly at each other and into the trolleys and into the tool bag – nothing! Back to the shop and a search in the corner of the stores revealed nothing, so concluding that someone had walked off with it, we tried to draw a tool bit from the stores, but those in stock proved to be far too big, being stocked for the general machine tools of G Shop and being of a section too large for the small clapper box or tool post of the portable shaper! Incidentally, the clapper box is so called because on a shaper it is hinged at the top and when the ram moves forward on the cutting stroke, the box is pressed firmly against the seating by the force of the cutting action. On the return stroke, the hinged box allows the tool to float and not drag its cutting edge backwards over the newly machined surface to the possible detriment of both, which would be the case with a rigidly held cutting tool. However, a wander around the shop was now the only possible solution, to see what we could scrounge! Still there was nothing that would fit, as all of the machine tools used the range of tools stocked by the stores. On our way round, we bumped into Fred, the chargehand, who asked how things were going. The fitter explained and Fred, with an exasperated look but not saying anything, took him by the elbow and guided him, with the two of us following in their wake, back to his cupboard. Opening a drawer, Fred produced a little box with a complete range of small tools which would fit the shaper, and we all proceeded rather sheepishly back to the Stamping Shop!

Setting the tool and testing it with a stroke or two of the ram, we were at last ready to continue, by this time perspiring freely in the heat of the day and the confines of the shop. At about 11.30 a.m., the chargehand appeared again and the fitter and mate departed, I thought a little too readily, for another job which had cropped up somewhere else, leaving me to continue to work, or at least oversee, the cutting operation with the small shaper, the instruction being to continue cutting, making sure that the complete surface was machined, the cutter already showing up the unequal wear by the patches of unmachined area showing particularly on the corners of the surface. The midday break came and went and, immediately afterwards, the fitter showed up again to see how things were progressing and then went off again, saying he would be back later.

I spent the afternoon gently cooking in front of the furnace, watching the slow movement of the little tool across the surface of the hammer base, while I sat on the inevitable block of wood padded with an old sack, taking the tool out for a sharpening before a start was made on the finishing cut.

I never did get to finish the block as, at about 4.30 p.m., the fitter returned and said it was time to start a clean-up prior to the holiday period, and anyway he would be working for that period, so he would continue and complete the operation the following day when some of the major maintenance was undertaken or at least started during the works shutdown.

I had received my marching orders from Fred's gang in the general apprentice move pattern, and my next port of call was to be a maintenance area workshop known as the 'Hooter House', the domain of Harry White.

THE 'HOOTER HOUSE' FITTING SECTION

It is probably the best bet at this point to place in perspective the area of the Hooter House and what it actually contained. To locate the hooter itself was not a difficult task when it blew, as it was mounted on a high roof and its blast could be heard over a radius of about fifteen miles, followed by a column of condensing steam above its anchor point. To get to the Hooter House itself and walking from G Shop, there were two courses open. The first along the road past the Manager's Office and R Shop as if heading for the strappy Shop, but turning right at W Shop instead of going across the road and into the shop itself, then follow the front of the shop along to the corner and, while the eight chimneys of the central boilers loomed on your right, the corner was approached on the left, and above that corner could be seen the hooter, like a pair of GWR locomotive whistles in shape but much larger, as though from a passenger liner. The other route was through G Shop and a portion of the Smith Shop at the rear of G Shop, out into the road and turn left then past the steam accumulator, a giant, black-lagged, dome-ended cylinder about 80 feet long and of 15½-feet diameter, and the coaling plant, which served the central boilers by firmly gripping a complete loaded coal wagon and turning it upside down to tip its load on to a belt which ran under the road and end-on along the grates of the central boiler complex. There was also an ash removal belt running the opposite way which deposited the dead ash into wagons for disposal, and in this respect I have a recollection of a water spray arrangement to cool the ash before it was belted into the wagons. Reaching to a height of about 80 feet, in total, the chimneys of the central boilers could be seen from several miles away. These were certainly not flimsy structures as one considers a metal chimney to be, but were made from several boiler shells joined together to obtain the necessary height! The fluctuating demand for steam which would be inevitable with such a size of works, was handled by the storage accumulator, allowing very economical use of the bank of boilers which were of Stirling type and which fed steam into the accumulator.

The Hooter House as such, did not really exist! There was a doorway into a short corridor or entrance hall and on the wall to the right was the large clock and wheel-operated steam valve which was at chest height, on a pipe which emerged from the floor and continued up the wall to the hooter mounted on the roof! All in all not very impressive surroundings for the regular emissions which controlled, literally, the timing of the life of Swindon and its surrounding villages. As the hooter was silenced during the late war, except to warn of the approach of German aircraft by a series of short blasts, and then announce their departure by one long, sustained blast, the populace of Swindon had had to rely on something other than regular blasts of noisy steam for the routine control of their daily lives. Now that a semblance of normality was returning to life, the works hooter was once again blasting its timely warnings over its old area. To be in the road passing the hooter when it actually sounded, was to be avoided if possible, and the white collar staff from the offices passing to and from work five minutes later and earlier respectively than the shop floor staff, could be seen consulting with watches and quickening pace if anywhere near the hooter when it was scheduled to blow. Not only did the noise make your eardrums vibrate, but the ascending column of exhausted steam, its noise and power departed, now disintegrated into its component water droplets which, if the wind was in the right direction, or maybe the wrong direction depending on your point of view, descended from a great height on to those scurrying beneath, and many a light suit or flowery summer dress has been caught in the sudden shower of rather oily rain!

Entering the Hooter House door, to the left, was the entrance or one of the entrances leading to W Shop, its length being a rather long rectangle of a shop stretching away in front of you. The work W Shop was generally that of machining locomotive cylinders on special boring machines, a variation on the conventional lathe. I'm not too sure whether these were operated by turners or machinists in the terms of demarcation then existing, but probably by machinists, as nominally the workpiece was static and the tool revolved! There was also a section which machined certain aspects of the locomotive (and bogie) frames, with regard to shaping, drilling and slotting. Although I did not work in the shop at any time, and I do not recall that it was on the circuit for training apprentices anyway, or at least for those engaged in the fitting, turning and locomotive erecting trade, I did pass through it on several occasions and to me it had a peculiar, distinctive smell!

Having entered the Hooter House door, with W Shop door on the left, a turn in the opposite direction to the right, opened up a completely different environment, although once again with a distinctive, and to any steam enthusiast, marvellous smell; the aroma of oily steam and warm lubricating oil which can only emanate from a steam engine!

The smell of the steam engine rose up subtly from below road and workshop level as the source of such aromas was met in a cellar room with no roof and could be looked down into, a marvellous vantage point for watching stationary engines at work. Although a door led immediately to an iron ladder down to engine house floor level, the best viewpoint was through one of several low-arched doorways which opened out in the outer wall at road level facing the eight chimneys of the central boiler complex, which were to the right as you entered the door to the hooter house. Stepping through those doors brought you into another world. You stepped on to a narrow iron balcony with a rail at convenient height for leaning your elbows, and in front and below facing you, end-on, were two horizontal compound double-acting engines, smoothly and almost silently, slowly turning their flywheels until demand for their services caused them to speed up; but speed up in a leisurely, dignified fashion, not in a great rush and panic and without any perceptible increase in noise!

The first thing which of course attracted attention was the pair of engines, but one soon became aware of other movement in the sunken room. In large recesses in the right-hand wall as you looked at the engines, two huge vertically mounted cylinders about say 6 feet in diameter and 10 feet long, one smaller than the other in diameter, seemed to rise and fall to no particular rhythm, but just moved gently up a short distance then slowly fell, to remain stationary for a few seconds before rising again, both rising and falling to any position between fixed limits. This room, with its engines and weights, for such were the cylinders, was the power nucleus of the works hydraulic system, the weights forming and maintaining the immense pressures of 750lb and 1500lb per square inch which ran through the low pressure and high pressure pipework of the system. The heavier of the two cylinders – riveted steel plates like a boiler shell, as indeed was the construction of both cylinders – weighed reputedly 40 tons, and was full of steel scrap!

It was fascinating to stand on the balcony, while below the two engines slid their polished piston rods in and out of their two tandem-mounted cylinders and the Watt governors reacted to every demand on the system by whirring a little faster, the balls increasing the radius of their rotation as the governor whirled faster to suit the sudden demands in some distant shop, and then descending on their hinged support arms as demand dropped, and the engines could once again proceed at their usual dignified speed. Everything was polished; handrails, copper and brass pipes, steelwork, and the governors, of course, looking like ethereal polished silver cones when whirling at full demand on the system. In explanation, the 'governor' controlled the flow of steam to the cylinders quite automatically by operating the control valve on the steam feed pipe, giving a smooth increase and decrease to the amount of valve opening and hence the amount of steam required. With a steam locomotive, if the regulator (the control valve of steam to the cylinders) is opened too quickly, the wheels tend to move or attempt to move again too quickly and will inevitably skid on the rails, giving no movement to the locomotive and stressing the mechanism, the regulator in this case being manually operated by the driver. The governor on the stationary engine gave a safe control over flow of steam and hence speed of engine, quite independently of any human factor when the variations of demand could have the engine responding in a very jerky and stressful fashion; smoothness was the key word.

There can be absolutely no comparison between such horizontal steam engines, now long gone, and the noisy, clattering, foul-smelling diesel engines used generally as power house replacement sources of power generation!

However, we have entered the Hooter House and looked in at the hooter steam control; we have had a glance through the doors on the left into W Shop and through the door and down the steps on the right into the softly hissing, warm and aromatic world of the hydraulic system engines and pumps and their counterbalance weights. Straight ahead lay another door through into a workshop containing another source of power, that of the local pneumatic system. In the centre of the room were two large, I believe two-stage, air compressors, which hammered away through all hours.

The compressor room area contained Harry White's gang, a small, closely knit group of some of the friendliest people I worked with anywhere in the works. The ages varied; there was young Jock, obviously a Scot, whose name I can't remember even if I knew it originally; there was Ken, who as I recall seemed to live cricket! Jesse, a large powerfully built but very quiet and gentle sort of person, I believe a lay preacher in one of the villages around Swindon, and then Dick and Alfie, a fitter and mate pair who seemed to know everybody and were two of the most cheerful characters I ever met. I worked generally with all of them, in no sort of order, but as required on the type of work they were to undertake, generally just accompanying them around to any of the shops covered and maybe taking out a bolt here or tightening a pipe connection there, but generally just watching.

One trip with Dick and Alfie was shrouded with an air of mystery when they stated that we would go to the A Shop complex without going through any other workshop or walking down beside the main railway line and crossing any bridges on the way! Alfie packed a few tools in a bag and Dick rummaged around in a cupboard and produced a powerful battery-powered hand lamp and off we set, heading in the direction of the running shed. The plot thickened! About the turn of the century, with the expanding Works complex requiring more and better services with regard to water, gas and electric power, hydraulic and pneumatic service mains, and with the top surface covered with shops, road and railway lines, the only alternatives left for siting the myriad pipework were either over or under! The latter was eventually chosen and a tunnel or passageway was commenced in 1900 to contain all the necessary pipework and mains supplies, making attention reasonably straightforward and accessible. Taking about three years to complete, the final tunnel was brick-lined and of 7-foot diameter internally and for drainage, sloped from both ends to the middle. Due to the layout of the works, the tunnel was not a straight line, but kinked in a couple of places with a further branch off in the direction of the iron foundry which itself occupied a long, rectangular shop adjacent to the main London to Bristol line.

Somewhere in the area, I believe, of the general stores, we went through a low metal door in an equally low brick structure, into a damp, dark, cold, brick cylinder, along the bottom of which ran the drainage channel covered by a catwalk. Dick went ahead with the hand lamp, its beam reflecting off the wet walls and sweating pipework stretching off into the distance, and with me in the centre and Alfie following along in the rear, off we set. Dick was a tall, thin man with a swaying walk on seemingly hydraulically damped knee joints, springing over thin legs with '10 to 2' feet. He often exaggerated the swaying walk which would then be copied by Alfie so that both of them walked in step as though just entering stage left for a comedy routine. Anyone looking along that tunnel from the other end would thus have seen what appeared to be three eccentrics following a bobbing light, all swaying from side to side in step and all whistling the 'marching to work' song from *Snow White*!

There were eyes watching us as we marched along approximately 2,250 feet of bricked shaft, and a number of little feet scurried away under the duckboard or into the shadows of the pipes which lined the tunnel. Sometimes Dick would stop and flick the torch down on to a stilled furry body which suddenly shot away past us into the dampness, dark and silent, through which we had just passed. The tunnel had been provided with electric light in its early days, but due to the very damp conditions, the lighting fittings and cables had been removed along with the power supply cables as they had been adversely affected to the point of becoming dangerous. The remaining power that was still contained within the damp walls was very considerable. The water main from Kemble ran along the wall to one side, along with gas mains for lighting and power supply. The tremendous pressures of the hydraulic mains – 1,500lb and 750lb to the square inch – also ran the length with branches here and there to the various shops en route, almost a potential bomb under and through the heart of the works, supported in steel racks placed at intervals and secured to the walls.

Occasionally the light would flick on to a pipe flange and a quick examination would be made of bolts and seal, but as everything seemed to be quite normal on this occasion and no work was actually required on anything, the whistling trio proceeded on its way, still the tiny feet dancing attendance as we passed. From the top of a pipe at chest level, the light would often reflect a pair of pink needles glowing, unblinking from the recesses of the pipes and brackets, the furry owner with the long tail wondering who were these three whistling, swaying madmen intruding into their silence. We passed the tunnel turning off to the foundry and negotiated the various turns, continuing the march with our boots echoing on the catwalk base of the tunnel. The light stretched its beam on into the dimming distance until stopped by a metal door, when the intensity of light increased by reflection from the end of the tunnel. And so out into the air once again in the vicinity of A Shop, and tunnel's end.

Having arrived on the far side of the A Shop complex, we had passed under the original area of rail sidings where that classic, and to a Great Western enthusiast, tragic photograph was exposed to show the rank on rank of condemned broad gauge locomotives awaiting conversions or scrapping in 1892. There was, until recently, a strange legend among the older inhabitants of Swindon in which some were convinced that when the yard (the 'Con Yard' or Concentration Yard) was extended by building up the ground to that of the level of the rest of the works, several broad gauge engines were buried in the tipped earth! How this started it is difficult to imagine, but the wheel had turned full circle by 1984 when much of the infill was in the process of being removed for use elsewhere. There has been no trace of any broad gauge locomotives and the area is being returned to its original level. The only items being exposed are the remains of the farm buildings covered when the massive tipping task was underway ninety years or so ago.

Blinking in the light, we stood for a moment until Dick suggested a look at the large air shaft with grille top which covered the now bricked-over course of the brook, which had originally crossed the area of fields. The water had been concealed by the huge amounts of infill to build up the 30 feet or so of depth to the edges of the reclaimed and levelled area, and there was one area which, because of its presumably largely vegetable matter content, had ignited by spontaneous combustion, the ground feeling warm under the feet and smoke whisping out of fissures in the surface, giving the ground the appearance of a volcano's edge. This was causing a very great problem as it was at this time spreading, and had caused great concern during the late war, as often little flickers of flame would shatter the inky curtain of the 'blackout', that wartime necessity of having no lights which could in any way guide or attract enemy aircraft. The spread of the fire blazing or glowing away underground was threatening the brick arch over the river which wound its course under the embankment, and several attempts had been made to pump water from the brook (which emerged from a grilled tunnel mouth very near the corner of the yard affected by the blaze), down through bored holes to the seat, but nothing had been successful. Eventually a bold move was made, really the only thing which could be done, and a huge chasm was mechanically dug on what was thought to be the edge of the burning area, in a half circle, to stop the blaze spreading any further and to isolate the corner affected.

We had just arrived at the airshaft and were peering down it when a voice said 'What do you think you are doing here?' One of the works watchmen had spotted us, but as Dick turned round, he said 'Oh! It's you is it', and had a short chat with us as Dick and Alfie were known around the works, but officially it was not done to wander about the Con Yard. During our wander round the yard I found an old wooden filing box, one of those used for storing reference cards in offices and stores, etc., and immediately thought of its use for my personal tools, calipers, scrapers and the like, and carried it as a prized possession back, on the surface this time, to G Shop. It served me until the end of my apprenticeship, being carried around on all future moves.

Another little wandering around type of job with the cheerful duo, was that of servicing the steam traps. These small bulbous fittings could be found over many of the drains outside the office blocks and shop offices, workshops, etc., throughout the works. The apparent function of these items was to remove condensation from the many yards of steam heating pipe that threaded the works, and I believe they had a small diaphragm inside which should have retained the steam but allowed the moisture to drain out. Some of these inevitably failed and we would be informed of a doorway or window being obscured by a cloud of steam vapour, entailing a visit and change of trap.

About this time I had purchased a new small lathe for home use, having made several enquiries about obtaining a Myford lathe and finding a waiting list of up to two years and a cost which would have kept me a pauper for even longer! A new or newish manufacturer had put a lathe on the market, the Grayson by E. Gray & Son, and delivery was from stock. I dug deep into my post office savings for the £26 required, and waited, almost with held breath, for the arrival of the large wooden crate which duly arrived after a couple of weeks and was speedily unpacked and returned as there was a £2 refund on the prompt return of the box; such were the difficulties of material handling and obtaining in those days of shortages. I mention the lathe at this point as one of the requirements which I thought I needed was a countershaft arrangement to enable the flat belt, three-step pulley on the headstock to be driven by the round belt from my existing small lathe drive, i.e. the treadle! I didn't consider a motor drive at this time as I had to start saving up again, although that was the goal eventually. Being in G Shop or its environs, I thought would be good opportunity, and also an unofficial extension of trade training, to design a simple countershaft and make it from odds and ends of scrap as what was termed a 'foreigner', or a little personal job completed really illegally at work! With assistance from almost everybody in the compressor house, I had a little bit of turning done here and a little drilling done there, with much filing and hacksawing by myself, and very speedily produced the metal components of the countershaft. I made the rest of it at home from bits of oak found in the shed and the whole thing worked for a number of years, long after the treadle had been sold with the original lathe, and the round belt pulley replaced with the V belt type to match that of the motor, the latter obtained a number of years later when my apprenticeship had finished and my bank balance had risen.

Among the moves in the compressor house to assist the staff as required, was one I remember with Jesse, who appeared to have the servicing of the cranes and hoists in the Boiler V Shop on his list of duties. It was with Jesse that I learned that in engineering, the most difficult thing to handle, at least in my opinion, is a chain! With a rigid component, even an irregularly shaped one, various bits of protuberances can be used as levering or pick up points; even the bogie or sacktrucks can be used as a lever to move things around and position or turn the item concerned. A very weighty bar can be picked up with comparative ease and carried by two men without problems, as can other rigid components be moved, lifted, carried and shifted with ease. A chain just flops! It's just like trying, on a far bigger scale, to pick up a blob of mercury between finger and thumb! A chain seems to run away from you whenever you attempt to move it. To load a largish chain into the bogie or sacktruck, it has to be moved a handful at a time, it can't be just picked up and plonked on. Having loaded most of it from one side of the bogie, one seemingly false move and the chain starts to majestically flow over the other side of the bogie just out of reach!

All chains had to be routinely tested, therefore replacements were continually being made so that no halt in production occurred, save that occasioned by the change over itself, and to this end I accompanied Jesse into the Boiler Shop to change what I believe was an operating chain as opposed to the main lifting chain, on the hoist near the firebox flanging press, and it was here that I experienced an example of how difficult, and even dangerous, handling a chain can be. The flanging area of the Boiler Shop was located in that corner which, in effect, backed on to the compressor house and housed two large gas-fired furnaces and two horizontal hydraulic presses, which resembled huge four-poster beds! It was on these presses that firebox throat and back head plates and smokebox tube plates were pressed and flanged, suitable dies being inserted top and bottom to conform to the required shape. The inner plates of the firebox were of copper and these were pressed and flanged cold, the periphery bent up, with the exception of the bottom edge, about 5 inches and at 90 degrees to the rest of the plate, the bend being a smooth radius.

Facing the flanging press area, a standard track of railway line stretched across the shop, and on the other side of the track, the bay stretched out with large radial drilling machines and the special tower structures for drilling the hundreds of stay holes through the shell of a new firebox. These towers had a counterbalanced drilling platform on which the operator stood to control the horizontally mounted drilling head which could, by horizontal movement of the tower and vertical movement of the platform and drilling head, cover any spot on the broad face of the side of locomotive firebox, say of an area 10 feet by 5 feet. The complete bay was also well provided with jibs and pulley blocks and the whole was covered overhead by a single carriage crane which ran on rails attached to the columns which supported the roof of the bay, the columns reinforced as part of the crane rail support structure.

Having loaded a live, snake-like chain into the bogie, quite a feat in itself, Jesse and I proceeded to the flanging press bay, a small bag of tools and a long length of rope also on the bogie, along with the now recumbent chain. Jesse had a few words with the operators in the area and from somewhere obtained a ladder. We swung the jib back against a column, positioned the ladder, and Jesse climbed up and undid the bolt or shackle retaining the chain end at the top, tying on a piece of rope. Holding the rope, he descended the ladder and lowered the old chain to the ground. I'm not too sure how it happened, but on pulling the replacement chain up over the pulley, something came adrift and the chain came down again like a python in an Amazonian swamp descending to wrap its coils around its next meal! I had the fleeting impression of falling coils dropping on to Jesse who, although a powerful man, was forced to his knees from the weight of the chain and the weighty blows as the coils dropped around his shoulders, fortunately missing his cap-covered head. Rather shaken and bruised, he recovered after a few minutes and the chain was successfully installed, but it certainly gave me a lasting impression of the difficulties of chain handling and a certain respect for an item which appears so innocuous.

On another occasion, attention was again required on a further piece of V Shop lifting tackle, this time on one of the overhead travelling cranes along one of the bays. This entailed us both clambering up the ladder at the end of the bay to mount the crane itself, and travelling with the crane, which as I recall was controlled from the floor level while Jesse examined some part of the mechanism which had been reported faulty. Signalling a stop and selecting a couple of spanners, he swung himself down on to the girder structure under the crane and adjusted something under the carriage which held the lifting mechanism; the clambering around looking very awkward and dangerous and suitably impressing me as an apprentice.

A small job in the compressor house with Jock entailed stripping the headworks off one of the compressors and renewing some of the valve components. My main lasting impression here is of the flat valve seats, which resembled in a much larger way the cutters from a food processor, those flat discs with ground and polished faces with the multi-shaped slots cut through in various positions.

A job undertaken I believe with this gang, though I can't remember now with whom, took us into the Rolling Mill. This was a quite fascinating place and one of those once-in-a-lifetime sights unless you actually worked in the steel industry itself, as it was quite possible that no other large industrial concern actually produced its own rolled sections at that time, it being easier to purchase them from manufacturers who specialised in that sort of work. A range of furnaces provided the raw material in billet form which was then processed through to a series of rolls, a line of eight feeding out on to a wide, long, plated floor over which the snakes of glowing, scaling bar flowed from the back of the rolls, considerably altered in cross-section from the material entering at the front.

The Rolling Mills had a rather interesting and unusual origin. Due to the difficulties experienced during the very early years of the company, the 1840s and 1850s, with the quality of metal used for the railway lines themselves, it was decided at the beginning of the next decade that what was required to solve the problem was a Company Rolling Mill.

No one at Swindon was suitably qualified for initiating such a venture, and so feelers were extended into an existing ironworking area for experienced personnel to not only create such a function but to operate it as a going concern. From South Wales were recruited not only the skilled and experienced operating personnel, but also the actual key founder of the mill, a Mr Ellis, who could not only supervise and manage an operating, producing rolling mill, but who became the major figure in its design and its construction when his proposals had been approved.

Accompanying Thomas Ellis were Welsh-speaking artisans from the established iron industry of South Wales, among Ellis's achievements must be listed the location and establishment of a small Welsh area, quite near the Railway Village, to house the influx of mill workers and their families. Bringing such a group to what was really a very tiny community must have created many problems, not least was the question of where they were to live when they first arrived, but this was solved (satisfactorily must be another question), by housing them in a rather forbidding structure which had been originally built on the founding of the works to house bachelor members of the workforce. This building had a rather chequered career incidentally, becoming next a Wesleyan chapel and later what is now the Swindon Railway Museum, now closed and replaced by 'Steam' GW Museum.

However, the Rolling Mill staff were eventually separately housed in a small extension of the Railway Village, itself now refurbished and preserved, and while off the main track of those visiting the village, still exists as Cambria Place with its little chapel in which originally the services were in Welsh.

First impressions of the Rolling Mill were that it was a rather dark, murky sort of place and you were never too sure where it was safe to walk due to hot material being on the move, or seemingly so, from all directions, whether glowing red, scaling or just hissing and steaming when spat on, but otherwise appearing as black, the spitting preceding placing the hand down to grasp or support. The visit to the mill was just to check on something which had previously been replaced, so apart from the fitter chatting to one of the operators and examining something on one of the rolls, there was really nothing to do. The rolls, those huge shaped metal rollers which worked on the principle of the domestic wringer used for squeezing the water out of the weekly wash, were driven by two horizontal steam engines, 28 inches in terms of the cylinder diameter. Apart from all of the attractions which the horizontal engine had for the steam enthusiast, and really as detailed previously in the sights, sounds and smells of the hydraulic house machinery, the most outstanding item of these engines were the flywheels which gave smoothness and momentum to the engine, and through a large gear train, to the banks of rolls which stretched out parallel to both engines. The flywheels were of cast iron and were of a 20-foot diameter; what a feat of casting that was! The whole engine group sat in isolation within a screened area which, needless to say, was the cleanest part of the mill, and the engine man received his operating and control instructions through a couple of special 'windows' or openings in the surrounding screen.

Compared with the noise of the Steam Hammer and Drop Hammer shops, the Rolling Mill was relatively quiet, the clank of metal and rattle of trolley wheels and the rumble of the rotating rolls just about obliterating the gentle hissing of the engine, the slowly rotating flywheels and the distinctive slow clanking rattle of rotating iron gears. The main gear driving each bank of rolls was about 6 feet in diameter and about 8 inches wide at its toothed periphery. The engines were then about eighty-seven years old, having been installed with the mill in 1860 (the life of these engines was actually 104 years as they were scrapped when the mill closed in 1964). Incidentally, reputedly the highest paid man in the works, on the manual side that is, was the chief shingler, charged with the quality of the finished product through the various rolls and incidentally the father of a school friend.

On another occasion I visited the Spring Shop, located to the right of G Shop, facing the door over the broad gauge turntable. The spring-making process was quite fascinating to watch as there were both coil and leaf springs used on a locomotive. For a leaf spring, a series of flat plates were heated and shaped in a slight curve and then assembled with a buckle or strap around the centre, the pre-punched plates held tightly in the shrunk-on buckle by means of a pin. The biggest of the leaf springs, the King class trailing coupled wheels with a total of thirty-four plates, was quite a weight to handle being about 18 inches high, 5 inches or so wide, and its longest top leaves 3 feet or so long, the top leaves having holes at the ends shaped to clear the spring hangers. Making a coil spring entailed heating the round bar in a special long furnace, drawing and flattening a portion of each end of the bar, already of the required length, pre-calculated and so cut and then withdrawing from the furnace while glowing red, gripping the flat end in a special set of rolls and rotating the rolls to wind-on the bar. The winding process was preset to ensure that the coils had the correct pitch, as with a thread, and the coiled spring was then heat-treated or tempered by immersing in special oil.

To test a spring for elasticity, it was placed in a scragging machine and literally bounced a number of times under the loads, or with a safety factor above the loads it was to endure when actually installed and in use on the locomotive. The term associated with the process was applied to several procedures throughout the works. We have noted scragging applied to removing the rag or sharp edges from nuts and carried out in R Shop; also the special press for removing the squeezed-out excess metal from a stamping made under a drop hammer, and here we have yet another use of the word on the testing of springs. A dictionary definition (one of several) gives 'scrag' as a noun meaning 'anything thin or lean with roughness', so its application to a human being as being 'scraggy' is understandable also!

My next moves, while of interest, were rather out of the run of a locomotive apprenticeship, being in the first instance just across the road from the Hooter House and behind the rectangular building housing the central boilers. The new short stay area was that of the garage which housed the very small section which maintained the run-abouts of the factory transport. As I recall there were only two fitters in this shop, the senior one I assume paid a chargehand's rate, andI do not remember there being anyone else although there could have been a labourer or mate. However, what I do recall is that everything was dominated by Harold, who appeared to me to have a dislike of most people and a pathological hatred of apprentices. Short-cropped, greying hair over a square face (his whole being resembled Peter Sellers in the later classic film *All Right Jack!*), I was greeted, when I tried to introduce myself, with the statement 'I'm not interested in your name! I call all apprentices John! Saves a lot of time! If you hear someone call John, that's you so come running!' His next question was equally short and to the point. 'Know anything about car engines?' I should have realised! I should have considered my answer but with such an off-putting introduction, I was beginning to wonder what I was being let in for, but I didn't! I said 'No! Nothing. I prefer steam engines!' I thought he was going to explode.

He threw up his arms in horror and said 'Good God, not another one!' turned on his heel and strode off! The other fitter who had been standing in the background came over and had a little chat, showing me where to stack my little box of tools in the bench and where to hang my coat, explaining away the incident of the introduction as 'Harold's not such bad old stick really!' Maybe not, I thought, but he certainly scared me!

Still associated with G Shop, the stay was to be short, but quite long enough, most of the jobs being quite small, allocated in one sentence and only once by Harold, and then supervised by the other fitter, whose name I don't remember as the presence of Harold seemed to dominate the shop! One job I do remember doing in addition to digging nails and bits of metal out of tyres, was that of attaching registration numberplates to several of the vehicles so that they could travel on public roads outside the works. The vehicles were very powerful for their size, being four- or six-wheel (double at the back), rather high up and with no protection for the driver except a cape-like sheet which could be attached to the bonnet cover and the back of the driver's seat. The capacity was two on the bench seat, and behind was a towing hook with a metal box over it to hold the pins and safety clips used for securing the standard, flat, two-wheel trailers used throughout the works. Built up on to the chassis, probably made as an additional feature actually in the works and attached to the vehicles on purchase, was a stout angle-iron framework which supported the towing hook at the back and a large square ¼ inch thick steel plate which completely covered the front of the vehicle, being about 4 feet by 3 feet and perforated with drilled holes immediately in front of the position of the radiator. I remember seeing, on several occasions, while an office boy, these vehicles using this metal plate to move wagons short distances in the stores yards. I had to drill and tap a couple of holes in the top of the plates on several vehicles and attach the number plates; I think the only comment from Harold when I had finished, being a very blunt 'Hmm! Finished it? Certainly took you long enough!' Apart from that small job, coupled with puncture repairs and steel splinter removal from tyres, the only other job was that of cleaning components removed for repair. Steering track rod assemblies and broken springs (quite a lot of these), various engine bits, sumps to be cleaned out and the like, gave me very dry, chapped hands, caused through the effects of the cleaning oil. I don't remember any form of protective gloves, which would probably have been scorned by Harold, but the drying effect of the cleaning oil was certainly undesirable, although the oil which resembled paraffin was a standard issue for that purpose throughout the works. I was not sorry when Harold approached and said, 'Next Monday, B Shed, mobile cranes!' and then as an aside muttered what sounded like, 'And then I suppose I shall be stuck with another one!' That was all that was said. The other fitter wished me the best of luck and really without a backward glance and certainly with a feeling of relief, I assembled my box of tools and odds and ends for the next move. Since my introduction to the trade, now about two years ago, when I had started in B Shed, some changes had been made regarding mobile crane repairs, (I didn't remember seeing the area on my first stay in the shop, although the site may have been there, and further developed in the intervening period). In B Shed were the three sections the locomotives down the right-hand bay adjacent to R Shop wall, then the tender section and, down the left-hand wall, the boiler bay. On my first stay in the shop I don't recall a fenced or partitioned off area specifically for mobile i/c engine-driven cranes but the boiler section seemed to have considerably reduced, and the end of the ex-boiler bay at the main line end of the shop now contained a special section partitioned off from the rest of the shop with what looked like new metal and wood partitions, brown painted, and with a wire mesh panel in the top section of each partition. It was in this section that the mobile cranes were repaired. In the shop at this time, incidentally, at the end of the tender water road, was a large steam crane under repair, and I think I would rather have been working on that! However, I reported as instructed, to the mobile crane section.

This section was a complete change from the barn-like garage, being a rather closely knit group who seemed to go out of their way to be helpful. Having work explained by being shown the manuals, and drawings by Geoff or Ivor, helped a great deal and the small jobs which were completed were commented on and chatted about, making a very good working environment. The cranes were what was called I believe the Jumbo variety, having a jib which was pivoted above the operator's seat with the winding gear at the back over a very large grey-painted counterbalance weight, which was itself above two smaller diameter, solid rubber-tyred wheels, which also did the steering. The jib could only lift and lower, the whole crane being required to 'slew' or turn with the load. It was one of these cranes that I had seen a couple of years before when still an office boy, trundling its way down between the CME's office block and the side of B Shed. I had just come up the slope from the tunnel entrance and was about to go in through the door by the west time office when I saw the crane and stopped to watch it. The old telephone exchange was then in the main office building, the new exchange being several years away in the future, and the web of 'phone cables came from the exchange and crossed the road about 12 feet up, to the wall of B Shed. The crane came trundling along with its jib up instead of the usual horizontal position, and ploughed straight through the telephone wires, stopping part way through when the driver (female?) realised what had happened. There was great consternation, people appearing from all sides with bags of advice, most of it conflicting. How it was resolved I'm not sure but I would imagine the lady did not qualify for a 'driver of the year' award!

After a very short stay with the cranes it was back to G Shop, so once again I packed my little box of tools and crossed the old broad gauge table to enter G Shop, turning immediately right inside the door and so to the cupboard of Cyril Wallington, right at the far end of the shop. Cyril was a very tall, quietly spoken character, a complete contrast to my stay in the garage under the tender care of Harold. I worked here with Norman, a younger, very chatty man, whose speciality at this stage was repairing the grab bucket gear of the various lifting appliances unloading sand and gravel, presumably at railway dock and wharf establishments. Norman had been in the RAF in the late war and regaled me during my all too short stay on Cyril's gang with various tales of exploits in the Pacific area of the war with the Royal Air Force.

One of the bucket grabs repaired had given trouble by seizing up after being in use for a short time, and had been sent back for further attention. What had apparently happened was that the pins which had been renewed during the repair, had been made, with the best possible engineering motives, with too good a fit in the holes, and while working very crisply and smoothly in the shop, tested and tried out by being attached to the overhead crane for a dummy run, when actually in use had seized up due to the sand getting into every bearing and pivot point. The seized pins had to be driven out, and the bucket was placed on its support ring with the bucket jaws up in the air. I should think about 5 feet off the floor. With considerable difficulty we drove out some of the seized pins, with Norman standing on a bench to reach some of the mechanism. I was standing by one of the bucket halves and moved sideways to get a better view of what he was actually doing, when he drove out a particularly tight pin and half the bucket came down like a big rat trap, the 8-inch-long bolted-on teeth on the bucket edge going right through the floor blocks and into the concrete base underneath, in the spot I had occupied a moment or so before! A rather shaken Norman got down off the bench and we chatted a little, although he was rather quieter than usual, and several others came over to watch as the bucket was eased out of the floor and back to an even keel. The new pins were refitted with greater clearances and no further trouble was reported.

Quite near where the episode with the bucket had occurred stood a large marking off table, just to the right of the entrance to the area of Fred Selby's gang, with a grinding wheel next in line along the wall. This in turn led to another small area behind the main shop, which also had lathes and fitting benches and was the area which I remember repaired the hydraulic capstans, one of which was located by the side of the old broad gauge turntable outside one shop door. The capstan was of course all that showed above ground level, apart from the cylindrical operating pedal of the control valve. Under the cast-iron base plate, which was about 4 feet square, was an interesting three-cylinder oscillating hydraulic engine driving the capstan crank and secured so that it was horizontal, literally hanging under the base plate. There was a tale that the chargehand explaining repair procedures to either a fitter or an apprentice, using as an example a repaired capstan with its mechanism exposed and connected to the hydraulic main for testing, had said 'Now, something you must never do is touch this valve while checking this clearance or you will lose a ow....! I b.... well have!' In short, he did and he had, lost the top of a finger between the casing and a cylinder!

Between this small area of capstan repairs and the main shop itself, in effect stretching along the row of arches, which supported the overhead crane, on the opposite side of the shop to that of Cyril's benches which themselves stretched along from the door to the shop end on the yard side, was the longest lathe I have ever seen. The headstock had, I believe, been raised from say 12 inches to about 18 inches centre height by the insertion of special iron block castings, the tailstock having been raised as well as in the same manner. The lathe bed was a feat of engineering by itself, being about 50 feet long, in fact it was so long that the end fitted into a recess in the wall of the Spring Shop next door! While I was in the shop, the lathe was in use turning a ram for a hydraulic lift, the workpiece being about 20 feet long and say of 18-inch diameter. It appeared to be in several sections joined together, although I'm not sure how, but it had to be supported by steadies at regular intervals to stop it from sagging (*see Plate 15*). On some of the longer items, I would image a 'roughing' or first cut on the basic metal could take several days to complete and the possibility of turning something of this length down to the wrong size doesn't bear thinking about! The work on the marking off table was undertaken by two men, one short and slim, bespectacled and with blue overalls always with an array of scribers and rules in the top pocket, and the other, a rotund, round-faced little man, also with an array of items in his top pocket, although this time a brown warehouse coat in place of overalls. The name of the former I don't recall but the latter I came to know quite well after Norman said on the first Friday, 'Better nip across to Bill Godbold and pay my tool club!' Further questioning revealed that Bill ran the Stratton

Tool Club whereby you could pay a small sum each week and when a particular tool was required, a visit to Bartrop's (now Sargent's Tool Stores) in Swindon with a special little order form from Bill (the amount recorded on your little pink folding card would be adjusted to suit), and the item could be obtained possibly at a slight discount. Without further ado I joined as well and continued for a number of years, regularly paying a shilling or so and chatting to Bill, a very cheerful, friendly sort of character, during my weekly visits. Bill also operated the large roundabout near the marking off table (*see Plate 13*). Also on Friday afternoon, the mate or labourer on the gang would, as in some long established ritual, clean our much smaller marking off table. I did not see this done anywhere else in this fashion, but on Friday he would tip an amount of cleaning oil, that paraffin-like liquid that had given me chaps in the garage, on to the tabletop, produce a clean sheet of medium emery cloth and a special large steel block. Placing the sheet 'sharp side' down on the oily surface, the block was placed on top of the emery cloth and the whole lot pushed backwards and forwards across the table top. The top came up clean and bright of course for the start of the week the following Monday, but over the years of continued treatment I often wondered how flat the surface would be in the future!

The next move after another short stay was in effect to the other end of G Shop. Cyril's gang had been to the right of the entrance door and my new assignment was to the left, the chargehand's cupboard being as Cyril's had been, in the corner of the shop along the wall facing the yard, and this time at the Manager's Office end. Fred Hawksbee had a similar row of benches, but it appeared that most of his staff were 'outstation' operators and from the nature of the work undertaken, were mainly concerned with turntables and their mechanisms. While the big locomotive turntables, located all over the system in works and running sheds, were dealt with in plate and angle structure terms by boilermakers, the wheels and locking arrangements were dealt with by fitters.

On arrival, it appeared the only other person on the gang actually still in Swindon, apart from the mate, was Ray Taylor, a newly transferred fitter from the Locomotive Erecting Shop who, as a journeyman, had completed his apprenticeship and been transferred from the pits to this new job. One of my first jobs was to assist him to 'move in~ as there was no one else on the gang at this time. We collected his goods and chattels from AE Shop and then cleared out a cupboard under one of the benches for his use. The first actual job for both of us was the cleaning up of some very large locking pins for one of the larger turntables. They were each about 2½ feet long, possibly of 4-inch diameter, and screwed for part of the length with a large coarse pitch square section double start thread. In screw cutting a large thread, or any thread for that matter, the start of the thread, commencing as it does from a square end or shoulder on the length to be threaded, always has a very thin wall and is always susceptible to damage, the same comment applying to the other end or run out of the thread. It is always the practice to remove this thin section before use of the screw, with the larger threads, as even a small amount of damage renders the thread inoperable.

We had several of these screws to do, about eight or ten, and they were very carefully handled to avoid any damage to any part of the thread. Mounted in copper 'dogs' or separate sheet copper faces, which pushed over the hardened vice jaws to prevent bruising or cutting the workpiece on the very course serrations on the face of the jaws, we chipped off the lead section for about ¼ turn of the thread. The new blunt end had a very short taper filed on it and was then smoothly rounded off and tapered downward quite sharply from crest to root of the thread. During the early afternoon Fred came along to see how things were going and said that what we were doing was correct, but that we were now to hang fire on the job!

I believe the finished screws had to be heat-treated, so we assumed that some problem had arisen and they could not now be handled at the Treatment Shop. At about 5 p.m., Fred returned and he appeared to be both shocked and annoyed that we had not finished them, but we told him, or at least the fitter told him, that we had followed his instructions to the letter and had slowed down as he wanted. This proved to be a case of incorrect instruction and/or interpretation. Both of us assumed that to hang fire was to slow down, but Fred had meant entirely the opposite and had wanted us to proceed as rapidly as possible! My memory of Fred is of a very annoyed chargehand, haring off round the shop looking for the gang labourer to move the screws we had completed and, being unable to find him, returning to the bench pushing a bogie himself, hastily loading the completed screws and disappearing into the distance in a cloud of annoyance and dust. We completed the remaining screws in some haste and to Fred's eventual satisfaction, but it shows how easy it is to incorrectly interpret the spoken word and do just the opposite to what is actually required.

In the shop at this end were several lathes, and a large planer. The machines which were located at this end of the shop included a couple of large capacity machines which turned the rolls for the rolling mill. The lathe which was certainly unusual was positioned to the left of the main entrance and roadway through the shop. As the right-hand side had included the lathe with the longest bed I have ever seen, so that on the left included the largest faceplate I have ever come across. The lathe itself was very old but still very much utilised and accurate, being in effect a very low-level short bed with extremely large tail stock of special design, and an equally large cross and top slide assembly, the whole being waist height on a level with the lathe centre. The main feature was the face plate which was probably of about 10-foot diameter and ran in what would be the gap of a normal lathe in the usual way, but which in this case was a railed off trench in the floor! The face plate was capable of being extended by bolting on special arms, and in this format must have been capable of swinging about 16 feet in diameter. Quite a machine and one of the oldest in the works. The largest items I saw being turned were some very large gear wheels, but these fitted on to the face plate and the extensions were not used.

As with all G Shop moves, my stay with Ray and Fred came to a rapid end and my next job according to the piece of paper waved by Fred, showed that a return to P1 Shop and to Chargehand Stevens was to be my lot, with a start on boiler mounting.

It is unfortunate really that my seven months' stay in G Shop did not produce some more lasting memories, but with only about a month on each gang and coupled with the very random nature of maintenance, many of the smaller jobs of the one-off variety did not remain in the memory or make an impression suitable for more detailed recall.

12
P1 Shop Again

The return to P1 Shop certainly occurred in better weather than I had experienced last time I had set foot in the draughty place. The Monday morning saw me with several other new arrivals, unhooking my check from the board and walking across the end of the shop to the cupboard adjacent to the top of the hoist, which brought the boilers through from the Boiler Shop, under the road, to re-emerge in P1 Shop for finishing work.

If the composer Handel had been alive at this period, or conversely if steam boilers had existed in Handel's time, I'm sure he would have dedicated his Largo to the new chargehand, 'Banger' Stevens. A tall man, to me at least very tall, as he towered above my 5 feet 3 inches, quite heavily built and with a small, spikey, waxed moustache, he moved with a very slow, measured step, so upright that his head seemed to be drawn back and his chin tucked in. His slow tread and carriage reminded one of the passage of a seventy-four gun ship of the line and when he approached, you knew how the French admiral Villeneuve felt at Trafalgar when Nelson appeared, as it was more of a 'bearing down on you' than an approach. However, he was a man of few words, and I think the only time he spoke to me was when he allocated me to a fitter whose name escapes me.

It appeared that various fitters on the gang specialised on various jobs, although it is quite possible that they could each do most jobs. My first move was with the casing brackets man. A locomotive boiler, subjected to all forms of temperature variations along its not inconsiderable length, is only attached and anchored securely at the front end! Not of course that it is free to move about all over the place at the firebox end, but it is secured there in a different way. While bolted in front to the cylinder saddle and not allowed to move, the temperature variations must be accommodated somewhere, and this is where the casing brackets come in! Marked off very carefully on the shaped sides of the firebox were two lines which coincided with top edges of the locomotive frames at the firebox end, one on each side of the box, ensuring that the boiler would be in a truly horizontal position when in place on the frames. Set to this line on each side of the box was a very stout, shaped bracket, often in two or more sections, of very heavy 'L' section, each about 1½ inches by 30 inches and about ¾ inch thick on the back section and about 1½ inches thick on the bottom of the 'L', which stood out possibly 2½ inches. In use, the bracket rested on top of the frames and was free to move under special clamps, longitudinally as the boiler contracted and expanded in its range of use and temperature variations.

Although sounding very straightforward, which in principle I suppose it was, the brackets themselves were, of necessity, very strangely shaped on the back face, which was bolted to the firebox. In Great Western practice, the firebox was of the Belpaire form in which the rectangular base of the box fitted between the frames then rose up to frame level, and then curved outwards and upwards, to finish considerably wider than the frames at the top of the box, which had curved corners and a relatively flat top. It was, in effect, roughly an inverted flat pear shape, but with a flat top and bottom, the box also in plan being wider at the front above frame level where the boiler barrel was attached than at the back where the firehole door was located.

The back face of the casing bracket had to fit the shape of the firebox and, when bolted into place, also fit neatly on top of the locomotive frame, and with its edges aligned with the frame. The line to which these brackets had to be fitted had, I believe, already been marked out by Banger before the boiler was allocated to a fitter for the brackets to be attached, as I don't remember being involved in any process of marking out; we just secured the plates to the box. A further complication arose with the stay ends! I mentioned that the inner and outer firebox shells were secured and strengthened with dozens of stays, screwed through both shells and caulked in by means of a specially adapted pneumatic hammer which had a hollow nose tool. The hollow end of the hammer fitted over the protruding length, very short though it was, of the ends of the stay, and proceeded to rivet over or drive the metal, not of the stay in a usual riveting procedure, but a ring of the actual boiler shell into and around the protruding screwed end of the stay. This left a little circular indent around each stay end.

The casing bracket had therefore to fit not only the varying shape of the firebox outer shell but also to fit over the protruding stays! I have the impression that the brackets arrived already shaped to fit the firebox and with predrilled 'blind' holes (i.e. not drilled right through the plate) to fit over the stay ends. Also predrilled were the holes through which the specially collared stud would pass when the plate was eventually secured to the boiler. The stays were of course located in set positions, and the plates could be pre-jig drilled to suit the anticipated protrusions, the recessed hole being considerably larger than the actual end of the stay. I'm not certain where these plates were actually prepared; it could have been in the boiler shop itself, but by the usual trade demarcation (i.e. they were not riveted in situ) a fitter had to drill the holes in the boiler shell and insert the studs, followed by securing the plate with nuts and spring or grover washers.

At this period, there were very few electric portable drills used in the works; in fact I do not recall ever using or even seeing one, all portable machines being driven by compressed air, the pneumatic main reaching to all parts of the works with all benches fitted with regular air points, the hoses being of the screw-on type, the brass union having two wings or ears which were pressed by thumb and fingers in the tightening process. There were small hand drills, in size similar to the present day DIY drills by various makers, but usually the drill used was very weighty, and was a two-man job to control, having two tubular handles, one either side of the body on the centre line, one handle having a twist grip like a motorcycle throttle control. The air line was connected to the end of the handle to which the twist grip was attached, and the very stoutly wire-wound rubber hose trailed off to the nearest air control valve and connection.

The sides of the firebox were whitened in the area to be covered by the casing brackets which were offered up and secured by finger clamps screwed on to the extremely short ends of the protruding stays, only possibly a couple of threads being usable. The predrilled holes through the bracket were now used as jig holes to mark through with a scriber on to the firebox shell. A big centre pop mark in the centre and four smaller marks to show the

P1 Shop – boiler mounting under the watchful eye of 'Banger' Stevens.

periphery of each hole showed the position when the brackets were removed, care being taken that the brackets sat well on the firebox and were not held up by a stay end which protruded a little too far, or a blind hole which did not quite give the clearance required by the stay end; in the case of the latter the edge of the blind hole was chipped out a little to miss the stay.

Drilling was by 'drill post and arm', the post being a round bar of about 1½-inch diameter forming an 'L' shape with a 2½ inches by 1 inch thick slotted base about 10 inches long. The arm was free to move up and down the post and was secured in the drilling position by a bolt screwed in at 90 degrees to the post, allowing the arm to be positioned anywhere up the post. A special hollow-screwed end stud was itself screwed over a protruding stay end and the slotted base of the post secured by a nut and washer on the top of the stud. The drilling machine had a pointed centre at its back end opposite the drill chuck, controlled by a star wheel handle which could be turned to screw the centre in and out. The lower face of the arm had a vast number of random shallow pointed holes, shaped to the centre point angle and, in effect, like very large, deep, centre punch (or 'pop') marks. In use, the drill was positioned with its drill bit in the centre of the marked out hole position and its star-wheel-controlled centre located in one of the holes in the arm, consistent with the squareness or angle of the required hole to be drilled. With the fitter holding and controlling the star-wheeled centre which gave the feed to the drill bit, and with the other hand on the twist grip throttle control, the apprentice's job was to hang on to the other handle like grim death while the fitter opened the throttle and the drill started to cut (*see Plate 22*).

The job required considerable concentration as several things could happen, usually at the same time! Firstly, if the drill jammed, and a ¾-inch or ⅞-inch drill is quite large, the drill stopped and the machine tried to go round! This meant that there was an almighty kick as the large machine twisted. The time this occurred was usually just as the drill bit was breaking through the material, having just about finished its cut, and in this case, of course, the star wheel centre was no longer tight into its hole in the arm, so the whole drill not only kicked, it twisted viciously sideways as it was not now supported at its back end and tended to screw itself forward up the drill's helical flutes. We were often working on low platforms of boards and portable trestles to enable a reasonable position to be maintained so that we were not trying to drill at chest height, and when the twist and kick came from the drilling machine we both had to do a little double shuffle along the boards to hold the drill for the split second before the air supply could be stoped. It would have made a good music hall act! Sometimes the drill stuck partway through, and then the process was to firmly grip the machine, or I should say grip it even more firmly than we had already been doing, and rock the machine around the drill by pumping the handles up and down; meanwhile the fitter opened and closed the throttle control, hoping to kick the thing back to life. This usually had the desired effect and the drill resumed cutting. Sometimes the kick was so vicious that the whole post and arm twisted round as well, in extreme cases pulling off its very short threaded piece of stay, so you were then both dealing not only with the wild machine but with a freely falling and weighty drill post and arm! The job certainly sharpened the reflexes and gave you very nimble footwork!

However, for all its hazards, the old boys in the shop said it was far better as a method than the old drill post, arm and ratchet drill, where the drill was fed by the centre post and arm method, but rotated manually by a ratchet handle arrangement. At the end of the day with this method, you were quite 'armless'!

Having drilled the holes, ¾-inch Whitworth taper taps and wrenches were produced and the holes were threaded to take the studs. These were of a special shape, having a collar about ⅞ inch or so in diameter around the plain body of the stud, and about ¹¹⁄₁₆ inch or so long, just a little less than the thickness of the back of the bracket. Tapping the holes was a straightforward sort of job, as was screwing in the studs for which a stud box was used. This was a short length of hexagon or sometimes square, heat-treated bar about 3 inches long, drilled and tapped right through the centre longitudinally. A hardened steel bolt was screwed in one end and the top end of the stud was screwed in the other end of the box. In screwing in the stud, the bottom of the box was not allowed to touch the collar, the amount of stud screwed in being governed by the bolt, itself allowed to contact the end of the stud and so prevent it screwing any further into the box. The opposite end of the stud was now positioned and started in a tapped hole, being screwed home tightly by means of a wrench or spanner which fitted the outside of the stud box. When screwed home firmly, releasing the bolt allowed the box to be easily removed by hand from the stud, which was now secured in place.

Having screwed in all the studs, now came the moment of truth; would the bracket fit over all the studs? In my experience, I would say that in most cases the answer was no! There always seemed to be several of the studs which would not go through the holes in the bracket or at least the collar part, the most important bit would not go through or in some cases would not even enter!

Given the difficulties of drilling and the shape of the firebox itself, this was not really surprising and the procedure was now to file out the holes in the bracket to suit the positioning of the rogue studs. At the base of most of the roof support columns along the edge of the traversing table road was usually a small bench of steel plate and angle iron, attached to the column and about 18 inches square, and on which was mounted a large-size leg vice, the old type in which the jaws do not open parallel but are pivoted between the jaw level and the ground, the front jaw held by a large flat spring to stop it from flopping when the vice is opened. Not being very tall and with nothing to stand on except my own feet and the wood block floor, I did not like the job of filing out the holes as quite a lot of pressure was required, particularly if the file was a bit ancient which it usually was, and I couldn't seem to get over or above the job to bear down fully. Once the brackets were fitted to the studs, they were securely nutted on.

A further interesting point which still confuses even to this day: as a war economy measure, someone had a bright idea in some far-removed Ministry Office regarding saving of metal. Most nuts and bolts of the day were to the Whitworth thread form and such sizes in imperial measures of ¾ inch, ⁷⁄₁₆ inch, ½ inch, ⅝ inch, ⅞ inch, 1 inch, etc. All nuts and bolts were hexagonal in shape, and made to set dimensions. Thus a spanner marked ⅞ inch, was suitable for a ⅞-inch nut, the dimension on the spanner referring to the diameter of the bolt or the hole through the nut. The genius with the economical turn of mind decided that it would be a good idea in the attempt to save metal, to make the nut to fit for example the 1-inch bolt, from the material and to the size of the ⅞-inch nut but to actually thread it 1 inch! Thus, at this time, bolts of one size could be found with the original full-size head and with a nut of the size below; conversely, an old full-size nut could be found on a new smaller headed bolt! It may have saved on the nut and bolt material but you now needed to take two sets of spanners with you to match the various combinations that could be found!

While on the tapping job for the brackets, I sustained a minor injury which entailed a visit to the outpatients section of what had been until the war, the GWR medical fund hospital. This establishment was really the forerunner of the National Health Service, whereby for a small sum payable per week by each employee and deducted from the wages, a full medical service was available without extra payment, including hospital, medicines and doctors, the latter either visiting the home of patients or actually visited by the patient at the Medical Fund premises in Faringdon Road. I believe the first payment I made as an office boy was 4*d* (less than 2p per week!)

However, the injury was sustained in reaching up to grasp the end of the tap wrench when changing grip in the to and fro motion of tapping a stud hole. As I reached up, my right elbow moved too close to the firebox shell and a protruding stud end with a sharp thread cut my arm quite deeply. A visit to the red box in the shop, accompanied by the first aid practitioner, saw a dressing wrapped round the elbow and a pass out provided from the office to enable me to attend for a checkover at the outpatients. It was a clean cut which was filled with some white powder which I believe had the new penicillin base, a new dressing applied and I was back in P1 Shop in no time. Everything healed well and quite quickly and I had no trouble with the arm at all, although I still have the scar to remind me of the incident.

One casing bracket fitted is very like any other casing bracket and a general move round the gang was a standard practice. While working on the firehole door mechanism on the back head of a boiler, my new mate and I spied Banger in full sail, gliding majestically across the table road in our apparent direction, so we both kept our heads down while watching his approach. He hove-to at the end of our particular stretch of rail line and anchored in the table road. A slowly beckoning arm and crooked finger had the look of a pennant signalling 'All captains report aboard the flagship', so the fitter dutifully complied, climbing down from the platform where we had been 'keeping our heads down', seemingly in vain! A short exchange of conversation and the fitter returned to the platform while Banger sailed away in the direction of his cupboard. 'Got a foundation ring in the AV first thing tomorrow,' said the fitter, 'we can sort out some tools before we go, shan't need much! Drill post and arm, the drill of course, hand hammers, round noses and diamond points! Should be about it. Oh! And chisels, musn't forget them!'

I was still a bit intrigued about what we could actually do with a foundation ring, that heavy, square section rectangular seal in the bottom of the firebox which closed the gap between the inner and outer firebox shells. All would be revealed on the morrow. For the rest of today, the back head fittings still awaited, and I continued with the firehole door gear. The door operating mechanism on a GWR pattern boiler was quite simple in operation and in attaching! The two cast-iron doors were hollow and ran between two horizontal rails mounted one above and one below the firehole orifice in the back head. The hole was formed by both inner and outer shells being 'belled' out, to come together in an outward facing, double, riveted edge where the two plates joined around the circular firehole. The orifice itself was protected by a heavy iron casting which covered the lower half of the hole and in section was 'D'-shaped, the shape fitting upside down over the riveted edges of the plates. A handle on the left of the firehole, attached by a pivot stud to the bottom door runner, operated the doors through a linked lever arrangement, in which levers pivoted to the doors themselves caused both to slide open or close when the lever was operated. A drop stamped plate flap was hinged to roughly clear the orifice when the doors were opened and an angled deflector plate was attached inside above the hole. The whole door mechanism was quite simple really, just retained in position by ordinary stamped black washers and split pins with relatively large clearances on the pivot studs and lever holes, running quite easily when operated. Although seemingly crude, the whole was designed for the specific purpose, the shape of the angled deflector plate for example was to direct the flow of air entering the box down towards the fire itself. In the event that the plate was not correctly angled or had become burnt and was thus too short, the air would pass, still cold, over the brick arch and into the area of the top of the tube plate, thus causing unnecessary stresses to the boiler. Regarding the reference to the brick arch, this was a fire brick structure within the firebox to direct (roughly as a simple description) the flow of the fire gases into the fire tubes through the boiler assisting combustion and 'smoke' clearance. The brick arch also protected that portion of the tube plate in the box over which the flame and gases flowed, thus avoiding a certain amount of scouring and corrosion of the stays and plates (*see drawing*).

The following morning saw us loading the items into the trolley or 'bogie' as it was always called, and heading out of the P1 Shop door opposite the hoist from the Boiler Shop, across the P1 yard, past the standing boilers on their special trolleys, bumping the bogie across the rails of the table road, and up on the other side to AM Shop.

Stepping past the partitioned end of AM Shop, the scene changed completely and the noise level differed. Gone was the hum of machinery and line shafting, the rattle of walking

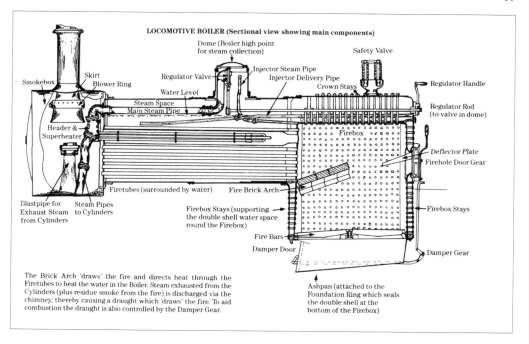

Sectional view of locomotive boiler.

crane gears and the crackling and flashing of the welding bay. We were back in a wider, higher version of the Boiler Shop. About 2 yards, in on the right stood a permanently operating punch and shears, the twin heads and cutters worked by a cam arrangement which gave the very small movement of the shear blade, angled at its cutting edge like something from *The Tale of Two Cities*, and the punch on the opposite side moving its hardened finger up and down about 3 inches through its guide, both sufficiently and quietly powerful enough to cut and punch up to about ⅝ inch, thick steel plate. To the left as the AV Shop was entered from AM Shop, the roof suddenly became very high indeed over one portion of the bay and in the clear space below, standing like some mysterious Egyptian obelisk of black basalt, was the 'Iron Man'! Some portions and components of a locomotive boiler and indeed of large cylindrical tanks, while readily if somewhat awkwardly handled separately during manufacture, reach a stage at assembly where handling is very difficult if the job is to be done efficiently. Riveting a boiler shell to the firebox is an example of the difficulty encountered, the security of riveting at the junction of the two items, say an 18-foot-long boiler cylindrical shell and a circular flanged rectangular firebox, having to be of the first order and it was this process which benefited from the assistance of the Iron Man, temporarily bolted together, the shell and firebox combined would be lowered carefully end-on over the upright iron finger, the very high roof at this point allowing the overhead crane, its travel limited, sufficient clearance to lift the boiler assembly, firebox first, up into the air and then carefully lower it so that the iron obelisk went up inside the boiler shell. A set of varying dollies was available for insertion in the head of the obelisk to suit the head diameters of the rivets, which would be used to permanently join the two items together, the temporary bolts being removed as riveting proceeded. The top of the obelisk contained a small platform on which the member of the riveting team stood to ensure the team operation both inside and out. The use of the hydraulic riveting facilities completing this very awkward job, the soft hiss and extreme power of the hydraulic system replacing the clang of the riveters' hammers, closing jaws on the red hot rivets inserted by metal tongs.

The riveters' hammers clanging away in other parts of the shop were still a feature of boiler work, although it certainly seemed to be quieter here than in the Boiler V Shop itself. One was also drawn inevitably to the flash of the arc welders, working somewhere on the many boilers in process of repair in this very large bay, and so wending our way with care, with me pushing the bogie containing our tools, we found ourselves in the middle of the shop in a relatively clear space looking at a foundation ring, mounted on its back on two very stout wooden trestles. The solid section ring was perforated horizontally all around by rivet holes, I should think of about ⅞-inch diameter in two closely spaced but staggered rows, and the upper surface of the ring which would normally be the underside in actual use, was completely ringed with ¾-inch studs, to which the ashpan would be attached. Some of the studs were in reasonable condition but many were either broken off or bent. It was these studs which we had to deal with. The object of the exercise was to cut off and drill out any studs broken or bent and to remove the drilled-out thread of the stud from the tapped hole in the ring.

I waited a minute or two while the fitter sought out the boilermaker chargehand to ensure we were looking at the correct ring, and that it was OK to start work. It was the right time and place, so the tools came out of the bogie and the air pipe was unrolled and attached to the nearest air valve mounted on one of the angle or RSJ roof support columns, trailing its armoured length a considerable distance across the shop. The first thing, however, was to cut off those studs which had bent and to chip flat those which had broken, making a flush surface with that of the ring itself. Usually a good stud was left standing within a small group of those to be renewed, and could be used to anchor the drill post and arm, but sometimes a run of broken studs meant that one stud at least had to be drilled out using a free standing drill. I think the term 'free standing' is a misnomer really as these drilling machines had a mind of their own, the users just hanging on like grim death and trying to push the machine forward at the same time to feed the drill into the material. However, first having cut the studs off level, a large centre pop mark was made in the centre of the now flat stud face, and the drill post and arm positioned to suit.

Drilling out the studs was accomplished after the same sort of struggle experienced with the casing brackets. The stud ends were screwed in tightly to the end of their own threaded portion, but the hole into which they had been screwed was usually considerably deeper to allow for the lead of the tap used to form the thread in the foundation ring, and this caused the same kicking and jumping problems with the machine as we had faced with the casing brackets. Having drilled out the core of a broken stud, the shell remaining in the thread had to be removed, the tapped hole being required for a replacement stud. Removal was accomplished with the round nose chisel and/or the diamond point chisel, the shell being driven in from the thread into the hole, and folding or collapsing away from the thread. The pieces were hooked out of the hole by a short length of welding electrode, the wire used in the arc welding process being flattened and bent into a ¼-inch hook on one end.

On reflection, I believe we had to remove all the studs from the ring as I do not recall screwing any back in, and again on reflection those which remained or those which would have been replaced, would have been further damaged when the ring was replaced and riveted back in to seal a fire box. The studs must have been replaced elsewhere but I have no idea where, as I was not involved in the fitting of any ashpan and damper gear during the course of my apprenticeship.

In addition to the clang of riveting hammers and the rattle of pneumatic guns, a pair of boilermakers were using a pneumatic rivet-cutting hammer on the next boiler. This resembled a longer, slimmer, pneumatic road drill, having a chisel blade at one end, a long thin body and a long 'T' handle at the other end. In place of the squeeze handle of a road drill, which resulted in an automatic series of rapid blows until the handle was released, the rivet cutter had a single short lever on the side which moved only about 5 inches to and fro from its pivot, giving a single sharp blow to the tool at each movement. Depending on access, the cutter could be suspended from a frame by a hook at its balance point, or could be used independently, but with some difficulty in the latter case. With one or two men at the rear handle, one operating the control lever, a third man in heavy leather gloves and apron and wearing goggles, controlled and positioned the chisel blade against the rivet head to be removed. Using a shearing action, the blows of the chisel deformed the rivet head, digging into the dome or pan shape of the head and causing the rivet to shear off under the head. If allowed free range, the head would fly a considerable distance, with great danger to anyone in the vicinity, but a portable screen was used of tubular and wire mesh construction; also the man who controlled the cutter had a stick with a sack wrapped around the end which he held against the rivet head in the direction it was likely to come off when the gun was operated. The cut rivet was then punched out, sometimes a difficult job in itself if firmly home.

We usually drilled out all the studs first and then did the chipping out of the shell, wearing the standard issue safety goggles, metal frames with wire mesh sides and a lens of glass (I'm not sure whether it was what is now called safety glass or was specially treated in any way), the lens being held in by a screw cap arrangement similar to the cap on a honey jar. A piece of black elastic with an adjusting buckle completed the goggles, allowing the elastic strap to be adjusted to fit the head of the wearer. The chipping out process also taught another lesson. To ensure that the shell of the stud collapsed inwards, the chisel had to be repositioned usually for each succeeding blow, the point staying where it was and the angle of the chisel itself changed.

It was quite a lengthy process to remove the remains of the studs, and while chipping out the shells, interspersed with chisel work and digging out the crushed remains of the shell, I recall playing Hangman with the fitter, chalking the little hanging figure on the foundation ring, completing a chosen word by writing letters between the stud holes. We had no visits from Banger so we had no problems! All stud ends were removed and the holes restored to their former tapped-out state, although often with a groove vertically down the thread in a couple of places where the round nose or diamond point had cut in, and then run down with a tap, and that was that! The tools were collected-air line rolled up, and with the drill post and arm all safely back in the bogie, the fitter disappeared for a couple of minutes to tell the boilermaker chargehand we had finished with the ring, then back to P1 Shop.

Several journeys were made to AV Shop to deal with foundation rings during my stay with the particular fitter whose name I cannot recall, but he was an easy going, friendly sort of chap, not one to wear overalls, I think, and taking everything in his stride with a rather casual sort of approach.

A change of fitter heralded a change of job and one of the most interesting was that of fitting the regulator and lever. All locomotives, indeed all forms of engine, have a main controlling valve governing, by manual control, the flow of the power source, whether steam or some form of oil vapour, petrol or diesel, to make the thing work! The steam locomotIve was controlled from the cab and in GWR practice, the regulator handle was mounted centre top of the back head, just below the fountain (of which more later), the control handle extending to the right when looking at the back head. The sliding valve of the regulator could be mounted in one of two very different positions, again in GWR practice being either in the smokebox or under the dome-mounted centre top of the cylindrical boiler barrel (*see drawing which includes safety valve and dome*).

In the case of the former, the valve chest or box in which the valve worked was directly connected to a very heavy manifold, which allowed the steam released by the valve to pass via the manifold back through the superheater tubes to become in effect a very hot, invisible gas, to return throughout the manifold and thence to the cylinders. The valve in this case worked horizontally and sideways, moving to and fro across the slotted seat when the lever was moved, in this case lifted, in the cab. In the case of the dome-type regulator valve, the seat was mounted vertically on an 'elbow' which reached up into the top of the dome; the flat valve had a slotted-faced box-like form having a smaller 'jockey' valve on its back, the latter opening slightly before the former when the lever was lifted.

In all cases, the valve,was fitted and lapped to its seat before the regulator assembly was despatched to P1 Shop for fitting, indicidentally a job which I did later on in my apprenticeship, so when received, the job in P1 Shop was to assemble the complete regulator valve to the dome or to the smokebox. It was very difficult in any case to get a header positioned on a light repair boiler in which the smokebox remained in place and the header and regulator box had to be bolted to the front tube plate. One of the first jobs with the regulator was to assist with the fitting of both header and valve box onto a Class 1 boiler.

One of the achievements of G. J. Churchward was to introduce a standardisation to limit the variations found at that time (*c.* 1900) in the types, sizes and shapes of boilers. This had the effect of reducing the complications of stores materials and even of the, activities required in boiler repairs generally. The boilers had known steaming capacities and so various styles of locomotives could be designed for specific purposes, utilising one of the standard types of boiler. However, the boiler in this case was still complete with its smokebox, so we approached the boiler to commence fitting the header and valve box, which had been delivered previously with a cover plate over the valve assembly to stop any dirt entering, and my first impression was how on earth are we going to get those great iron castings into the smokebox and mounted on the range of protruding studs. I was soon to find out!

A tubular frame trolley on four iron wheels with built-in steps and a wooden platform was pushed along the track to the front of the smokebox. The boiler had previously been levered on its trolley under a pulley block and jib, a chain was passed around the header and it was hauled up on to the platform. A rope sling or sometimes an eye bolt was attached to the header in such a way that it was balanced reasonably well, and could be removed once the header was secured into place. We dragged the header casting as near to the open smokebox as we could and the chain of the pulley block was then passed down through the chimney opening and pulled at an angle to the smokebox front, where the hook was secured into the sling around the header. It was now a case of sliding the header and lifting with the pulley block to get the whole thing over the lip of the smokebox and suspend it below the chimney opening awaiting the next phase. Having lifted it inside the smokebox to the approximate level of the studs on which it was to be positioned, the struggle started! Within the confines of the sides of the smokebox, two struggling individuals could be seen, bodies curved to the shape of the box, one either side of the header, attempting to lift and push the holes in the casting over the studs. As the header had to go back towards the tube plate, the pulley block had to be operated to (a) allow the length of chain to be extended so that the header would actually go back far enough, and (b) retain support for the header should something occur and we had to release our hold.

The problem at this stage was the fact that in extending the chain to get the header back far enough, it also in effect lowered the header below the level of the studs! So, with both of us wrapped around the curve of the smokebox – the fitter operating the pulley block control chain, and myself with a nut in one hand waiting the opportunity to screw it on one of the studs to hold the header in place – we had to now physically lift the header and push it those last few inches over the studs! This latter move was the most difficult of all as not only were our bodies curved round the top of the smokebox, but our legs were equally

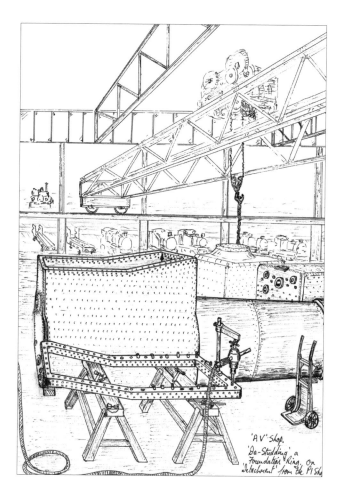

AV Shop – 'de-studding' a
foundation ring.

curved around the bottom of the box, the wheeled trolley now pushed under the box to cover the blast pipe hole in the bottom (one slip and one of us would have disappeared like the Panto magician) where the exhausted steam would finally be discharged to blast its way out of the cylinders and up and out of the chimney.

Once in place and secured with a temporary nut, the business of washering and securely nutting the header into place was a straightforward job. The main thing on fitting the valve box was to ensure that prior to struggling with the casting and the pulley block, you had remembered to clean the boiler seat and position the pre-cut joint or gasket over the studs. It could be a little disconcerting to find that when everything was nutted and secure, and two sweating persons emerged from the smokebox, the asbestos-based joint was still sitting, pristinely white on the platform! The next thing was to remove the sling and the pulley block chain and it could be equally disconcerting if the sling had been positioned round the component in such a way that it could not be removed with the casting bolted in place! However, such things are always discussed and with the individuals actually concerned, we had put the joint on first and could remove the sling!

The regulator rod was of about 1½-inch diameter and in length reached from the box back through the boiler to the back head where it protruded through the special gland and through the regulator housing. In passing through the boiler barrel, the rod also passed through the centre of the main steam collecting pipe, which ran from the header, back through the boiler barrel and curved rather sharply upwards to the high point of the boiler, the front end of the Belpaire firebox, the steam collecting point. A plain bearing and hole at the point of the curve allowed the rod to continue its course to the back head. At the back head the rod had a square end with a split pin hole, both square and hole to suit the regulator handle. The valve end had a shape very like a rimlock door key, a simple, short rectangular section of about 4½-inch by 1-inch, the latter parallel to the rod itself, the whole forming a chunky 'T' end.

The rod, lying alongside the boiler trolley while the struggle with valve box and header was going on, was now lifted and carefully fed through the valve housing and on through the boiler to the back head where its squared end protruded. The idea was that the 'T' end fitted snugly in the back of the valve while the squared end at the back head held the regulator lever correctly distanced from the face of the gland. In practice it was often the case that this did not happen as intended, depending on the actual repairs the boiler had undergone, and the rod could be affected in either or both of two dimensions. In the first place it could be too long or too short, only sometimes a matter of ½ inch or ⅜ inch, but nevertheless of incorrect length. The second problem was a little more complicated in that it concerned the relative positions of the square on one end and the 'T' section on the other. The rod, complete with the temporarily assembled regulator handle attached to the square had to conform quite obviously to the requirement that when the handle was in the down or off position, the valve was shut. Having ascertained the required length of the rod and made a note of the change to be made, the valve action was carefully checked by the fitter, wrapped around inside the smokebox at the valve end, with me operating the regulator handle at the other. Very great care was exercised in this operation as the valve passed over the slots in the valve seat like the blades in a hedge trimmer, and any undue movement or sudden action with the regulator handle could shear off a finger tip cautiously probing the valve and its seat. I know all regulations with respect of safety say you must use a metal rod for such operations but in practice it was often the case that you just could not get the feel or sensitivity from some inanimate chunk of steel, and so fingers were used!

It was often found that with the handle in the closed position, the valve was still partially open, or conversely with the valve shut, the handle was not down to its off position. The rod then not only required adjusting to correct length, but twisting to enable the valve and handle to both be aligned in the closed position. In smithing terms, the rod had to be jumped if to be shortened and drawn to make it longer, the related instruction shown in chalk, written on the periphery of the rusted metal surface. A simple, say '⅜ C' or '⅜ AC' chalked on the 'T' end indicated the amount of clockwise or anticlockwise twist required in inches to set the valve position.

Having then carefully checked and rechecked the requirements of getting the rod to fit, it was carefully withdrawn and placed on the inevitable bogie or two-wheeled sack truck, the typical shop hybrid. Transporting upwards of 20 feet of steel rod on a two-wheeled truck has its problems, not least of which was that of negotiating the tunnel and slopes adjacent to the hoist in P1 Shop itself, to get through into the Boiler Shop and on to the Smith's Shop.

The rod would be dealt with a short distance into the shop where, as with the Carriage & Wagon Smith's Shop visited as an office boy, the shop comprised a long rectangle with the forge areas forming bays down each wall and a row of small steam or pneumatic hammers down the centre. The hammer driver serving the bays adjacent to where we deposited the rod was a rather hefty female, one of the few still remaining at this time, but one very much in charge and capable of handling the hammer. Being a 'hot shop', it was still advisable to watch where you walked, and where you extended a hand to pick up a bar or forging, as the innocent-looking black rod you were about to pick up may have only just been put down and had cooled only as far as black heat! Having taken one rod to be altered, there was another to be returned to P1 Shop, having been dealt with previously. So, leaving with instructions written on our rod concerning the jump and the twist, we departed with the other rod for a colleague working on another boiler, having first spat on the rod to ensure its coolness before handling!

In the case of a domed boiler, the dome itself was the high point of the boiler where the steam collected, and the vertical length of pipe to which the regulator valve was secured was the main steam pipe to the cylinders, the valve up in the dome being well above the water level. Generally (but not always), a domed boiler, in the GWR sense, was one in which the steam was used in a saturated condition, meaning that it was not superheated by being passed through special pipes of smaller diameter back in the direction of the firebox through a special group of fire tubes (of larger diameter than the ordinary boiler tubes) en route to the cylinders.

The boiler with the header thus possessed a manifold to which the superheater units could be attached, each tube group passing back into the boiler fire tube related to its position on the header. Actually attaching the superheater assemblies to the manifold was possibly a boilermaker's job, as I don't recall handling a unit or being involved in attaching any to the header. The regulator handle would be tapped on over the square on the rod end and the pin put through and secured, after being again tried for position of handle related to the valve. Although attending to only a comparatively few rods, I can't remember any of them being returned to the Smith's Shop for further attention, although I suppose there may have been occasions when such was the case. However, handle on and valve OK, and the small plate cover was replaced and nutted over the valve box, a straightforward job preceded by the asbestos-based flexible joint. Nuts on covers were tightened diagonally opposed in the tightening sequence, so that one side of the cover or seat did not pull down unevenly, causing a break when the opposite side was eventually fastened down.

Diagonal tightening was generally the rule for all covers, the large dome cover having a flat flange and dished centre portion, all hidden under the lagging-filled outer dome cover, distinctive and gracefully curved, on the finished boiler. The dome was actually a cylindrical extension of the boiler shell, attached vertically and riveted securely to a special saddle, shaped to the boiler top. The cover was a straightforward end for the vertical cylinder, held by a large number of studs at the top orifice and held by an eyebolt screwed into the centre of the dished portion and the sling of the column mounted pulley block and runner. An old sack sufficed to sit on or kneel on the boiler top, and the routine of diagonal tightening of the nuts seemed to go on indefinitely as the cover slowly pulled down over the clean and lightly oiled regulator valve underneath.

The same procedure of diagonal tightening was applied to the safety valve, lifted by sling and positioned as with the dome cover, over a ring of studs in the special saddle ring fitted to the coned, cylindrical boiler shell, and the nuts applied and tightened while sitting on the inevitable old sack draped over the cold metal. It was a general practice, mentioned previously but not applied to the safety valve, to file the outer edge of a face or seat to ensure that it pulled down really tightly in the centre, and in this respect it was also usual practice to keep a special file for the job. If a new file was obtained and usually they could only be obtained by handing in an old one at the stores, it was the 'done thing' to mark one of the faces of say a square file with chalk in the teeth about ½ inch at the handle end, and to keep this face for brass face filing or indeed for any non-ferrous filing. Once used on steel and while still cutting steel, the initial sharpness disappeared and cutting brass became more difficult, the file tending to skid over the surface, considerable extra pressure being required to get the true 'feel' of cutting.

A small episode which I seem to recall as associated with one of the P1 Shop fitters, was that of a special job in the brass foundry, repacking or attending to a gland of one of the hydraulically operated axlebox bearing moulding machines. These were horizontally operating rams which at the end of the ram had a cast-iron mould half, the other fixed half forming the semicircular shape of the bronze bearing shell, which was eventually pressed into the top of an axlebox. Once in and secured, a press fit, the surface was given a thick layer of white metal and then machined. The moulding machine when used had its metal bearing faces whitened to prevent the hot molten metal from sticking, and I believe had to be pre-heated before casting could commence, done with the usual gas pipe and open jet. Once moulding or casting had started, the heat from the molten bronze itself kept the dies at the right temperature. As I recall it was a repack of a hydraulic gland which formed the job and this required a special gland packing because of the pressures involved. Instead of the usual type of gland packing, similar to asbestos string impregnated with graphite used on the steam glands, the packing comprised a special leather 'washer' impregnated with an oil of some sort, and moulded into a special 'D' section ring (like a circular canal). The thickness of the leather was shaped off at an angle on both sides of the top of the D to form a sharp edge and, in practice the D was placed open side down so that pressure forced the D to open against the sides of the gland where it was restrained, and made a very secure seal; in effect the higher the pressure, the tighter the seal. However, the bogie loaded up with the odd tools, and the job formed an interesting diversion from the usual boiler fitting routine.

There is an associated episode with this gland packing saga. In the boiler shop, there stood a very large hydraulic press for forming the inner firebox tube and back plates and, one night, during night shift operations, the gland blew out. This press was the preserve apparently of G Shop, and was not the responsibility of P1 Shop at all, but it appears that the particular fitter who was known to deal with other hydraulic problems such as that of the foundry moulding machines, happened to be on nights that particular week, and so he was approached to tackle the job, unaware that it was not really his responsibility.

Having completed the repack effectively and speedily, he resumed his own job in P1 Shop, now of course delayed by the amount of time spent in the Boiler Shop, and so, at the end of the shift, he duly reported events to Banger. What was actually said of course I don't know, but during the day Banger made the necessary enquiries regarding the price for the job, as having been an odd, one off type of event, there was no piecework number in his book against which the hours could be compared and recorded. The piecework checker in the office also had to do a bit of chasing round and 'phoning, presumably after Banger had been told that it was really the G Shop, which should have done the job in the first place. However, that was now really irrelevant as the job had been done and a payment was required! There must have been a very interesting exchange of conversation between the powers that be in both G and P1 Shops, and a few raised eyebrows and unanswered questions regarding repacking the press in the Boiler Shop. When the fitter reported for the next night shift, he collected his written instructions as usual from the clip by Banger's cupboard, and must have been very surprised to read that he was to take it easy during the shift, with only very minor jobs to do. The price for the job already established by G Shop and existing for press gland repack was so high in relative terms for the hours expended, that the fitter had earned his money several times over for the shift in question when the job had occurred. Such was the variation in setting values of money based on time claimed by the piecework system, but the argument was that of the usual swings and roundabouts, although in reality it semed to be one of 'he who knows the job and argues more forcefully gets the price relative to the strength of supervision'.

However, the period of assembly of regulator and safety valve, of fire hole door gear and water gauge, of casing brackets and foundation rings, was coming to an end, and on receiving sealed orders from a majestically still sailing Banger Stevens, I found my next port of call was AM Shop, but there seemed a little uncertainty on actually where, and one assumed the usual almost standard moves on to the axleboxes or the rods.

The axlebox section was quite a large portion of AM Shop to the right of the check board, and comprised roller transporters snaking between the benches and roundabouts where the boxes had the bearing section machined. Against the right-hand wall, again entering by the check board, stood an enclosed bay of small gas-heated crucibles and metal-topped low tables where any item which required a layer of white metal, a solder-like bearing material, was handled. Prior to an axlebox being machined and even before it went to have its layers of white metal applied, it had to be prepared to receive the white metal, not only on the bearing for the journal, that semi-circular bronze insert pressed into the top of the axlebox body, but also the two side bearings or slides where the box slid up and down in the locomotive frame horn cheeks. The horn cheeks were the two right-angle brackets which formed the bearing surfaces for strengthening the axle slots in the locomotive frame, which itself was only about 2 inches thick, the cheeks increasing this thickness to about 5 inches.

The bearing surfaces of the axlebox where it ran between the cheeks was of machined white metal applied to a serrated bronze surface in the form of a plate about ⅜ inch thick, studded and riveted to the cast-steel machined surface of the axlebox. The job of the apprentices, and there were always several on the gang, was to attach the bronze plates to the slides of all new axleboxes. The steel slots formed on both sides of the box were drilled out all over with a set pattern of tapped holes, the holes matching those in the drilled and countersunk bronze plate. A length of screwed rod, the black variety with a roughly squared section on the end, was then screwed into each hole using a wrench differing from the standard pattern issue tap wrench, comprising a stem centre section with a square hole to match the squared end of the screwed rod, and two integral round, polished steel handles. In some cases the wrenches were single-ended, as it was not possible to get a complete turn on the wrench due to the proximity of another screwed rod sticking up from an adjacent hole, but usually the 'T' wrench was applied. Having screwed in as many rods as possible, the section of the box looking like a porcupine, the rods were cut off just above the level of the bronze plate. I have seen these rods cut off with some difficulty with a hacksaw, but there was a small pneumatic machine available, resembling an electric pistol grip drill, but with two very short angled blades in place of a chuck, the blades coming together when the finger trigger mounted in the handle was squeezed. This easily cropped off the ⅜-inch diameter of the black screwed rod, leaving a rather sharp chisel edge projecting, but the whole exposed portion of cut end was soon flattened and riveted over into the countersunk portion of the hole. Progressing around the plate, cropping off first and then riveting over, the plate was soon secured rigidly to the groove of the axlebox. Prior to white-metalling, the boxes were mounted on a special fixture attached to the shaper, and each faced slot was serrated lengthwise, the newly exposed 'V' slots of bronze forming a good key to the white metal which was then run on. The boxes were taken in batches to the white-metalling bay and there the serrations were tinned or coated with a brushed-on layer of white metal, changing the yellow of the bronze to silver, and forming the base on to which the thick layer of white metal would be cast.

A clamp placed around the axlebox groove formed the well into which the white metal would be run, the metal scooped from the retorts by means of long-handled ladles. The retorts resembled the old-fashioned domestic copper or wash boiler, about 20 inches in diameter with a domed bottom, under which was a gas jet and the whole could be covered by a metal, loosely fitting lid. On removal or pushing aside of the lid, the gently fuming layer of silver metal had a skin over the top which reminded me of my grandmother's jam saucepan at the height of the fruit season and, as with the jam, this layer was gently eased aside with the ladle when an amount was required, the skin, on being moved, forming ridges which changed colour as they formed and reformed on being pushed back to reveal the clear glossy silver metal underneath.

When cleaned and fluxed with a brushful of the fluxing acid, the white metal adhered very firmly, and if care was not exercised, could stick to any clean, warmed surface, particularly

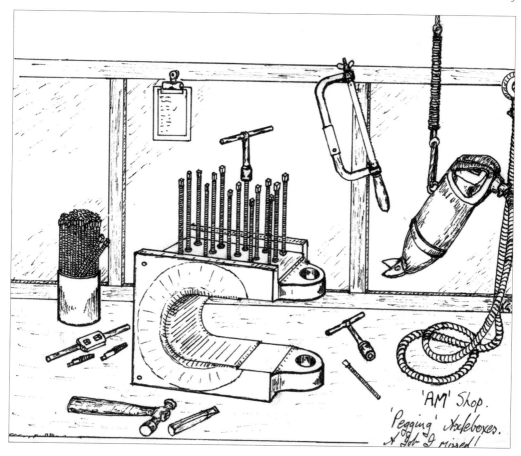

AM Shop – pegging axleboxes.

a machined area. To avoid this, any area or clean surface where white metal was not required was usually dabbed with whitening, which stopped the white metal adhering and could be easily brushed off afterwards. When watching, and of course particularly when working with molten white metal, great care had to be taken to avoid splashing, so aprons, gloves and goggles were essential, even so it was possible to get a splash somewhere on your overalls which you felt when it had burned its way through.

Many items were white-metalled here, not only the axlebox components but the connecting rod bearings, cross heads and quadrant blocks and slippers from the reversing gear, all transported to and from the bay by the transport group or for local items, the shop labourers, so as apprentices we did not really have any lasting business in the bay. However, there was usually some occasion or other which entailed a short visit and as I recall, it was usually a rather hot, fumy sort of atmosphere which didn't encourage you to stay if you had no pressing business there.

Right across the other side of the shop in the short section that overflowed into a portion of AE Shop, and mentioned during my stay on Harold Sawyer's turning gang, was the area which dealt with the rods, the locomotive connecting rods. New rods were machined, as mentioned, at the opposite end of the AM Shop, but rods new and old were dealt their final processes in this area.

At this stage there were no rods, in Great Western practice anyway, which were designed to receive a ball or roller race as a bearing, white-metalled bronze and ground steel, hardened pins being the order of the day. Most bearings were thus white-metalled and machined. In new rods and in some but very few repairs, a new bronze bush would be inserted, but generally the old metal was run out and a new white metal core run into the bearing end.

There were two machines adjacent to the rods gang, just across the gangway against the wall of the stores and the locomotive test plant, which were specifically for machining the con rod white metal bearings (*see Plate 27*). One of the machines was operated by the father of yet another school chum of mine named King, and both machines worked on the same principle. A long narrow bed on to which the con rods could be bolted, had at each end an assembly which had all the characteristics of a drilling machine but which had been built to the same standards of rigidity as a milling machine, the 'quill' or vertical spindle holding the cutters being supported right down to the cutter itself. The whole quill assembly had the usual vertical and horizontal adjustments, the rod being set up for machining by various bars and dial gauges before being firmly clamped under the cutters, also firmly locked in place, the cutter head using, I believe, a single point tool like a small lathe tool, not a milling cutter as such.

The setting measurements relating to the centre distance between the two end bearings of each rod, had to coincide exactly to the centre distance between the axles of the locomotives to which the rods would be fitted, and to this end I believe the rods would be machined to fit a specific locomotive, the measurements forwarded from the AE Shop inspectorate and obtained by use of special optical equipment designed for the purpose (about which more later). Whitemetal is very soft as a lead-based material, and was machined at quite high speeds, although surprisingly a white metal bearing will also wear a hardened steel pin, while itself showing probably little wear. The rod ends were bored out and radiused to suit the diameters of the crank pins to which they would be fitted, and again the measurements would be supplied to the borer, being taken from the actual wheels and not from the nominal measurements shown on the drawings.

It is always a wonder to me how the reciprocating and revolving masses of the locomotive stayed together when travelling at high speed, particularly the more obvious items such as the connecting rods, the side assemblies often taking three or four men to lift into position over the crank pins when the whole was put together in the Erecting Shop. Nowhere I think, did this become more apparent than when a locomotive was running on the test plant, to me the most spectacular sight in the whole of the Locomotive Works. To witness from close quarters, an 80-ton 'Castle' class locomotive travelling at 70 miles an hour while standing still, was a sight never to be forgotten, but one which unfortunately appears to have now gone forever. The locomotive, firmly anchored at both ends and the wheels running on rollers which could be weighted to provide a load, could have the safety valve just open and blowing, a fierce blast and exhaust beat sending a solid column of steam exhaust and smoke up into the coned base of the extension chimney, which reached from just above the swaying engine, up through the roof of A Shop; the column of exhaust continuing for a short distance as a solid jet before dissipating into the winds blowing in from the fields across A Shop roofs.

The wheels, 6 feet in diameter, appeared as a solid disc, no spokes being visible and the flailing connecting rods a blur as the wheels revolved, pushed around by a further blur at the cylinders where the crossheads were flashing backwards and forwards, pushed by the invisible pistons. Most of the sensations of a travelling-at-speed locomotive were all encased in one large, noise-filled vibrating area, punctuated by an occasional blast on the whistle to signal commencement of a test phase, but to the driver and the fireman, the cooling air flow of actual travel in the open was missing, and it was apparently hard, hot, dusty work to travel thus and not really go anywhere! Indeed, I think I recall a large electric fan positioned at the back of the cab over the coal bunker (no tender was used in the test plant) in an attempt to keep up at least some semblance of a cooling breeze. Various pipes led from the cylinders, boiler, valve chests, etc., back to a specially equipped and constructed rail coach which contained a range of testing and recording instruments and which was standing on a stretch of rail line adjacent to the test bed. The coach, the well-known dynamometer car, was often seen actually running as part of a train to record various running data and could be connected to a locomotive other than on the test bed. A problem of the test bed was that there were a number of conditions of actual running which could not be simulated by a static test, at least during that period, the problem of wind speed and cross winds.being but one of several. We shall of course never know now how the computer could have been linked to the locomotive on test, and what other fascinating facets of locomotive control and management could have been brought to light almost as a by-product of the test! What a fascinating avenue of conjecture that leads to! However, a rumbling, swaying locomotive on the test bed was a sight now locked in the memory of those who were privileged to actually be there when such events occurred. The smell of oily steam still lingers!

In the rods area of the shop there could on occasions be seen an individual, indeed several different individuals who each resembled a miller, having white hair, white faces, white hands, overalls and boots. These were the boiler laggers who worked just down into AE Shop along the same bay of the shop; those unfortunates who spent a lifetime removing and replacing the 2½-inch-thick layer of asbestos-based material which formed the insulation over the actual boiler, covered by the painted and glossy outer skin of thin sheet steel when under the public gaze.

In these days of such concern over the use of asbestos, the contrast in its use, when now examined, is almost bizarre by comparison. With the outer skin removed, a boiler presented an off-white, crumbly appearance, the off-white of the asbestos stained in various colours of rust and oil. Removal was a question of sticking in a scraper with a longish handle and just levering off slabs, which broke at random and reproduced on the inner curved surfaces the shape of the various rivet heads around the sections of the boiler and firebox. The air was full of the white particles and as the pieces were thrown down on to those which had gone before into the special trolleys, a rising puff of white fog mingled with that already hanging in the air of the vicinity. The slabs and bits of asbestos lagging which had missed the trolley would hit the floor and break again, to be eventually picked up and pushed into that which had found its mark, and the lot would be trundled round to the mixing tanks. These resembled metal coal bunkers, those which are used by householders for the storage of domestic coal, having a metal lid which was more often than not broken at the hinges. The lumps of lagging would be usually manhandled from the trolleys into the bunkers, and there pounded and jabbed again to break them down even more, an amount of new lagging in the form of a bag of particles being split open and poured in, the final shake of the bag to ensure that it was empty, adding to the blizzard of white particles now going in all directions. A hose water spray and a paddle and shovels, and the remixing commenced, the snow storm slowly abating as the dry fibrous particles became water-saturated and broke down into a grey-looking plaster-like consistency.

Once mixed, the soggy plaster was shovelled out of the bunker into the trolleys and pushed round the bay to the boiler to be lagged. Surrounded by trestles and plank platforms, several buckets would be filled from the trolley and with large trowels, the snowmen would commence application to the boiler. In retrospect, what must have been a very unhealthy job was accepted as part of the routine of the shop, the only visible signs of protection being the wearing of a simple face mask over nose and mouth, used of course only by the actual laggers themselves, and then I believe only when actually removing the lagging in its dry state. I seem to recall the boilers being then steamed to dry out the lagging, and I have a recollection of a gently steaming boiler as the moisture dried out of the asbestos, but where the steam came from to actually fill the boiler itself and so warm it up for drying out, I don't know; probably a layed-in steam main from the general circuit.

I have seen, on several occasions, individuals passing through the bay actually grab a handful of the plaster, form it into a 'snowball' and quite illegally throw it at some unsuspecting character walking in front! The casual way in which the lagging was treated by all concerned shows just how little was known about its dangers forty-odd years ago!

13

AM Shop

The move from P1 Shop and the reporting to AM Shop arrived and with a little trepidation, the checky was approached to consult his list for the new check number and destination. Would it be the tap-tap-tap of the hammer riveting over the studs in the axleboxes, or the rods with a piece of emery cloth wrapped around the polishing stick and the application to those parts of the rods which needed a final clean up before being despatched to the Erecting Shop?

I was very pleased and rather surprised to find it was to be neither of the two moves anticipated, but to the fitting benches at the opposite end of the shop where the reversing gear was repaired, and quite near the plano mills which machined the connecting rods. Harry Jarvis had a rather small gang comprising three fitters and three apprentices, and was one of the three fitting gangs whose benches formed three separate little areas or bays to the right of the main through walkway to AV Shop, stretching from the rear of one of the plano mills to the partition wall of K Shop welding bay. Harry's gang was the first of the group; then came Charlie Bailey's area, and against K Shop partition, the group of Harold Angell, with the old joke that their singing was better than their fitting, although over the years this had probably worn a bit thin, being still trotted out at Christmas time!

Harry Jarvis was a quietly spoken character who seemed, on occasions, to have breathing problems. He didn't interfere with the jobs going on but he was always there; in essence, I suppose, good supervision. The three fitters (I seem to vaguely remember a fourth but I can't put a face or name to him), dealt with the three main functions of the gang. Caddy Jones, a Welshman who resembled the conductor Sir Malcolm Sargent, although he was not as tall, dealt with the eccentrics and eccentric straps. John, who I believe had originally hailed from Wales in his very early days, dealt with the reversing levers and racks, and finally Colin who was leading hand, dealt with the reversing screw gear and associated long-reach rod, which connected the screw or handle to the weigh shaft and quadrants.

The bench area formed a D shape with the open end to the gangway. The centre of the area was taken up by a pair of long and high metal angle trestles which supported all of the long-reach rods, while under the trestles were stored, awaiting repair, the reversing screw castings, covers and handles. A space at the inner end of the rods allowed access to the rod ends for changing and fitting the pins to the fork ends of the rods, and also to the small gas-fired hearth which was attached to a roof support column, being built into the angle-iron section, as the columns in this shop were fabricated and not cast-iron rounded pillars as in the older parts of the works. The closed end of the D was taken up by Harry's cupboard and a storage rack, the rack sandwiched between the cupboard and a small marking off table, and with a narrow gangway in front opening on to and in line with the outer two gangs in the block, both of which were set out in roughly the same way. The bench where the screws were dealt with was single-sided, and backed on to the larger of the plano mills, taking about half the distance from the gang to the chargehand's cupboard, the other half being a double-sided bench where Caddy dealt with the eccentrics and straps.

The area was well provided with overhead runners and pulley blocks and the items repaired were stacked by the gangway side of the plano mill, where they were collected by the night staff who also delivered another batch of items for repair. It was not often that repaired screws or levers were collected during the day unless one was wanted urgently, having been delayed for some reason in the repair process, when the actual fitter from the Erecting Shop would come out with the mate or apprentice and take the item required.

It appeared that, at that time, Colin had two apprentices on an overlapping basis, so one, John Packer, was already 'in residence' when I arrived. Allocated a bench cupboard, I stowed away my box of tools, calipers and such-like from my turning days, which were to prove useful also during this fitting period. The first job in the morning was to strip down the reversing screws which had come in overnight, some still warm and showing residue from the 'Bosh', a large covered tank of caustic soda solution which gurgled and bubbled away in AE Shop, and through which most components destined for repair had to pass before being forwarded to the various repair shops. The screw consisted of an iron casting with a flat base and a raised bed, was 'T'-shaped, and sloped from the handle end down towards the front, the handle end having a solid vertical section which carried the rear bearing for the screw and the star wheel rack into which the catch of the handle fitted when the gear itself was set for the various positions of the valves controlling the amount of steam to be allowed into the cylinders. The front of the casting had also a raised portion in the form of a bridge, which contained the bearing for the other end of the reversing screw itself. The open bridge allowed the long-reach rod to move relative to the position of its supporting slipper, the movable nut controlled by the action of the screw to which the rod was attached by means of a pair of brackets attached to the rod end, and having bronze-bushed holes which were supported by trunnions on each side of the nut portion. The nut itself had a 'T'-shaped portion at the base, which fitted over the sloping bed and which was white-metalled, forming a smoothly functioning action when the bed was lubricated. An indicator finger screwed to the top of the nut ran between the slot formed by the graduated indicator plate which fitted over both raised end portions of the casting, and was parallel to the sloping bed, a cross line on the finger indicating the position on the indicator plate of the valve setting, whether in forward or reverse gear.

The subject of steam locomotive valve gears is a complex and fascinating one, and there are a considerable number of variations, all doing basically the same thing. In essence, and completely without toothed gears as such, the steam engine, when running or stationary, has the same problems as the motor car. First, when starting, or rather before starting, the decision has to be made whether a backward or forward travel is required. Having decided, and exactly as with the motor car, a slow start is necessary to start the mass moving, i.e. in low gear with slowly applied maximum power. Once moving, the low gear can be altered to maintain the travel with the minimum of effort, as with the car through second, third, and finally top gear. Differing from the actual toothed gear type gearbox of the car, the steam locomotive has a smooth arrangement which gives, within a range, a virtually infinitely variable ratio without disengaging the drive, as with the clutch of a car, and without the grating of toothed wheels in a special gearbox! This is achieved through altering the length of travel of the valves which control the entry of steam to the cylinders. In essence, steam entering the cylinder at one end pushes the piston along the bore. The steam is then cut off by the valve and again, due to the valve position, enters the cylinder at the other end, pushing the piston back in the other direction, the cycle being repeated again and again.

One of the properties of steam, discovered in the early years of its use, was its capacity to be used expansively. In other words, it is not necessary to admit steam to the cylinder for the complete length of the stroke of the piston. Steam admitted at the beginning of the stroke, and then cut off at a predetermined position of the stroke of the piston, continues to expand and do useful work, although of course its effectiveness diminishes from the point of cut off, although that effectiveness does not immediately stop on cut off.

The two uses of the reversing gear were thus the obvious one of forward or backward travel, followed by the control of the valve stroke determining when steam was admitted to the cylinder and control of the point of cut off, from which point the steam was used expansively. The reversing lever served the same purpose as the screw, being equipped with a catch arrangement, as with the handle on the screw, but acting on a double-sided rack, between which it pivoted with its arc of movement governed by the length of the rack and the hardened notches into which the catches fitted (*see Plate 3*).

The motion required to move the valves over the port faces, allowing steam to enter the cylinder at the correct time in the sequence was by eccentrics. This mechanism acted in the same fashion as a cam, being a circular casting which, when mounted on the axle, while rotating with it, was off-set, allowing an outer ring or strap attached to a rod to rotate with it, but at the same time giving a reciprocating motion to the rod. In other words, while the eccentric transformed rotary motion into reciprocating motion, it could not transform reciprocating motion into rotary motion in the way the normal crank can.

To strip the screw, the two covers were first removed, the number of the locomotive chalked on the inside of each cover, and both were placed on the floor under the trestles laden with the associated long-reach rods, the latter being sometimes placed on the trestles by the night shift transport personnel, and sometimes left on the floor alongside the plano mill on the other side of the bench. The nut was removed from the handle end of the screw and the handle driven off its key by the use of the lead hammer, a tool with a head made of white metal and available in a hand size or sledgehammer size, the smaller version being used to drive off the handle. Just in front of the rear bearing, a screwed collar around the screw itself, retained by two taper pins, had to be next removed, the two pins punched out and the collar unscrewed, the collar being of about 4-inch diameter and 1 inch thick. With the collar removed, the screw could be unscrewed from the nut of slipper, which was then placed aside for transport to the white metallers to have a coating of metal run over the sliding guide slot in the base. The screw and nut were compared for wear, and the nut could be removed from the slipper, but this was only rarely necessary as both screw and nut were quite deeply case-hardened, and generally there was not enough play in the thread to warrant renewing.

The bronze bush in the bridge end often wore considerably, and this was tried when stripping was in progress by using a flipper gauge, consisting of an adjustable length of rod mounted at the sharp corner of a 2-inch length of 2 inches square corner steel angle section, the rod adjustable by means of a thumb screw in and/or out of a socket welded to the angle. In use, the open 'V' of the angle was held tightly against the underside of the reversing screw itself, and the flipper gauge adjusted to just touch the slide section of the bed at the bush end. When again positioned and tried at the handle end of the screw, if the bush was considerably worn, it was likely that the gauge would not flick under the screw across the bed, usually in these circumstances not going under at all, but jamming tight between the bed slide and the screw if forced. With a badly worn bush, the gauge would not even jam, but would just stop when touching the slide at the handle end. Bushes were stored in a rack at the side of the chargehand's cupboard and, with the old one driven out by a dolly and lead hammer, the new bush was inserted, again by lead hammer.

A special reamer with a long extension was used to open the bush out to the size of the screw end, the extension passing through the back bearing of the casting and its square end socket fitting over the square end of the reamer, which was of about 1½-inch diameter. This job was usually done by Colin after the apprentice had driven out the bush. Most of the bushes used were predrilled for the oil hole and when the small batch order for replacement was delivered, the bushes would be centre-popped at the expected position of the oil hole and taken to the driller for the holes to be drilled. The drilling machine was a small pillar drill, floor-mounted and located at the corner of the three-gang bay or section, where K Shop welders' bay came to the main gangway. The driller was a character nearing retirement, rather tall, with cap and spectacles, and with the reputation for being awkward. His favourite statement seemingly was 'Too busy! Come back tomorrow!' By one of those demarcation arrangements, any bush actually installed in a component could be drilled for the oil hole by the fitters, but a 'loose' or new bush not installed had to go to the drillers, a branch of the machinists group. There was, on the gang, a small pistol grip pneumatic drilling machine which sounded like a dentist's drill when in use. The slipper was sent, with several of its fellows which had been stripped at the same time, to the white metallers, where the worn antifriction slide metal was run out, and a new coat cast into the 'V' grooves. On return from the metallers, the screw was replaced in the casting and the flip gauge used to determine the amount to be machined from the new white metal. Another gauge was set, this time a thumb-screw controlled plate gauge, to the width of the slide itself, and then slipper, screw and both gauges were taken across to the centre of the shop to the machinists' gang for the slipper to be set on a shaper and the white metal machined off to the sizes set on the gauges. This was a machinists area with two double-head shapers, vertical and horizontal mills (one I remember worked by Tommy Smith, who later became chargehand), and several drilling machines, one of which was worked by a neighbour, Mr Jones! The shapers, as well as machining the slippers, also dealt with locomotive motion bars, those two heavy slides which carried the crosshead, and which often had to have the location slots (where the pair of bolts secured the front or rear ends to the cylinder casting), machined after being built up with welding. Weld material, deposited to build up brake hanger beams, was also machined to size on this section.

On return to the benches, the slipper was now fitted with the screw to the slide on the casting, and while the object was to scrape a bearing and fit on the slipper, it was often necessary to use a course rasp on the white metal, initially to reduce the amount to be scraped off. While the slipper was being fitted, the handle was being attended to by Colin, who was usually several handles ahead of the screw being repaired. The handle was a drop forging consisting of a central boss and two rectangular section arms, each of which had a projecting handle from the shaped smaller end bosses, one of the handles operating a spring-loaded catch which fitted into the star wheel rack attached to the handle end of the casting. To protect fingers from getting caught in the rack, a pressed-metal 'dish' was welded to the handle, its 1¼-inch-deep rim curled back over the teeth of the rack and just clearing the periphery.

The locking catch worked in a dovetail slot on the back of the handle, a spring and plunger operating in a drilled hole down the length of the related rectangular arm, drilled crosswise at the top for the ⅝-inch diameter pivot pin for the case-hardened handle. A small shaped plug sealed in the plunger mechanism, being screwed into the top of the handle, and retained by being stamped with an old No. 1 number stamp across the join of the thread, showing when the final clean up with emery cloth exposed the fine ring of the thread line on top of the handle end.

The catch sometimes required renewing, but often it could be repaired or reused. The slot in the top where the round nose of the handle fitted, giving the necessary movement along the dovetail into the rack, could be built up with weld deposit, refiled to shape, and re-case-hardened. A visit to K Shop welding section and a wait of a couple of minutes were all that was required, one of the welders, Norm Cox or Ron Lawrence, usually stopping his work for a moment or two to dap an electrode into the end of the slot with the catch held down to his metal table top with a bit of scrap steel angle used as a weight. A hand held in front of the face protected against the arcing flash and any spatter that came from the struck arc, then back to Colin and the handle under repair. Sometimes the handle split at the top where the top cap screwed in, the little bridge of metal where dovetail ended and screwed plug hole began breaking away, and welding was again resorted to, to insert a roughed-out bridge length for later filing and reshaping.

At the tongue of the catch where it fitted into the circular rack, the wear could be eliminated by heating the tongue to bright red heat in the small gas hearth and flattening it out slightly, then, at a second heat, tapping the glowing tongue into one or two of the slots in the circular rack, tried in the rest to make sure it fitted snugly and then cooled in the water tank, about oil drum size, which stood in all its rusty splendour by the gas hearth. To ensure hardness of the catch and its pivot pin, particularly if the latter had been renewed, a tray of yellow case-hardening compound was always kept near the gas hearth, into which the red-hot pin or catch could be rolled, the case-hardening powder melting and spitting and being absorbed into the surface of the metal as carbon, giving a hardened layer when the item was quenched in the water tank, accompanied by a very pungent smell.

With the spring and plunger assembled in the handle and the offset 'V' end of the plunger round the correct way (otherwise the handle could not be assembled), a deft move with an old screwdriver pushing down on the top of handle nose and the spring depressed, and the handle slid forward into the slot of the pre-positioned catch. This was quite easy once you had the technique, but it was quite a struggle the first time round. It was then a matter of tapping in the pivot pin and inserting the small taper pin in the face of the pivot slot to retain the pivot pin.

A pair of taper pins that required particular care in insertion were those which held or retained the screwed collar on the screw itself. These were first lightly driven in with the screw held in a special sheet metal clamp in the vice and then sawn off leaving about a

¼-inch length protruding from both sides. Every apprentice who worked on the gang, and who was required to saw off those pins, without fail, at some time during his stay, cut his little finger or the little finger side of the hand when cutting off those pins! Just as the saw completed its cut and shot forward when the pin end separated, the cut end was in the right place on the secure pin to do the maximum damage, which it inevitably did!

The trunnions on the slipper occasionally wore to such an extent over the course of several repairs that 'welding-up' was required, a layer of weld material being applied in K Shop welding area and the trunnions turned down again to the correct diameter. The bushes in the fork ends of the long-reach rod would be changed or reamed out to suit the new diameter of the trunnions, and while the fork ends themselves were closely fitted into recesses at the rod ends, it was often the case that the two retaining bolts had worked loose and the rod ends and/or the forks themselves had worn badly where they fitted together. It was a regular thing to have the edges of the fork ends welded up so that with hammer and chisel and then file, the rods could be squared up, and the fork ends refitted. If the rod end recesses were particularly badly worn, they were also welded and remachined, being taken to the shapers of Ted Dafter's gang in the centre of the shop, he being a rather round, short man, who always seemed to be cheerful and chatty.

Long-reach rods for the tender locomotives were usually in one piece and, while following the course of the weigh shaft lever (about which more later), prescribed a dipping motion when operated. The length of the rod required support as it could not be made sufficiently thick to stop it flapping sideways, and to this end a bracket was attached to the locomotive running board with an open-topped slot about 1 inch wide and about 9 inches deep, down the centre of the 5 inches by 3 inches solid rectangular bracket. Halfway down the slot was a hole for a special case-hardened bolt with an oil hole drilled in its domed head and through to the ground body of the bolt in the centre of the slot. When assembled, the bolt was located by a feather under the head to ensure the oil hole stayed on top, and the body was provided with a hardened steel roller, about 2 inches in diameter, which ran inside the quadrant-shaped hole machined in the wider section of the centre of the long-reach rod.

On some tank engines, the rod could not be assembled if in one piece, and so was made with a join in the middle. It was more often than not found to be the case that at some stage the bolts had worked loose in the joint and were very badly worn, the bolt holes being in some cases virtually twice the length of the nominal diameter. How on earth the driver obtained a correct valve setting with the centre of the rod folding and scissoring when operating, goodness knows, it must have been solely experience and skill in listening to the exhaust beat, as the position in the notches of the rack would have really signified nothing. In such a case, for repair, the rod would have been bolted with two temporary bolts through two of the four badly worn holes, and then the two halves of the rod aligned into the correct position. Two deep centre 'pop' marks would be made, utilising the trammel with its two hardened points adjustable along a rod, and positioned at a known distance, say 2 feet, one centre 'pop' mark on either side of the joint. The rod was then taken apart and sent for welding, the holes to be completely filled in, and then sent for shaping, to machine off excess weld material on the rod faces. On return a rub with a file to remove burrs and sharp edges, and again using the trammel and its known dimension, a couple of bolted clamps were adjusted around the rod ends, relative to the trammel distance, to hold the rod ends together in what should be the required position to give correct overall length. With the clamps finally tightened, the joint position would be re-marked out as per the spacing on the drawing, a large pop mark made in the centre of each hole position, and a circle scribed around it with dividers to give the periphery of the holes, and again the periphery line was centre-popped in four places, like the main points of the compass. With only the pop mark in the centre, once a large drill starts cutting using the pop mark as a starting point, any wandering off centre is lost to view once the initial centre pop has been removed by the drill point. With the four compass point pop marks, a check can be made on the drill accuracy.

The clamped and marked out rod was then removed to the drilling section of the machinists' gang in the centre of the shop, and usually to Mr Jones, my neighbour at home, in particular.

The drilled rod was also deeply countersunk on one side for the heads of the special bolts which, apart from being a light drive fit in the holes, had a thin hexagon head which was also countersunk, the nuts also to be retained by split pins through the nippled end of the short bolts. I later found, while working in AE Shop, the reason for the bolts being in such poor condition and loose in the holes more often than not when returned for repair. It was really a design fault, I suppose! While it was easy in AM Shop to make sure the bolts fitted closely, when the time came to put the rod into position, there was no room to enable the bolts to be tapped in for the light drive fit, and they were always filed so that they could be inserted easily. Coupled with the problem of access to tighten the nuts, it was inevitable that, at some stage, looseness would increase and rapid wear would result! However, that was the design and that's how they were assembled.

Having fitted the two fork ends of the long-reach rod and rubbed a file over the bronze bush ends in the forks, the rod then awaited fitting of the pin to the other end which connected it to the lever arm of the weigh shaft, part of the reversing mechanism which supported the lifting links and the quadrants, the latter connected to the eccentric rods. With the exception of the lever, the other items mentioned were dealt with by the next two gangs down the bay, Charlie Bailey's and Harold Angell's.

Some rods, those which had the joint in the middle, had an integral fork end to fit over the reversing lever (as opposed to the separate fork ends used with the reversing screw), and at the other end, another fork with bronze bushes and a plain cylindrical pin with a flat head. These pins were retained by an ordinary split pin and a clip over the flat head, held by two $\frac{3}{8}$-inch diameter screw-in hexagon bolts. Other pins for the fork ends were of different design, being tapered or coned where they fitted into the fork with a parallel section for the bush in the centre. The pins could be of different diameters to suit different size bushes in the weigh shaft arm, being ground to clean up the centre diameter. Once fitted into the coned holes of the rod-end fork, they very rarely wore or worked loose, being pulled in tight by means of a threaded section and a large castle nut and split pin.

The thread portion was soft, while the centre section and the cone were case-hardened and it was the practice to change the bush in the weigh shaft to suit the diameter of the newly ground pin, taken down to the next size step. The pin could be reduced about four times, with bushes to suit, and the bushes themselves were knocked out of the weigh shaft arm by dolly and lead hammer. The shaft end was held over the hole of a small cast-iron cylinder, loosely placed on the floor blocks, the top of the cylinder reinforced with a $\frac{3}{8}$-inch thick circular steel plate. Reputedly, the cylinder was part of the brake gear on, or rather from, one of the French railway engines purchased around 1906 from the French railways by G. J. Churchward, when the research was being undertaken into compounding, applied to locomotives, resulting in the successful 4-6-0 locomotives of the GWR.

The pins, as they were removed from the rods, were checked, a size restamped on the soft end, and taken over to Norman, one of the two operators of the cylindrical grinders on the opposite side of the through gangway. A tall, cheerful character, he would assemble the pins on one specific day of the week, and concentrate on completing them all, moving from the machine to return them to the fork end, giving them a light tap into the coned holes in the rod ends. Some new pins replacing those scrapped as being badly worn or below size when cleaned up, were ground on the cone and refitted with the larger diameter of the head or top cone standing about ⅛ inch or ³⁄₁₆ inch above the coned end.

The quadrant at the centre of the rod sometimes required welding, as the hardened steel roller seized on occasions and really chewed out the metal of the quadrant, particularly if the wear on the seized roller was indiscriminate due to variations in the depths of the case-hardening of the surface. The rod was taken to K Shop welders' section and built up in the worn area, then, depending on the amount of weld required, shaped or chipped with hammer and chisel to give a flat face, which was then marked out, using a template and centre popped along the marked line for slotting. In a rack by the chargehand's cupboard was a pile of templates of quite thick quadrant shapes and sizes applied to the range of long-reach rods for the classes of locomotive then existing. The template was stamped with the class shown as, for example, 28XX or 69XX, etc., and often accompanied the rod to the slotters, so that the machinist could check the slotting as it progressed.

The apprentices and Colin dealt with the rods which were used with the reversing levers as well as the screws, and on occasions the apprentice helped out with the levers, but not very often. Levers were usually handled by John, a rather quiet but friendly expatriate Welshman, long removed I believe from the land of his birth. The lever repair bench was on the opposite side of the rack which held the long-reach rods, and that was where John usually stayed, only coming round to our side of the rack en route to the adjacent marking off table at tea break times to sit with Colin, Norman, Dennis and George, on the usual sack-covered wood blocks or home-made benches.

The reversing handle was quite a straightforward mechanism, comprising a long lever pivoted on a brass bush at the bottom with a further bronze-bushed hole about 2 feet above. A centre section consisting of a very thick-walled short slot, contained a pair of catches, which worked up and down in the slot, and the tongues of the catches were fitted to the double-toothed rack castellations between which the handle pivoted. The front bolt of the two which held the rack in place, separated by distance pieces to form the gap for the handle, had an extended portion with a knob on the end, and was intended for use as a footstep to enable the driver's foot to give a reinforcing push when the lever was operated.

The slotted box section which contained the catches was tapered toward the tongue section of the catch, the catches being retained by the sides of the catch-operating lever, which was in effect a three-sided box, a pin going through the two open sides and through the catches, themselves slotted through the centre. An integral spindle on the top of each catch retained a coil spring, the whole hidden when the box was assembled. A pivoting hand lever at the top of the handle was connected to, and operated the catches (*see Plate 3*). The catches were filed to fit the taper in the box slot in such a way that when fitted, using red marking paste to ensure a bearing in the slot, the tongues protruded just below the bottom of the box slot and the catches fitted snugly without play at the end of the tapered slot. The box was case-hardened but, in spite of this, it wore on occasions and had to be 'closed in' when it was heated to red in the gas hearth and squeezed in the hydraulic vertical press which stood at the end of the bench, but which was really, I think, on Charlie Bailey's territory, although we used it on occasions. The box itself was often heated and annealed, then filed to clean up the worn faces in the slot. Then it was reheated, liberally coated in the slot with case-hardening powder, which was allowed time to penetrate; the box reheated, and the whole reversing handle plunged handle-end first into the water tank adjacent to the gas hearth, being left in the tank for ten minutes to cool off. The gas hearth, although only about 12 inches square on the outside, being of plate lined with firebricks, had two slots cut to accommodate the body of the reversing handle while the box section sat inside the hearth in the path of the gas nozzle, which could be propped up into several positions.

One job which didn't require the use of the hearth was that done by the other gang member, 'Caddy' Jones, another expatriate Welshman, but still with links in the old country; quite a character! Usually very blunt and straight to the point. Caddy dealt with the eccentric straps and sheaves. The sheaves were the means of imparting reciprocal motion to the valve gear from the rotary motion of the axle to which they were attached, the straps forming large bearings, in effect, which were rotated around the periphery of the eccentrically set sheaves. The strap was in two halves, joined by a pair of bolts and distance pieces and lined with a semi-circle of white metal, not run-in in liquid form to adhere to serrations, as with many applications, but inserted into the slightly dovetailed shape of the inner side of the strap halves in the form of pre-cast white metal inserts. The half strap was placed open end up in the vice and a white metal section fitted into the groove was thus exposed, the fitting entailed filing the sides of the white metal section to make sure it entered the groove. The liners were also filed on the ends to bring them level with the two joint faces of the strap halves, a distance piece about ⅝ inch thick made of bronze, and with a cast-on white-metalled section to coincide with the strap liner being filed flat and positioned on the joint face. The top half of the strap was then positioned, itself also complete with a fitted white metal liner, and the two bolts inserted and pulled down tight to form the complete strap. Still held in the vice and also supported by a sling from the overhead pulley blocks, the white metal liner was now hammered hard to spread the metal into the dovetail of the outer strap, this being only a very slight dovetail, and it appeared in some older straps that the groove sides were actually parallel and not dovetailed at all. The metal was thoroughly hammered with the vice being undone, and the strap rotated on the sling to complete the circle. The completed strap was then sent for machining.

The sheave or inner part of the bearing was of cast iron, and contained a pair of integrally cast circular bearings, suitably shaped to fit into and retain the straps, positioned eccentrically around the large circular centre hole which clamped tightly to the locomotive axle. The sheave and its two offset bearings were in two halves, held together by four bolts set in recesses in the casting, allowing the two halves to be positioned by a key let into the axle 50 per cent, with the other half locating a keyway on the inner half-hole of a sheave section. The sheaves were very rarely worn badly or damaged in any way, and were just cleaned up with emery cloth, occasionally having new bolts fitted. When assembled, the diameter of the sheave was noted and the white metal of the strap bored out to suit on one of the machinists' gangs at the other end of the shop, the sheave and straps awaiting transport to AE Shop for actual assembly on the locomotive.

The eccentric rods which were attached to the straps were of 'T' shape, the 'T' being attached by two studs to the straps and the single fork end fitting the reversing quadrant. The rods were dealt with, as was the rest of the gear, on the next gangs down towards K Shop welders' bay. As with the scraping and fitting of the reversing screw slipper, another item which required fitting, as such, was the bronze quadrant block or die block, which slid in the reversing quadrant slot, the long, vertically mounted, slotted quadrant ensuring by its rocking motion, the correct valve travel.

The quadrants were ground in the slot on a specially adapted spindle grinder, the small grinding wheel rotating at several thousand revs per minute and traversing up and down the quadrant slot. There were varying types of valve gear in use throughout the various railway regions and, as previously mentioned, varying types or adaptions of types on the Great Western itself. For many years it had been almost as tradition that all valve gear was hidden between the frames, certainly a fact commented on at some length when the *King George V* locomotive made its historic trip to the USA in 1927, the differences of inside and outside valve gears being very noticeable when exhibited against the massive American locomotives. With the Stephenson valve gear, two eccentrics and the valve spindle was attached to the quadrant block (or die block) indirectly by what was called the intermediate valve spindle. The quadrant itself moved over it in an arc, depending on the position of the reversing screw or lever in the notch which determined the valve travel by lifting or lowering the complete quadrant over the die block. There was an adaption of this gear to suit the GWR outside two-cylinder locomotives by the introduction of a rocking shaft, which took the motion of the eccentrics via an intermediate rod to the end of a 'U'-shaped rocking lever mounted in brackets, open side down, to span the locomotive frame and give a lever connection on the outside of the frame for the drive to the valve spindle (*see drawing*).

A similar sort of adaption was used for the four-cylinder locomotives but, in this case, the valve gear was of the Walschaerts type. This was usually an externally mounted gear, driven by an intermediate crank arrangement attached to the outer end of the axle, but in GWR practice, the gear was mounted internally and a single eccentric substituted for the external crank. The expansion link or quadrant was supported by trunnions and was oscillated by the movement of the eccentric; it was not lifted up or down as in the Stephenson gear over a die block. In the Walschaert gear, the die block itself was moved in the slot of the expansion link by means of the attached radius rod, itself connected to a combination lever and union link, the latter attached to the crosshead, and the former to the valve spindle. The combined motion of the various levers driven by both crosshead and eccentric, gave the correct valve settings at correct lap and lead amounts to the valve itself. The motion of the inside valve gear was transmitted to operate the valves of the outside cylinders by a rather ingeniously designed rocking lever, in this case not working over the frame as with the two-cylinder arrangement, but horizontally through the frame, only the fork end of the rod and its attachment to the valve spindle being visible (*see drawings in Chapter 15*).

The valves, as such, could be one of two main types, depending on the class of engine. The small tank engines with inside cylinders had slide valves of basically flat 'D' section operating between the cylinders, themselves fitted between the locomotive frames. The larger locomotives had piston valves, working in cylindrical valve chests as opposed to the rectangular valve chests of the slide valve, with its flat, slotted, steam ports on the flat valve face. An inside crank axle could be quite crowded, taking into account the cranks themselves, the thick slabs of the crank webs, and then the attachment of two double eccentric sheaves. When in operation at speed, there was quite a weight of metal on the move, with the rotation of crank webs and eccentrics and all of the associated rods and levers of the valve gear.

I mentioned earlier on, the apparent smallness of the gang in terms of manpower, which was only about seven, including apprentices, chargehand and the gang labourer, the latter a rather round man. Ben appeared to be rather rotund but, being rather short, it was a false appearance as he was very solidly built, with a large round bald head and powerful shoulders and quite a sense of humour. At the other end of the shop, in the vicinity of the white metal bay, and covering an area against the outer wall of the shop, was a two-man team, which I believe was attached or in some way associated with Harry Jarvis' gang. The pair were equipped with a special gas hearth, floor-mounted, and an array of lifting tackle in the form of swing jibs, straight runner rails and various heavy duty pulley blocks, certainly necessary for one of the heaviest fitting jobs in the shop, augmented by the power of the walking crane in that area. Bert Morkot and his mate were the builders of crank axles, a job where the weight of the product rapidly increased as the pieces were assembled.

A crank axle was built up from several sections, all pre-machined to very close limits to enable the almost immoveable shrink fit method of assembly to be applied. The axle comprised nine separate pieces, being the centre section, turned with a seat on both ends and machined with a long keyway between the end seat sections, two pairs of crank webs, the journal section to fit between the webs, and the two outer axle lengths on which the wheels were pressed. To start the assembly, a crank web, about 4 inches thick and complete with two finely bored holes about 8 inches in diameter was positioned over the centre section of the special hearth, and the gas nozzle arranged so that its circle of jets played all round the inner surface of the hole, which would be then expanded by the heat with a sufficient amount to allow the insertion of a short cylindrically turned connecting rod journal section of the crank axle.

The heat was absorbed by the metal and the bright steel of the bored hole soon started to change colour; straws, yellows and blues, radiating from the gas jets. Bored with an interference shrink fit, i.e. slightly smaller than the web end of the journal section, it was very important to know when the heat had sufficiently expanded the metal to allow the journal end' to be inserted into the hole smoothly; any sort of burr or hesitation was fatal as the cold journal would cause the hole to contract with the journal still not home fully. If this occurred, the only recourse was to machine out the journal, so tightly was it gripped. Fortunately, such problems were rare and the journal was usually fully inserted in the hole without problems.

The final matching of wheels to axles was undertaken in AW Shop, which was the most westerly shop of the A Shop complex, stretching across the entire end of A Shop building which, in order, house the AM, AV, AE and finally AW Shops.

In the area formed by the plano mill and the cylindrical grinders was another machining area. Frank was usually the chap here to do some of the general drilling that arose, and near his radial drill was a small machine which dealt only with drill sharpening, and a second which sharpened milling cutters. These were quite fascinating to watch in action, and I must admit I passed some of my own very blunt drills from the garden shed through the system while the opportunity afforded itself!

The drills were mounted by operator in a small 'V'-shaped fixture mounted at the side face of the revolving grinding wheel (you cannot grind a drill properly on the curved periphery of a grinding wheel) and, particularly with the larger diameter drills used by the drillers themselves, were ground semi-automatically by means of the machine hand wheels, which presented the drill to the stone with a reciprocating, twisting motion to obtain the correct clearance on the cutting end behind the actual cutting edge. On removal from the fixture the larger drills were 'backed off'; this entailed the operator holding the drill manually against a corner of one of the revolving wheels, and grinding a radius in the drill end to thin the point and give additional clearances.

A further interesting tool grinding was the sharpening of the big milling operation cutters, particularly those from the plano mills. The cutters were hand-rotated on to a stop, which located the cutting edge for the approach of the small, very rapidly rotating grinding wheel which just touched the tool edge to keep its sharpness, before being rotated against the stop for the pass along the next cutting edge.

I often watched the drill and cutter grinding procedure while en route across the end of the shop to the stores to change a lead hammer or a file; the lead hammers quite quickly becoming deformed due to their softness, which of course also deformed the shape of the hole where the handle fitted, and then care was required, or suddenly the head flew off halfway through the delivery of a blow! While waiting at the stores for a replacement item, I often had a quick look at the work of the adjacent maintenance benches.

There are always occasions in a large Works, particularly in a heavy industrial environment such as the railways, when accidents occur, and none is more serious than damage to an eye. One character of AM Shop was 'Crocker' Howell, a very chatty little man who had at some time lost an eye, but who nevertheless knew or wished to know, the ins and outs of everything going on in the shop, and who was often involved in most furious arguments or heated discussions about any subject you cared to mention, or about the doings of anyone in the shop, his eye blinking and watering as the argument progressed. You either got on with Crocker or you didn't, and fortunately we had some very good heated chats on occasions, but always with a friendly atmosphere.

The tragedy of the loss of an eye cannot be overstressed, and in his case was the result, so I was told, of someone else using a hammer and chisel and chipping the 'nipple' off a bolt. Bolts, as mentioned earlier, were either forged black or could for more particular work, be turned from bar. Where the bolt was cut from the bar length when turned, some bolts were made specially to be driven home by blows of a large hammer, a real drive fit in the holes, and to stop the hammer head damaging the top of the bolt, a fairly large diameter nipple, or raised centre portion, was left in the centre of the head by the turning process.

In driving the bolt home, the hammer blows were directed at this raised portion which, in consequence, was distorted and dented, and when finally driven home was cut off neatly with a chisel to give a smooth bolt head without burrs or damage.

This definite raised centre portion was not to be confused with the small nipple or pip left on the head of an ordinary bolt when the parting-off tool, separating the bolt from its parent bar, finally parted through and the bolt broke off, the nipple then being unable to support the bolt any further. The nipple should stay on the end of the bar but this was not always the case, and depended on the tool used. Sometimes for a light drive bolt which could be relatively easily tapped into its hole by a hand hammer (although it was often the quite wrong practice), the parted nipple was used as the drive site for the hammer, a couple of blows serving to drive in the bolt, flattening the nipple which often then just fell off, again leaving an unmarked bolt head.

I was putting the four bolts in the joint of a reversing rod and the bolts had the remains of the nipples still on, not being designed as such with the larger raised centre. A blow or two with the hammer and the oiled bolts sat down firmly in the countersink. A quick blow on one bolt and I felt something strike my eye, immediately blotting out vision and leaving just a blur through which I could only distinguish light! Panic! I dropped the hammer and called out. There was a flap as I stepped back with a hand pressed to the eye and a very concerned fitter examined it, having prised my hand away. I still couldn't see very well but what had happened was that on the last blow, a large blob of oil had shot up from under the bolt head, straight into my eye, where it had spread across the eyeball! A trip to the little red box with the first aider and a wash out and I could see as well as ever, but at the time it was certainly a shock, and certainly something never forgotten.

One morning we had a message, or at least the fitter had a message, passed on through the Inspector to the chargehand, and then to the fitter, that a locomotive in steam at the running shed, and waiting, apparently, to go out, had been found to have a broken catch on the reversing screw handle. The tongue which entered the star wheel rack had apparently broken cleanly off and it was a great puzzle to know how this could have happened, the theory being that someone had belted the handle with the firing shovel! The running shed was virtually at the other side of the works relative to AM Shop, so a lengthy walk was anticipated. Loading up the bogie with the necessary tools and even a spare handle complete, the two of us set off, with me pushing the familiar transport.

Working in the engine shed was a vastly different environment to that of the machine shops of the works, but here, most noticeable of all, was that smell of hot oil, coal and steam which, to the steam man, says it all!

A few enquiries and we were passed on through the shed with its smoky, dim sort of atmosphere with breathing locomotives around us, spluttering and coughing now and again as if impatient to be off, with little whisps of steam and trickles of water from drain cocks and injectors. We found our quarry, boiler simmering in gentle impatience, and climbed aboard, its firehole doors shut tight but still warm in the cab. The handle was tied with wire, looped around the two small bolts which held the covers in place at the rear end, and how the locomotive had been worked back to the shed could only be guessed at; locking the handle with wire to obtain the valve setting must have presented some problems.

It was decided to fit a new catch, so the fitter removed the taper pin, pivot pin and handle, and lifted out the old catch, cleanly broken off across the tongue, the only occasion I ever saw one in this condition so it must have been either a fault in the metal which wasn't apparent, or quite a hefty blow which did the damage. The catches were carburised so that heating and then quenching activated the impregnated skin, causing the catch to surface-harden when quenched. Too much filing of course could easily remove the impregnated layer, so the filed tongue was usually recarburised with a yellow case-hardening powder after suitable heating. In this case, the heating was by oxyacetylene torch wielded by one of the residents of the shed, and the fitted catch filed up in a massive old fashioned leg vice, was refitted to the handle. A piece weighing about 8oz had knocked out a mechanism weighing about 70 tons! It was a little heavier to move a connected reversing screw actually on a locomotive than on the bench in AM Shop where the slipper sailed up and down the slide with no effort at all, but it now worked correctly and locked into position securely.

Colin sought out the appropriate person and reported that the screw was now OK to use. I cleaned and assembled the tools and piled all into the bogie for the return journey. We left the shed to a parting toot on a whistle from somewhere back in the murk and haze, and still the little whisps of steam spurted and little water trickles ran over the dark dirty layers of grime, making shiny bands over the waterproof floor covering.

A further small job took us later into AE Shop itself. One of the fitters from the shop turned up one afternoon with his apprentice in tow, carrying a pin from a long-reach rod, which he said would not go through the bush in the lever on the weigh shaft. It appeared that the bush had been changed but not reamed out to suit the pin diameter, so consulting the stamped size on the pin end, I sorted the reamer and wrench from the cupboard under the bench and we both took a walk with the AE Shop fitter back through AV Shop, across the first engine bay, over the traversing table road to Stan Lewington's gang where we, or more to the point I, reamed out the hole which I should have reamed out when the rod and lever were in AM Shop. It was quite straightforward as the lever was accessible easily from the running board, so the job was not really a problem, just, for me at least, a pleasant little trip among even more steam locomotives although these engines were much quieter than those in the recently visited running shed.

One job which came in very occasionally to Harry's gang and fortunately coincided with my stay, was the refurbishing of a Weir pump. These pumps were mounted on the right-hand front running board of a class of small side tank engines which were required to run over some of the lines of the Metropolitan Underground section in London. As such, the exhaust steam was not allowed to blast its way out of the chimney, but was passed through a condenser system and fed back into the water tanks for reuse. This created its own special problems as far as a steam locomotive was concerned, although easing the problems in the tunnels themselves. Not least among those problems was the difficulty of lifting hot water to feed the boiler, against the pressure in the boiler of course. The GWR injector could not effectively create the vacuum system at the nozzles to project the water forward and through into the boiler feed pipes, so the alternative was the Weir pump, used extensively in this form and in a number of sizes in a marine or maritime capacity. Most steam ships had a Weir pump somewhere in the engine rooms for steady, reliable pumping of some auxiliary function. In the case of the locomotive, if it was itself scheduled for repair and overhaul, then the pump went through the same system.

The pump stood about 4 feet high, and was in two main sections, the bottom portion being the pump, with suction and delivery valves, all mounted in a very sturdy base casting. From each side of the base casting and extending upwards from integrally cast sockets, reached a circular solid steel rod of about 2½-inch diameter, to the top of which, again attached by integrally cast sockets, was attached the steam cylinder and valve. A piston rod combined with a pump rod operated from top section to bottom section, and the valve gear comprised a very simple, short beam action, connected to the piston rod and pivoting from a bracket off the two round uprights, its outer end connected to a valve spindle. In action, the beam, about 5 inches long, performed a very simple rocking motion about its pivot point, halfway between steam cylinder and pump box.

The bottom section was a fairly conventional pump, but the steam cylinder, while straightforward in itself, had the weirdest valve I have ever seen. The valve rod was connected to what appeared to be a conventional slide valve, but the valve itself, which operated vertically through the rocking action of the small beam, was itself mounted on a cut-out recess in another valve, this time a horizontal, hollow, sealed ended cylinder which ran in a quite naturally horizontal steam chest, a distinctive portion of the Weir pump itself. The cylindrical valve had various strangely angled steam ports connecting with its hollow interior, which in turn led directly to the steam ports covered by the flat valve, or conversely from the flat valve, through the cylindrical valve, to the cylinder.

On stripping down, the pump section was found to require cleaning out and the valves reseated with a little grinding paste, the pump ram and bore being OK but, at the cylinder end, while the cylinder itself showed next to no wear at all, the cylindrical valve was ridged in places and the bore of the valve chest was also worn with the same ridges. It was decided, I'm not sure by whom, to have the steam chest bored out to clean it up, and the valve itself sleeved and the ports recut to suit. The cylindrical valve disappeared up the shop into one of the turning gangs, while the valve chest and cylinder end of the pump went in another direction for boring. I have since pondered on the effect of enlarging the steam chest in this way, on the efficiency of the design of the engine, but at that stage it was just accepted as the only alternative. A sleeve was made and, I believe, shrunk on to the outside of the cylindrical valve and duly returned to the gang for marking out the steam ports. I was not present for the marking out, so how these were matched to the originals now covered by the sleeve, I don't know, sufficient to say that when returned from being milled, the original ports were aligned to the new ones in the sleeve. An interesting feat!

The pump was reassembled and a special flange attached to the steam inlet, a flange kept by the chargehand for the purpose, and specially adapted to take the screwed end of an air line from compressed air main, a branch of which ran down virtually every roof support column in the shop, the small pipe terminating in the standard air valve with the small, flattish hand wheel disc pinned to the valve steam. With everything steamwise well oiled, and a drop of water in the pump, the air valve was cracked a term for being just opened a small amount, and we waited! With a little hesitation, the piston rod slowly moved and the valve beam lifted its end in the opposite direction. A further hesitation and the rod started to move in the opposite direction. Rather haltingly at first, as if wearing some of the stiffness out of the various components, opening the air valve had the pump chuff-chuff-chuffing away quite merrily, various visitors from the surrounding gangs wandering over to have a look. We kept it on the main and, on occasions, nipped across and turned it on for a few seconds, just to watch it work! A special command performance for the Inspector, Jack Evans, and then the pump was disconnected and placed aside ready for transport to AE Shop to be re-erected on locomotive. That we thought, was the end of that. But it wasn't!

A number of days later we had a call to the turntable at the corner of the A Shop complex and bordered the other side by the Iron Foundry and Pattern Stores, where a certain small tank engine, in steam, had a feed pump that wouldn't feed. We loaded up the inevitable bogie with an oil can and spanners, etc., and off we set, straight up the centre of the shop, clattering over the iron duct plates, out of the end door by the check box, and turned right straight down to the turntable. We climbed on the running board and looked at the now warm pump and had various verbal exchanges with the outside fitting gang representative who had been attempting to get the pump to work. There was much discussion, clattering of spanners and liberal oiling, but still nothing moved when the steam was turned on. It was decided to have the pump removed and taken back into the shop. That caused a few comments, to get a job returned as it didn't work, and was rather an embarrassment to all concerned.

At first our surrounding colleagues thought it was another pump in for repair and expressed great interest, which soon cooled when it was understood to be the same one which we had already dealt with. Unloaded once more, and standing on its base near the air line valve, the flange with the screwed connection was once more attached and the air line connected up. With the despairing comment 'Let's have a go to find out why it won't work', the valve was cracked open and immediately the quiet chuff-chuff-chuff was heard as the pump very smoothly started operating. We tried all sorts to stop the pump operating! We opened the air valve fully when the pump rocked away on its base, right down to the merest crack of the valve when the rod only just moved, but move it did, quietly and smoothly. We turned if off for a time and then crept up on it and opened the air valve suddenly; try as we could, we could not catch it unawares and it smoothly and quietly chuffed back at us at all times.

The fitter called the chargehand who removed his cap and scratched his head. Then the Inspector joined us, followed by Dick Johns, the foreman, then a general procession of Running Inspector, outside gang chargehand and the outside fitter, and all agreed that the pump worked. The transport was called, the pump hoisted aboard and off to the locomotive waiting by the turntable, and that we thought, was that. But once again it wasn't! Within the hour the message came that there was no move from the reinstated pump, so out we all trooped again to the small locomotive now hissing in impatience, the rain gently falling and steaming off the hot pump, and the equally hot outside fitter. The fitters fiddled and oiled and the air got bluer and bluer, but still there was no sign of movement.

In exasperation, the fitters finally straightened up from the crouched position on the running board and the outside fitter, staring balefully at the silent pump, exploded 'Why don't you start? You old ****!' and gave the valve chest a hefty bang with the spanner. With a slight cough, we were rewarded with a gentle chuff-chuff-chuff from the persuaded piece of stubborn mechanism which had at last decided to work! With steam on and off several times, everything now ran as it had in the shop, and this time we heard no more of the Metropolitan engine and its weird Weir pump!

Time was running out for my stay in AM Shop, and eventually the paper arrived indicating a return once again to R Shop. I was rather sorry to leave Harry's gang as I had enjoyed my stay. The work was interesting and the working atmosphere very friendly; Harry, Colin, Caddy, John, Norman on the grinder, and the two fitters from the nearby marking off table, Norman and George, being one of the 'matiest' groups I ever worked with. Great leg pulling and arguments often developed, always with a friendly atmosphere, on all sorts of subjects, with various notes and comments chalked on the back of the bench on the chipping screen frame. All taken and given in good humour.

However, Monday would see me back in R Shop.

'AM' Shop.
Harry Jarviss
The Weir(d)! Pump.
'We tried creeping up on it'

AM Shop – the repair of the Weir pump.

14

Back to R Shop Again

Leaving home a little earlier on the Monday morning to cover the slightly longer distance from home to check board, timed to the split second of the last blast on the hooter, the board cover came down with a bang to find a little group of us, checks in hand, waiting for the checky to consult his list and tell us where we had been assigned. 'Hmm. Gibbs!' Running a finger down the list and across the page. 'Marchment's!' This was no surprise as most apprentices, or many apprentices went on to Tommy Marchment's gang (although pronounced 'Marshman', I believe it was spelled as above). Tommy was a little tubby fellow who resembled, to me anyway, an owl! Wearing a brown warehouse coat instead of the usual overalls, he had a round face with a sharp pointed nose and thickish spectacles, a small mouth and a chin tucked well in. Two other apprentices were already at his cupboard when I reported. 'Gibbs?' he said, 'I've got no record of that name! Are you sure?' 'Certainly,' I said, 'that's what I've just been told!' I was advised to go back to the checky, which I did. 'Gibbs,' he said, again consulting his list. 'Marchment's! Told you once!' So back I went to Tommy. 'Better make some enquiries later about that,' he said, 'in the meantime let's get you started!'

I was allocated to one of the fitters, a youngish chap who said he didn't get an apprentice usually so he seemed pleased at any rate. I stowed my box of odds and ends in the wire mesh fronted cupboard under the bench and the fitter started to explain the job. The large base casting of the safety valve had to be placed on the bench, and the studs and valve pillars checked, nuts 'run on' to make sure the threads were not damaged. Two valve spindles were selected (I was familiar with these as I had spent five or six weeks about 40 yards from this spot actually turning them); two valves were seated by scraping and grinding paste and when a nice, unbroken dark ring showed around the valve seats, the bridge was put on over the valves and valve spindles complete with coil springs, and the nuts checked down. Adjacent to the chargehand's cupboard was a low test and setting rig where the valves were actually set. A large dial gauge gave the pressure, and with the complete safety valve base clamped down, a hand pump supplied the water pressure from a small tank below the rig. The springs were 'weighted' by screwing down the nuts and thus tightening the bridge piece to compress the springs. Pressures up to 280 psi had to be restrained, the 280 pounds from Hawkesworth's 1000 class locomotives, and if a sudden jet of water appeared from a valve before the required pressure was reached, the valve was called, very inelegantly, a 'pisser', and one of these always led to a cheer from the other gang members as it meant stripping down from the rig and reseating the valves, then trying again.

Seating in the valves commenced and break time came when the usual beverage was brewed, and we all sat on our small wood blocks or on the benches and consumed our sandwiches, the food usually gripped and eaten still in the paper bag in which it was carried to work. Just after the break, Tommy came up with a man in an ordinary jacket and trousers and said to me 'You are Ken Gibbs aren't you?' When I said I was, he then said 'You were given the wrong instructions, you should be on Bill Dawson's!' On that, the man in the jacket said, 'Yes, that's me! We wondered where you'd got to! Collect your odds and ends and we'll go!' Actually, 'go' was not very far, just along the same row of benches. This again was rather a small gang and I was attached to Ken, yet another little stockily built individual with very bushy fair eyebrows. The product of this job was the regulator valve. As previously mentioned, there were two general patterns of valve, one the vertical design for the domed locomotives, and the other valve set in the horizontal valve box which was mounted in the smokebox.

I recall a couple of other apprentices on the gang, but I believe these were moved off at intermediate stages. 'Sam' Eylett and 'Vic' Stevens, the latter an old school mate of mine, and the former among the apprentice group with which I had started in the Scraggery. I didn't know at the time that my stay on Bill Dawson's job was going to be much shorter than usual, being terminated rather abruptly, but the work itself was most interesting.

I was set to work on the vertical type of regulator valve, the main valve seat being vertically cut in the large cast steam 'elbow' or valve body, the flat face of the valve being scraped first to a surface plate and red lead paste, the paste on the surface plate showing the high spots on the valve face. These high spots were carefully scraped away and the valve tried again on the surface plate. A regular close pattern of reddish spots on the valve denoted its flatness and it was acceptable as the master for use when scraping a bearing on the valve seat of the large casting. The jockey valve on the back of the main valve was treated in the same way, first being faced to the surface plate and then used to ensure the flatness of the seat on and through the back of the main valve.

There was always a considerable amount of scraping to do, considering the machined or relative flatness of the valves to start with, but the significance of this did not leap out at the time and things just ticked along, scraped bearings being checked by Ken, and everything progressing smoothly.

One of the jobs which came on to the gang was the request for a main valve and jockey valve for a locomotive under repair in one of the outstation sheds dotted around the region, and I duly faced up a main valve to the plate and, accompanied by its jockey valve, it went in a neat parcel over by the check box for despatch. About a week later, Bill Dawson came up to me holding the valve and jockey, explaining that it had not been done properly, as it was blowing through badly and would have to be faced again. Ken was rather annoyed, and I was none too pleased either, but there it was, a duff valve! Ken checked it with the surface plate, said he couldn't find anything wrong with it really, but gave it a very fine scraping so that the spots of red were even smaller and closer together, and off it went again!

Within a few days it was back again, this time I think with a rather caustic letter! Ken had a look and tried it on the plate, then Bill tried it and so did the Inspector. All came to the conclusion that it should have been OK, and that the actual valve seat must have been at fault. We were all grouped around the small marking off table near to Bill's cupboard, just looking at the rejected valve sitting as forlornly as we felt, next to the red surface of the small face plate. Out of curiosity, I pulled my 12-inch steel rule from the leg pocket of my overalls and held it diagonally across the face plate, and at the same time Ken produced a 6 inch steel rule and slid it quite easily under the centre of my rule. The master surface plate was hollow! Probably used continually from its receipt when new, and throughout the war years, the plate was so badly dished that on return to O Shop tool room, it had to be remachined before it could be rescraped to the required flatness of a surface plate, a range of spots per square inch when tried against another plate being the criteria for acceptance. There were two ranges of quality for the flat surface, a jobbing plate having less spots per square inch than the tool room variety but both being acceptable standards.

Faced to another plate, the valve face was certainly domed; no wonder it had blown through on assembly, being rescraped and surfaced and again this time finally despatched, and the valves which followed certainly required less scraping to get them flat! The condition of that plate was a conversation topic for several days, with both Bill and Ken very puzzled on how no one had questioned it before, and it was probably only the fact that the separate valve had come in from outstation that the problem plate had been exposed.

Both Ken and Bill were very quietly spoken and showed generally good consideration and assistance to apprentices, or at least that's how I found them, and I quite enjoyed my stay on the gang, short though it was. Unfortunately, the stay was short as I came in one morning and started the usual valve scraping, and by about break time I had a pain in the stomach which I put down to indigestion. Back after midday lunch, having eaten nothing, I had a change of job temporarily, at the far end of the row of benches, up by the lads still banging away on piston heads and plugs, with the job being to straighten some bars which had bowed when being heat-treated. There was a small fly press on the end of one of the benches and a small marking off table adjacent, at the foot of which was a stack of the round bars for checking and straightening. The object of the job was to place the bar in 'V' blocks under the press, rotate them to determine concentricity, and lightly use the press to remove any distortion, placing the bars aside on the floor again when finished. I found it becoming increasingly difficult to stoop to put them down again. By about 4 p.m., I was in considerable discomfort, so walked back down to see Ken and told him I was going to get a pass out and go home. I remember having a considerable job climbing the steps to the foreman's office to obtain the necessary permision, then through to the clerk's office for the small pass out docket. I walked home, getting slower and slower, and I remember sitting on a wall of someone's front garden, en route, in Jennings Street, for several minutes, then finding it very difficult to start again. However I got home, having taken much longer than usual, and slumped into a chair. My father arrived home about 5.30 p.m., and one thing leading to another, I was consigned to bed and the doctor was called. Taken to hospital about 5 p.m., the diagnosed rotten appendix was removed a couple of hours later and that was that for about nine weeks! The end of my stay with Ken and Bill Dawson and the end of my fitting section of the apprenticeship. The next move would be erecting, the final stage actually working on the locomotives themselves!

There was to be a further intervening delay, however, again not known at the time, but the nine weeks 'on the club' as the saying goes, was not really wasted time. The evening classes I had been attending, 7 p.m. to 9 p.m., three nights a week for the winter period since starting the apprenticeship, had been pointing me in the direction of the National Certificate, but the further I progressed, which wasn't very far incidentally, led me deeper and deeper into, to me, the unfathomable depths of integral and differential calculus and the like, and a decision that, while I liked machine drawing, which I was quite good at, and science, with which I also managed to cope, the subject of mathematics as such, left me cold. I much preferred the practical applications to be found in the City & Guilds courses, which included an evening in a workshop at the technical college annexe, and engineering type problems with which I could identify. Prior to my appendicitis then, I had just ditched the 'National' course and started from the beginning with the City & Guilds Machine Shop Engineering course, the session commencing during September. The date of the operation was 19 October and the first thing I requested to read a couple of days after was *The Model Engineer* magazine which I had been then purchasing quite regularly and read avidly from cover to cover, even the small print in every advertisement. Waiting for the healing process, and with the City & Guilds course in mind, I had a colleague bring me his notes from evening classes and also the homework which I did at leisure during the days when I couldn't move around too much, also copying out the notes at the same time. I had purchased Chapman's book, *Workshop Technology*, and this also became required reading, much better I thought than dry-as-dust calculus!

The college annexe was on the estate of the Goddard family, who up to pre-war had been the Lords of the Manor, but the house was gone and the grounds were filled with ex-army huts, from which the troops had departed and which had been taken over for use as additional classrooms. The teachers for the evening sessions were generally suitably qualified personnel from the Great Western Railway drawing office, supervisory or management positions. The first year classes were generally packed solid at the commencement of the session although like everything else, whether academic or sporting, the first wave of enthusiasm cools, and the hardcore of those sufficiently interested remains. Learning about the compositions of steels and alloys of copper, machining techniques, machine tool design and application, with calculations to suit indexing heads, etc., was to me fascinating, and left the National Certificate 'Stresses in a Warren Girder' and the like, far behind! Not knowing really the requirements of the first year course, I read far in advance during my period off work, but the more I read, the more interesting it became.

Reading Chapman and other technical books, interspersed with listening to the twice daily episodes of *Mrs Dale's Diary*, I spent a leisurely couple of months while the rather large hole in my stomach healed. I made arrangements to commence work again on the Monday, being duly signed off by the doctor, and on the Sunday went out on my small motorcycle for a spin round. I had an old hand change O.K. Supreme, converted to foot change, and I could now kick start it without problems. My intention to go for a spin round terminated in just that way, because on the way home I turned a corner near the local cinema, the centre stand of motorcycle came down into the road and I joined the cinema queue, bike and all (and I'd already seen the film)! I caught my foot between the foot rest and the kerb and scraped a lump out of my shoe and my foot. I mounted again and drove home, washed my foot and stuck a bit of plaster over the scrape! In the evening I went for quite a long walk with another colleague and on the Monday morning I reported as required to B Shed where I had started my apprenticeship three years earlier. I was this time allocated to the locomotive side of the shop where the smaller tank engines were dealt with and commenced work on the end pit by the door into R Shop, just across from the small bay where my grandfather had worked on the buffers, just before he retired about thirty years before.

Apart from sorting out brake hanger brackets and assembling pins, washers and split pins, I do not remember much about that day as the pain in my foot got worse and I had a job to hobble about by the end of the afternoon shift. After sleeping very little that night, with a foot getting visibly larger as I watched, the first move the following morning was to go to the outpatients department of the GWR Hospital, visited before when I cut my arm on the boiler stay in P1 Shop. A rocket from the doctor for neglecting a badly crushed ankle which had a large hole scraped in it, and the instruction to 'Come along to the end cubicle when the nurse has dressed your foot.' I went along to the cubicle, as instructed, and the doctor said 'Now, you young idiot, take a good look at that!' That's what you could have done to your foot by neglecting it! 'That' was the biggest leg ulcer I have ever seen, the elderly gentleman sitting quite quietly watching me as I watched nurse proceed to clean and dress the massive raw area. Suitably impressed and a little subdued, I murmured the right things and turned to leave, when the doctor asked me how I was going to get home as I had a job to walk. 'Oh,' I said, 'I came on the bike!' I thought he was going to have a fit, but I explained to him that it was easier to ride than to walk, which I had great difficulty in doing. He accepted in the end that that was probably the best way of moving, but said 'Take special care and I want to see you at the same time tomorrow. That hole has to be kept clean!' That cleaning proved to be quite painful!

AE Shop and Loco Erecting

After a number of regular visits to the GWR outpatients department, the frequencies between visits getting longer and longer, and my home study work continuing along with the episodes of *Mrs Dale's Diary*, I eventually had a clean bill of health and instructions to start in the steam Mecca, AE Shop, on the following Monday. That was another five weeks gone by, making about fourteen in total. A couple of chargehands had received papers showing a move on to the gang and then a move off, but with no one of the name turning up at all. That proved to be the longest period of my working life that I was ever off sick!

However, due to the problems of the appendicitis and the wound that it had caused, I had a letter from the doctor, endorsed by the railway doctor, that I still had to have a lighter job for a few weeks on starting in AE Shop. This proved rather interesting as I was placed first with the fitter and mate who operated the Zeiss frame alignment instrumentation, a move not usual I believe for apprentices. So, reporting first to the foreman, having had a little red tab 'See Foreman before Starting' hanging with my check, I went down into the shop to find Harry Bown and Charlie. Looking along the rows of steam locomotives in all stages of undress from just bare frames to virtually complete beings, resplendent in new paint, I first had to locate the special handcart adapted for transporting the items of the Zeiss equipment. The handcart was quite distinctive when compared to the usual iron-wheeled bogies or sack trucks in common use, and was a high bed cart on large wood-spoked wheels, its bed transformed by the addition of wood blocks of various shapes and sizes and various other clamping pieces of wood, shaped to hold the rods and collimator of the viewing apparatus and with a wooden lockable box across the handles at the back of the cart for the dial gauges.

The movement inherent in the reciprocating and rotating masses of a steam locomotive were such that any misalignment of such items, although not sufficiently misaligned to cause a malfunction, nevertheless could cause fractures and twists which could lead to undue wear and fatigue in the components affected. Locomotive practice at the time included the use of plate frames cut out in the appropriate places to house the axleboxes which themselves were supported by special reinforcing angle brackets known as horn cheeks, very solid design bearing surfaces firmly riveted to the openings in the frames. Apart from the actual stripping pits, the activities of Harry and Charlie took them to virtually anywhere along the circuit pits on that side of AE Shop wherever a wheelless frame stood, and which could be destined for the special grinding of the horn cheeks to the dimensions ascertained by the use of the Zeiss equipment.

There had previously been a system whereby, in effect, one group or gang took a locomotive repair right through from stripping to steaming, but a reorganisation in about

1933 had introduced a circuit of repairs with special gangs doing one facet or stage of the repair and the locomotive being passed bodily on to the next stage or group of operations. The A Shop complex had been constructed early in the century, around 1905/06 and, at that time, and I believe for a number of years afterwards, had been the largest locomotive repair shop under one roof in Europe. We have briefly looked at the areas covered by the AM Machine section, AV Boiler section, and brief reference has been made to AW Wheel section, leaving possibly a good third of the shop as AE Erecting section; the latter stretching along on the main line side of the shop parallel to AM section, then being separated by AV bay with a blacksmith area at the main line end before coming to the AE erecting pits proper.

Three traversing tables plied up and down the three main bays which were at right angles to the main line outside, and while all bays were important and formed part of the shop the third of the three traversers served the bays which were of the greatest interest to many of those who worked, and I would say all of those who visited the shop. Here along the sides of the traverser track were the double-length pit facilities for the main steam locomotive repairs. Standing there was quite a fascinating environment. High roofed, with 100-ton-capacity cranes running above each bay under a vast area of glass, the impression of size and space seemed to be magnified. Wherever you looked, steam locomotives stood, including those on the New Work pits, all clean and red-lead painted, under the care of Bill Dando, the young fitter of 1927 who had accompanied the pride of the Great Western, *King George V*, to the USA and international fame, and who twenty years on was now one of the little tubby men with marvellous memories of steam.

Diagonally opposite, at the mainline end of the opposite bay, were the pits allocated to stripping the locomotives on entry to the shop for repair, an area of dirt and grime, where overalls were worn with tightly closed cuffs, collars done well up to the neck, trouser bottoms tied tightly around the boot tops with string and an array of hats worn at all times and, when working, pulled well down to keep out that very dirt and grime. In effect the circuit started here, the stripped locomotives passing on down the bay to Ron Glass and Harold Gardener, then across the table to Stan Lewington for the final touches before going up to the valve setting plant, which itself was backed by a high girder structure which carried the replica *North Star* locomotive of the early years of the GWR at Swindon. Stan Lewington's gang was in the centre of the bay, and on the end nearest the main line was Harold Rayer's area, the gang for light repair or special items which did not warrant entry to the circuit. This was the area of the works then which formed the centre of the world for the steam enthusiast!

Starting as I did on the Zeiss equipment, and on a date which was not an apprentice shift date, caused a little comment and questions from various people although my contemporaries, the apprentices in the group with which I had started, were themselves in the shop and of course knew me.

The equipment and associated items performed two main functions. It could very accurately measure the amount (if any) that the centre line through the bore of the cylinders fluctuated from the 90 degrees requirement of squareness, through the centre line of each pair of axlebox openings, i.e. the horn cheeks, across both frame sides. It could also, by means of dial gauges and rods, measure accurately and ensure the distance between the centres of the horn cheeks, for example the three pairs of boxes for the main wheels of the 4-6-0 locomotive, or the four pairs for the 2-8-0, and thus obtain the centre boring distances for the bearings in the associated connecting rods. Any deviation from squareness, as defined by the equipment, on any pair of horn cheeks was rectified on a specially designed bed to which travelling heads containing surface grinding wheels were attached. A pit had been converted in the repair circuit and set up by the use of machined and levelled plates, to form in effect a giant surface plate. A frame set and clamped level on this bed could be subjected to the attentions of the cantilevered and oscillating surface grinders which accurately removed sufficient from the offending horn cheek face to ensure its squareness, not only with its opposite of the pair, but also to conform to the 90 degree angle requirement with the cylinder bore (*see Plate 30*).

The large open shop was often, or at least appeared to the uninitiated, to be deserted at the midday break; so quiet did it appear after the 12.30 p.m. hooter had blown to signal the start of the meal period. The pits were certainly empty of personnel but by benches and around corners, individuals and small groups consumed their sandwiches and drank their enamel mug of whatever beverage was to their taste. It was from such a break that Harry and Charlie returned to their cart and proceeded to assemble the equipment for checking the next locomotive on the list. The microscope was set through the cylinder, its three graduated arms accurately centring the tube on the cylinder centre line and the rods produced to determine the exact distance between the centres of the cheekblocks for the axle positions. With the brackets clamped and screwed on near the horn cheek openings, the micrometer dial gauges were the next items to attach to the rod ends in the brackets. Each member of the team asked the other if he had already taken the dial gauges out of the box and if so, where had they been put. No one had them, nor had they been taken out of the box, so where were they? A walk back to the last locomotive frame on which they had been used drew a blank, the fitters there, while they had seen them in use, had no idea where they were now and all insisted that the dials had been removed with the rest of the equipment when the handcart had been loaded and taken to the next frame. The Zeiss equipment was about sixteen years or so old at this time, having been acquired about 1933, and was well-known in its use throughout the shop, so all knew of the dial gauges when asked, but no one had seen them. It was becoming increasingly clear that the only possible explanation was that they had been stolen! Without them, the Zeiss equipment was inoperable, and the items were so obvious with their special fittings that whoever had them must have only a vague idea of any use other than for the equipment for which they had been designed. Reported to the chargehand and then to the foreman, the enquiries produced nothing, so the works security people were notified.

The 'security', as such, at this period was not the sophisticated, uniformed staff one now sees at the gatehouses and drop barriers of the many firms now resident on the trading estates around the industrially developed sites, but was a system of watchmen, who undertook patrols around the area of the works, recording the journeys by special time clocks positioned at the strategic points of the route. These men were the watchers at the gates and the various rail crossings, often sitting alone in a small hut at a particular crossing of the main lines which ran through the works, stopping those unauthorised to cross and often preceding those who had authority to do so, as a measure of safety. The head watchman was notified and enquiries began. All those in the vicinity were approached to ascertain if anything suspicious was observed during the break period. Many of course were not there at the time, having gone home, but those who had stayed were to rack their brains for anything which they may have seen.

After a number of enquiries had been made, a boilermaker who has been sitting on the pits side of the benches, facing down between the locomotives where the cart had been resting, recalled seeing a person approach the cart, rummage through the box as though looking for something, but could not say if anything had been actually taken. The description given fitted that of an apprentice who had been seen in the shop, but who did not actually work there at that time, and enquiries were stepped up. Tracked down and confronted, he eventually confessed and, when police visited his home, a fair amount of odd mechanical and electrical items were found, not connected for a particular project but just acquired as being useful; items which included the dial gauges in question. That apprenticeship was terminated forthwith!

My own stay with Harry and Charlie was of very short duration, about a couple of weeks and I was then moved from the main pits section around to the gang of Jack Adams along the bay which dealt with bogie repairs, but in this case Jack dealt with injectors, those vacuum-creating assemblies which sucked water into the boiler against the boiler pressure to keep the level topped up without the use of a pump. I was placed with Reg, a little, chatty man who always seemed to be on the move, going somewhere or doing something, but again my stay was to be quite short as I believe apprentices were not usually placed on this gang nor indeed do I recall, on this side of the shop, although I may be wrong on this count. We were quite near to a plant called 'the Bosh', and the distinctive smell often wafted over when the doors of the shop were open. The Bosh itself was in effect, a building within a building, and housed the plant used for cleaning all the components which came from a stripped locomotive; these were of course the components of the mechanism and did not include the boiler. Special metal-sided small wagons were used, running on the standard gauge rails, into which was placed all of the assembled items, forming a wagon load, from a particular locomotive. The wagons were about the size of a locomotive's four-wheeled bogie and had loose bodies, very stoutly constructed, which sloped inward at the bottom to a very strong steel mesh base. In use, the loaded trucks were shunted along by the traversing table capstans, under the powerful hoists of the Bosh itself, and the bodies lifted complete with contents, dumped in a large rectangular tank of a steam-heated caustic soda solution, which bubbled away like the mud geysers in an American national park. Hot water jets from hoses could be directed at the more stubborn deposits, with the application of the occasional scraper for the more solid, stubborn lumps, but generally the caustic soda and the heat worked well. A final rinse and the wagon of components emerged grey and steaming slightly, from the other side, the components quite hot to the touch, but now clean enough to handle in the Repair Shops. Sometimes in the Repair Shop a little of the adhering mixture of oil grease, dirt and caustic soda solution had formed a jelly-like deposit in a crease or hole of the item and, if on cleaning it out, it got on to the inevitable finger with graze or cut that all fitters and machinists seemed to have, then it really stung.

Everything found its way into the Bosh, from the largest component to the smallest separated nut and bolt, the latter in small baskets dipped with the wagon body load. Quite near our bench was a small area which had, I would imagine, developed during the late war, and was dedicated to the reclamation of nuts, bolts, screws and small items which, although used for various locomotives in a general way, were not or could not be specifically numbered or identified as belonging to any locomotive. The small area was quite crowded with metal bins and containers and formed a general open U shape, with a bench across the closed end and storage racks forming the sides and positioned in the open centre. This was the 'old boys' area, where those with a disability, caused through accident or age, sat on home-made or acquired chairs or stools, and with a steel block or plate in front of them on the bench, spent their time salvaging and matching nuts to bolts, or anything else threaded into a mating screwed item. There were about up to half a dozen working away very steadily and there was a continual tap-tap-tap of hammers as nuts were started on the threads of bolts, and then held by the bolt with nut on the plate and lightly hammered as the bolt was rotated, the light hammer blows keeping a 'flat' of the nut on the plate. As the bolt was rotated, so it screwed itself into the nut and the light hammering ensured that any burrs on either the nut or the bolt were flattened, enabling the nut to be run on or off the bolt with ease. Although crowded with bins and containers, the area was generally quite neat as such with the bins labelled in chalk to define the contents which were again returned to service but with discretion, depending on the component concerned, certain items of strategic importance demanding and receiving new bolts or fastenings every time. These were often the bolts used for temporarily positioning an item prior to final bolting or riveting, and were then often retained in the toolbox for future use for a similar job. I have an idea those employed on this reclamation work were allowed to leave five minutes earlier than the rest of us to allow for disabilities and the problem of being caught in the usual mad rush when the hooter signalled the end of the shift.

Apart from having to change an exhaust injector, I was not really long enough with Reg to get into any pattern of work, but we did take an injector round to the pits, or at least it was transported round, while we followed with the tool bag, and Reg directed our operations for removal and replacement.

However, again out of the apprentice sequence of changes, came the instruction to report round to the pits and to Harold Gardner. Arriving with my small box of tools and rolled overalls on the Monday morning, I had a little chat with Harold and was introduced to Alf, who was to temporarily be my 'mate'. The significance of this didn't occur to me immediately, and Harold came with us down to the pit on which I was to work. Standing there was a boilerless, wheelless frame with the cylinder castings exposed on the top, over the steam chests and valves, and on the ground by the side of the frame a large air-driven drilling machine with the post and arm familiar to me from the processes of P1 Shop and other shops throughout the course of my apprenticeship.

It appeared that the casting had cracked, whether a stress-crack I don't know, but this was probably the case and was not unknown for the type of locomotive, nor for the location of the crack. The welding of cast iron is, or at least was at that time, a difficult process, although it was done with oxyacetylene to broken or cracked reversing screw brackets, but the process was out of the question for such a large, immovable mass as the inside cylinder steam chests in question. A practice had developed for repair of such cracked castings in situ, the method being to drill a large number of holes all around the crack and to screw in steel plugs. This introduced weldable material to the area of the crack and, well screened to protect everyone from the brilliant light of the powerful arcs required, was electrically welded over the top to form a large patch of weld material, possibly surface alloying with the cast iron but having the penetration strength required due to adherence to the weldable steel plugs. The top of the welded area was then cleaned up by the use of the air-driven grinding wheel, either the circular or cup wheel machine being used, depending on availability.

However, asked if I was familiar with the type of drilling machine, I said that I was, and Harold pointed out where he thought the first holes should be drilled, freehand, to enable them to be tapped first and a special stud screwed in temporarily so that the drill post and arm could be mounted, thus making the job of drilling the rest of the holes that much easier. We hoisted the machine on to the cylinder block and I connected up the steel wrapped air line to the valve on the roof support column adjacent, and said to Alf that we could do with a sack or two to kneel or sit on, on top of the casting. He said he would get some and departed at speed, returning a minute or two later with some sacks and a couple of large balls of cotton waste, used in vast quantities throughout the works for cleaning and issued to each man, one ball a week, for such cleaning purposes.

With the sacks suitably packed, we proceeded with the drilling, manually holding the drill for the first scattered holes for the attachment of the drill post and arm. The short drill had been put in the chuck to the depth of hole required (it had been probably broken previously and was therefore shorter than as issued). Having drilled the holes, hanging on grimly to the machine as past experience dictated, Alf handed me the taps and tap wrench and I proceeded to tap the holes. The drill post and arm were mounted on the special stud and drilling proceeded with no particular problems, taking us up to the break period and the consuming of sandwiches and, in my case, my usual cup of cocoa. We started drilling again after the break, and slowly the area around the crack began to look like a honeycomb, covering the general space indicated at first by Harold. My first indication that something was odd about the whole situation came when I started to tap out the remainder of the holes, mentioning that with another set of taps and wrench we could complete the job that much faster as Alf could also tap some of the holes. His comment that he wasn't allowed to do any such thing puzzled me at the time but I just thought there may be some medical grounds for such a problem and didn't push the matter any further. However, just before midday, Harold came back to see how we were getting on. Apparently all was well and we had a further chat, during the course of which he said that he understood I had been with Harry and Charlie on the Zeiss equipment as he had often seen me with them, and also for a period around in the other bay with Jack Adams, and asked me when had I finished my apprenticeship.

When I told him I still had about ten months to do to finish, the penny dropped for both of us. Due to my arrival in the shop and moves out of phase with the general pattern, Harold had thought I was a Journeyman, finished with apprenticeship, and he had temporarily given me a fitter's mate and a first job of drilling out the reinforcing holes in the steam chests as an introduction to the gang and its work. He called Alf over and we had quite a chuckle together. I now understood why he wasn't allowed to tap out any holes, but that was that as far as my brief period as a 'journeyman' was concerned, and I was marched off down the line of pits to Ken Allen, with whom I was to work for the next ten weeks or so.

Ken was a rather tall, slim, quietly spoken person with whom it was very pleasant to work, and I soon settled in, although it was certainly a change from my short 'journeyman' stint! The main work of this part of the circuit, as affecting us, was the fitting of motion bars and preparation and insertion of driving wheels and axleboxes.

The motion bars are the two large, horizontal guide bars between which the crosshead slides. The frame of the locomotive was set on specially designed stands, the top of each stand being a flat-bottomed fork, the width of which was slightly more than the thickness of the locomotive frame itself, which sat firmly on the bottom of the fork. The stands supporting the frame were adjustable so that the frame could be set absolutely level and, once set, the stands could be locked in that position to ensure the frame remained level; the base of the stand shaped like a buffer head with the stem supporting the fork. Knowing the frame was set level, the lower of the pair of motion bars could be attached, and usually once shown how to do the job, I carried on with the left-hand bars and Ken took the right-hand side, popping round now and again to see how things were going.

The bottom motion bar was set level with a spirit level, being bolted with two bolts to the cylinder gland cover and supported at its open end by two more bolts through a massive steel casting riveted to the frame. A flat distance piece of brass or bronze plate separated the shaped end of the motion bar from the supporting steel casting, and it was the thickness of this plate which was the adjuster to ensure the bar was absolutely level. With the bar bolted securely to the gland cover of the cylinder, the hard part of the job was to judge (a) how thick the plate had to be to ensure the bar actually was level; (b) if it wasn't level, how thick the distance plate should be, either thicker or thinner; and (c) how much should be taken off and where, to achieve a level bar, once a likely plate had been selected.

In each case, the motion bar bolts had to be pulled down really tight to simulate an actual final position, and the fewer times that had to be done, the better!

Having selected a distance piece, which could be yellow brass if an old one or bronze if one of the later sort, the piece was placed on the floor and surface ground manually with a cup-wheel grinder, a small air machine driven as with the familiar air drilling machines. It was quite awkward grinding these plates as you either knelt or bent over, operating the grinder over the plate's surface and trying to take off an even amount. Sometimes it was necessary to hold the plate down by putting your toe on a corner, and then being very careful not to grind your shoe! Then came the job of trying it under the motion bar, pulling down the nuts and rechecking. If it didn't do the job, you then released the nuts and removed and tried again (see p. 198).

The requirement and the difficulties of grinding or reducing the plate to the correct thickness had long been appreciated and presumably from a suggestion with supervisory backing, a machine had been obtained; by the look of it, it was a home-spun product, which incorporated one of the cup grinders and a compound slide table with a clamp for the plate. This was an innovation at this time and was operated by Stan, who had very recently been pulled out of the pits to work in a corner of the stores at the end of the bay, presumably with the sole job of grinding the plates for motion bars. It was a bit of a job to trot down with a plate and say 'I'd like 15 thou. off the plate', then wait while it was done, reassemble the bar, and pull down the bolts, only to find it should have been 20 thou., and tapering to the back outside corner! I have the impression that the job of grinding did not last too long and Stan was returned to his previous duties, not from any failure on his part, but due to the not-too-successful concept of the whole procedure. Stan was usually looking rather harrassed when a plate was taken for grinding, and with two or three waiting, his ruddy face was usually deepening in colour as the pressure mounted. If a wait was entailed while he dealt with someone else's plate, it was just as quick to go back and use your own cup wheel grinder on site, so given the several limitations, the whole concept apparently died a natural death. To me, setting the bottom bar was difficult enough, but that was only the start! Having set the bottom bar, you then had to set the top one! Held by the usual two bolts on the cylinder cover, with a distance piece, the job was to get the top bar parallel to the one at the bottom! The same procedure was adopted, fitting distance plates and grinding, but now complicated by use of a flipper gauge to which the top bar had to be set above the bottom one to give the true parallel distance between for the crosshead. This meant the usual trial and error procedure of bolting and unbolting the top motion bar, grinding the plate, reassembling, then checking with the flipper gauge and feeler gauges, the flipper on top of the feeler leaf, to determine the differences affecting parallelism of the two bars. A certain amount of clearance was required for the actual crosshead, and it was always a time of hopefulness followed with some relief when Ken announced that the bars were now acceptable and the chargehand was approached for another job.

A fairly smallish job was that of fitting (to certain locomotive classes) the valve rockers in their bearing, and this again was usually a two-sided job, Ken doing the rockeer on one side of the frame while I assembled the rocker on the other side. With GWR policy of all valve gear inside or between the frames, the motion of the eccentrics had to be transferred to the outside valve spindles, and this was achieved by the rocker.

A bracket containing a large, white-metalled bearing was riveted to the top edge of the frames towards the front, the bearing cap secured by, I believe, six or eight bolts. The rocker itself consisted of a long cylindrical (and hollow) bearing about 15 inches in length, terminating in a large radius running up into the arm positioned integrally on each end. One of the arms was at 90 degrees to the bearing surface, the other inner end considerably

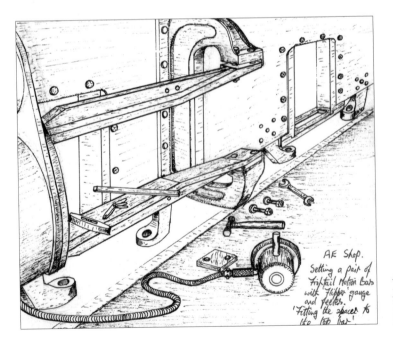

AE Shop – setting a pair of 'fishtail' motion bars with feelers and flipper gauge.

off-set out to about 30 degrees from the vertical to meet up with the gear from the eccentrics. The assembly had to be carefully done so that the well-oiled bearing rocked easily within the bracket without any play, and the bolts could be pulled down tightly on to special shims to give the free movement, and also, in due course, some adjustment when removal of the shims allowed the bearing to tighten up.

A job which, in its later stages at least, required a certain amount of team work, was that of wheeling. As work progressed on a frame, so the time arrived when the wheels had to be fitted and these had, during the course of work on the frame, been dealt with in the AW Shop, where the bearing surfaces would be cleaned up and repolished, the crankpins given attention and the wheels reprofiled or retyred. As the frame moved down the shop, the wheels would be returned and positioned on the line of the pit where wheeling that particular frame would take place. About this time also, a trailer would arrive and a set of axleboxes would be offloaded adjacent to the wheels which would be chocked to stop any movement. The wheels and boxes would be conveniently placed under the inevitable pulley block and runner swinging off the roof support column. An eye bolt screwed into the top of the axlebox was hooked to the pulley block and the box lifted on to its appropriate journal, suitably red-leaded to check on the bearing surface of the box. The white metal of the box was scraped as required to ensure a good bearing, and when obtained, the bearing was cleaned off and oiled, and the keep fitted to the open bottom of the box, thus retaining it on the axle. I recall only doing this job once, although involved in wheeling several times, as apparently it was normally undertaken by the night shift, the wheeling procedure following during the day using the already prepared wheels.

For wheeling, the horn ties had to be removed. The ties were the heavy flat forgings which fitted over the studs in the bottom of the horn cheeks, recesses in the flat ties locking over the rectangular bottom of each cheek, the two studs diagonally positioned at the bottom of each horn block.

With the ties off and placed at the side of the pit, the overhead crane was called, and rumbled its way slowly down the bay towards the frame, a massive double chain and hooks slowly swinging from the hook of both hoists. Stopping above the frame, the double chains were parted and a hook positioned on each end of the buffer beam at front and cab end, the crane man looking up and motioning with his hand to the driver to take up the slack. The chains slowly straightened as the weight came on them and the hooks moved and locked against the buffer beams. A further signal and the hoists started winding up again, the weight of the frame now fully taken by the crane, but still with the frame in the forks of the support stands. A quick check that the hooks were secure and the frame balanced, another hand gesture from the slinger and both hoists started their smooth clanking, winding action with the frame gently rising up out of the stands. As the frame cleared, the stands were rolled away to one side, out of the way, and the frame continued its ascent up to about 8 feet where the hoists were stopped and the frame gently swung on the chains above the pit.

Previously acquired from the last pit on which a wheeling had taken place, Ken and I carried a couple of long steel pinch bars out towards the waiting wheels which were carefully pinched along a pair at a time, to the general position in which they would have the frame lowered, so that the top of the boxes entered the horn openings. When the wheels were positioned generally in the correct locations, a quick visit was made to adjacent pits for assistance as 'one-man, one-axlebox' was required. With the boxes fully manned, we all stood in the pit, while the slinger signalled the frame down to a position just above the axleboxes, where it swung slightly as the hoist brakes were applied. The wheels were now positioned finally, 1 inch forward here, 3 inches back there, until it was felt that the boxes would enter without a problem. A nod from Ken and the slinger signalled the crane driver to lower the frame while we all stood in the pit, guiding our axlebox into the cheek slot, looking up at the very slowly descending frame. It was quite an experience to stand in the pit while a frame, complete with boiler, was lowered above you. Often a sudden jolt and a cry of 'Whoa' would signify that a box had caught an edge of the cheek block and tipped over slightly, locking itself in the opening. The whole frame would give a shudder as it stopped, then released itself and slowly rose again a couple of inches to allow the box to be freed and righted, prior to another lowering attempt. Once the axlebox had entered the cheek opening, it was just a question of watching it as the frame descended the full depth of the box, with no more jolts or hesitations, and shuddered to a halt with all boxes safely home. Cries of 'Thanks' and our helpers rapidly left the pit and returned to their own varied jobs on the gang, while the slinger signalled the hoist on down and the large hooks released themselves from the buffer beams and swung together with a 'clank' as the hooks met on the ends of their chains. Pulled clear and signalled up, the gently swinging hooks slowly ascended as they were wound in, the chains appearing to shorten as hoisting continued while the crane rumbled away up the shop.

Having got the wheels in place, the next job was springing up, attaching the massive leaf springs to both axlebox and frame, but first the boxes had to be sealed in by the replacement of the horn ties. The horn ties, removed for wheeling, were now manhandled upwards on to the studs protruding from the cheek blocks and hammered into place with a foreshortened or strangled large lead hammer, the ties fitting closely over both studs and the square ends of the horn cheeks. Grover washers, a split ring type of spring washer, nuts and split pins secured the horn ties which would not be removed again untilthe wheels had to be taken out, hopefully hundreds of running miles into the future, so everything was really tightened up. The horn tie was cut out in the centre where it spanned the opening between the horn cheeks, so that it would clear the box and spring buckle junction.

Deposited at the end of the pit line, adjacent to the table road, the required number of springs would, by this time, have been delivered by trailer from SP Shop where they were made, repaired and tested. The leaf springs were about 2½ feet to 3 feet overall length of the top leaf, down to about 12 inches for the short bottom leaf and about 5 inches wide, the leaves reducing in length from top to bottom of the stack which could contain up to about thirty-four leaves and be about 15 inches high when stacked, all retained by a special suspension buckle or strap around the centre. The buckle had an integral pair of rings formed at the top which entered the bottom of the axlebox hanger, where it was retained by a round pin about 2½ inches in diameter, the rings on the buckle being a close fit over the matching lug on the bottom of the axlebox hanger. The springs were collected from where they had been dumped by the table road and moved by two-wheel standard bogie to be positioned near the openings between each pair of wheels, on the edge of the pit.

A search round for several unused pit planks was next made, the pit plank being a very stoutly constructed wooden platform of two say 12 inch by 2½ inch elm boards strongly cross-braced underneath by being bolted firmly to two or more cross boards of the same size. The length just fitted between the rails of the pit, thus forming an extension of the floor level across the open top of the pit. The planks were either walked, dragged or carried back to the pit and with one of us behind and one in front, part-dragged, part-carried under the wheels, and positioned between the first driving wheel pair to have the springs fitted.

Scrambling out of the pit again, the next quest was for a spring trolley, a very low small strongly constructed frame about 8 inches square with small roller wheels, the open centre of the small frame just fitting the square section end of the central strap of the spring. With the spring settled in the trolley, its dead weight was fairly easily manipulated and moved between the wheels and on to the pit plank, thence into position under the opening in the horn tie and between the two dog leg brackets that descended from the frame, one each side of the axlebox opening in the frame.

The spring hanger bolts were about 2 inches in diameter with a split pin hole through the bottom threaded end, the heads resting one each end of the top leaf of the spring, which itself was protected from wear by the positioning of a pair of specially shaped thick washers, under the head of the hanger bolt, a ridge on one washer fitted into a groove on the second washer, so retaining them in one position. Under the hanger or dog leg bracket, the length of bolt was such as to accommodate a special cup of pressed ⅜-inch or ⁵⁄₁₆-inch plate which held a sandwich of india rubber pads, each about ⅜ inches thick, separated by thin steel plate discs about ¹⁄₁₆ inch thick, with a ⅜-inch-thick plate sealing the cup, and then being followed on the bolt by the nut, lock nut and split pin.

Large, short steel plate spanners were available for pulling up the nuts to tighten against the washers, but this was just to take up slack as the final setting came later in the repair procedure when the locomotive was taken outside to the weighbridge and a process of putting the weight on the spring occurred. With each pair of wheels on a separate scales, with the locomotive standing on the weigh table, each scales were connected to a weight dial on the adjacent control panel. The springs would then be pulled down so that the weight of the locomotive, showed as being evenly distributed to predetermined requirements, giving the correct reading on the dial associated with each pair of wheels. A lot of work had to be done before this stage was reached, however, and having got the wheels in place and the springs up, the coupling rods had to be put on.

The rods, again delivered to the pit during the sequence of repair, would be lying now alongside, and again the teamwork necessary would require the recruiting of several fitters from the adjacent pits to give a lift with the rods. Prior to the recruitment drive, the wheels had to be checked to ensure that the crank pins lined up, otherwise the rods could not be positioned, so these, with some difficulty, were pinched round a fraction; and although it was best to ensure the crank pins were aligned when wheeling had been completed and the crane was still hooked on, the weight could be taken and the wheels moved to suit. On a 2-8-0 locomotive, the coupling rods when joined together were about 20 feet long, and the weight was considerable, so half a dozen of us would be required to lift the rods at a given call of 'Hup' and then a step forward to position the rod ends over the crank pins. The bronze, white metal bearings, not split as such, formed a solid ring, so often a little persuasion with a large head hammer was required before the rods were completely home over the crank pins. Ball and roller journals were not used at this stage, and in the driving on process with the white-metalled bushes, I often saw little slivers of white metal being

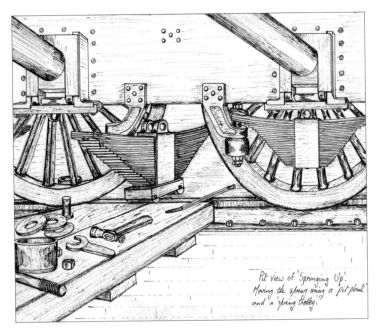

Pit view of 'Springing Up'. Moving the spring using a 'pit plank' and a 'spring trolley'.

AE Shop – Springing up. The heavy leaf spring moved into position under the locomotive, using a small spring trolley and a pit plank.

planed out of the bearing by the end of the crankpin as the rod was driven on but, with a diameter of about 6 inches to 8 inches, it seemed to have no effect on efficient running. Lubrication was by felt pad in the bearing, the oil coming from a reservoir machined in the con rod over the journal bearing and fed by the usual wire trimmer, which was, in essence, a wick arrangement, the journals always well-oiled in any case before the rods were positioned. Finally, with the rods on, the retaining nuts, large flat special items, were screwed on to the journal ends and themselves secured into place by set bolts screwed through.

From the stripping pits on down this bay, a frame would often be seen with a very strange accumulation of machinery in one of the cylinders. A rather tall, dark-haired and thin-faced man operated this machinery, Mr Robinson, who was a neighbour of mine.

The machine in question was a portable cylinder borer and was probably a home grown piece of mechanism, designed and built in the works. It consisted of a large hollow boring bar arrangement supported in the gland of, I believe, a converted back cylinder cover, and utilising in the front the studs which supported the cylinder cover at that end, and over which was securely nutted the driving head gear of the machine. Power was obtained from a suitably adapted and converted air drill of universal fame and use within the works, which was connected by a steel-wire-wrapped air line to the nearest air valve on a roof support column. Once set up and with the air turned on, the continual whining drone of the air drill seemed to go on and on as it took seemingly ages for the small cutter to rotate its way along the length of the cylinder, the lead screw slowly turning and progressing the cutter forward into the cut and along the cylinder bore. The machine appeared to work well for all its 'Heath Robinson' appearance, and a good bore was obtained, part due, I suspect, to the quality of the cast iron it was cutting. No lubricant was used as the cut was very slow, so very little heat was generated to require a coolant, as such, and one of the qualities of cast iron being that it is virtually self-lubricating when machined. It was thus cut dry, so no problems of fluid being required at the tool tip were inherent. To ensure uniformity, the opposite cylinder was given the same treatment, so once Mr Robinson set up shop, he was with you for quite a time.

I am not sure whether a cylinder was rebored and used just as bored; somehow I don't think it was, but was bored out for the purpose of being relined. This relining was a very interesting process. When Mr Robinson had departed, he was often followed by a pair of characters pushing what looked like a modern day cylindrical rubbish skip, being a steel tank about 5½ feet deep and about 2½ feet in diameter, surmounted with a gallows-like jib and standing on a small iron frame cart or trolley. From a second accompanying trolley would be selected an approximately 18 inch by 30 inch cast-iron thin-walled cylinder liner, which would be attached to the special small hoist above the tank by means of a fixture so designed to hold the cylinder liner in a vertical, hole-down position. Donning goggles, hats, thick rubber aprons and long gloves covering both hand and arm up to the elbows, the lid of the tank would be removed and immediately strange fumes, in the form of vapour, would flow out of the tank and slowly curl down over the rim and down the outside of the tank's surface, quickening in flow as the cylinder liner was slowly lowered into the tank. This was a tank of carbon dioxide in liquid form, the objective being to freeze-shrink the cylinder liner so that it could be inserted into the newly bored out cylinder where it would thaw out, and on doing so, expand inside the bore and tightly grip the machined surface. After a set period in the tank, the lid was removed and the strange fumes again curled and waved in swirly patterns over the edge, the hoist carefully operated and the cylinder liner withdrawn.

With special tongs and lifting frame, the liner was rapidly inserted into the cylinder. Any delay or obstruction could be very serious as the liner rapidly started to warm up and expand, the metal of the cylinder itself at a warm temperature after spending a quite long period in a warm workshop. Once home, the liner rapidly thawed and expanded to become an absolutely immovable part of the cylinder material. I don't recall the liner being bored out again, the inner diameter and finish suitable as it stood for use as the actual cylinder bore. There was the odd occasion, of course, where things did not go according to plan, and I recall seeing a frame with a fully lined cylinder on one side, and a liner on the opposite side protruding about 3 inches from the face of the cylinder, just outside the length of the ring of studs which would have secured the head. This was the situation requiring the attention of Mr Robinson again, so back he came with his trolley-load of equipment. The protruding end of the liner had to be cut back to enable him to get the head gear of the borer in place again, and the liner was chipped back to expose the level face into which the ring of studs was screwed. Boring out proceeded as before, the remains of the liner shell eventually breaking up and being extracted in thin curled wafers of brittle cast iron. This heralded the return also of the Inspector to check the bore once again to ensure the measurement for the new liner was correct; a procedure followed by the return of the strangely fuming tank and its operators, who now performed a one-off with the replacement liner.

About this time occurred an accident up on one of the stripping pits where a young fitter had his jaw smashed, I believe while working on the night shift. Some locomotives were fitted with a two-wheel leading assembly known as a pony truck, coming within the 2-6-0 or 2-8-0 etc. classification, usually goods or mixed traffic locomotives, as opposed to the four-wheel bogie of the 4-6-0 locomotives. While the four-wheel bogie was a separately attached and pivoted assembly, the pony-truck often had an attachment which connected it to the spring system of the lead pair of wheels. This took the form of a compensating beam, a very heavy rectangular section solid-steel forging about 7 feet long, possibly 10 inches by 4 inches at the centre, tapering still in rectangular section, towards each end, one of which had a large hole for a pin and the other a very solidly forged, downward-pointing fork end with a rounded bottom to the slot, again to latch over a round pin. The beam was mounted along the centre line of locomotive, between the frames, and its removal entailed one man outside the frame and one inside or between the frame, the latter standing at the end of the beam and confronted by a solid line of pit planks, positioned to take the weight of the released beam, a good supply of wood packing blocks also in evidence. Standing in the pit with the pinch bar pivoted at chest height on packing blocks, and used as a lever to support the end of the beam, the various pins were removed but the beam appeared to have stuck somewhere. While attempting to work the beam loose, and while repositioning the bar, the beam suddenly freed itself and fell on the end of the bar, pivoting it in the reverse direction and driving the end out of the operator's hands and up with a crashing force into his face, smashing his lower jaw and knocking him backwards down the pit. There was always danger just round the corner when large engineering components were involved.

There was also the hidden danger, not realised at the time, but even more deadly than the directly visible accidents, harrowing themselves to those involved and those who witnessed. The dangers of the use of asbestos, so freely used in the construction and protection of the locomotive itself, to retain the heat of the living steam, had deadly effects on some of those involved, one of whom was the quietly spoken, gentle Ken, who was to succumb, thirty-five years on in the future, to the minute but awesome particles.

The last locomotive which I had assisted to wheel crossed the table road with me as I changed gangs to that of Stan Lewington, again a legend! Craggy, pointed face, cap pulled well down, brown warehouse coat over a medium build, head tucked down between his shoulders like a bird of prey, the whole personality surmounting very large, polished brown boots, which reputedly had so many studs that the soles were almost solid steel. This was the finishing off gang, where motion and boiler work was completed along with the smaller ancillary items such as the cock gear and outer painting. Without its bogie or pony truck, the wheeled and boilered frame, now that the cab had been fitted, looked rather tipped up with nothing supporting the front end. I started work with John, a quite tall, heavily built young fitter, who lived somewhere outside Swindon, coming to work on the local 'stopper' which picked up from some of the nearer stations, now all long since closed. Having already had the connecting rods fitted, the frame still had that eyeless look when viewed from the front as the cylinder covers were still off, awaiting the pistons. Piston rings were fitted to the bore of the cylinder, leaving the usual angled gap, and then positioned with levers over the piston head which had been delivered with the head, I believe wrapped in sacking, and positioned with its rod uppermost on the floor blocks adjacent to each cylinder.

It was the apprentice's job to oil the cylinder head studs and make sure the nuts ran on freely, there being about eighteen to twenty studs to be so treated. On one particular locomotive we dealt with, the two bottom studs had, for some reason, broken off, so we had to resort to the air drill and the post and arm method of removal. Care had to be exercised whenever a stud broke off in a softer material, particularly when the usual steel stud was broken off in a bronze component and, to a lesser degree, in a cast-iron item. The broken stud was filed flat to the surface of the surrounding material, and then extreme care exercised in centre popping the exact centre of the steel stud. The problem was caused by the fact that if a drill happened to be blunt or sharpened slightly off centre, or the centre pop hole was not bang in the middle of the stud, the drill ran off into the softer surrounding metal and then you really had a problem in getting it back in the stud centre! The damage that could result to a massive cylinder casting from such a seemingly simple job can be imagined! Drilled out successfully, the remains of the shell were chipped out and replacement studs obtained and inserted using the stud box.

With the cylinder bore well-oiled by brush and oil can, the piston was ready for insertion into the bore of the cylinder. The rings were closed by the usual strips of metal to clear the studded face of the cylinder, and the piston pushed home with a carefully positioned foot! Once in, great care had to be shown when moving the piston again (to be avoided if possible) until connected to the crosshead, and thence to the connecting rod joining crosshead to crank pin. The legend 'rings go up' was often seen chalked on the cover or cladding on the cylinder and spelled out the danger of inadvisedly moving the piston too close to either gland or front cover. A piston, when fully connected and running, has to change direction at either end of the cylinder on the reversing stroke, and obviously never touches or comes near the covers. An expansion gap for the steam inlet and exhaust, cushions what could be an almighty blow, which of course cannot occur due to the length of stroke/radius of crank pin throw ratio. Without the restriction imposed by the rod connecting the crosshead to the crank pin, there was no restriction on the movement of the piston (with added weight complications if connected to the crosshead) in sweeping the full length of the cylinder if pushed hard enough. It was here that the difficulty could occur! The piston rings, restrained by the bore of the piston in the 'swept stroke' of normal running, would expand quite suddenly due to their springiness, and lock solidly in the steam port orifice if the piston had been moved too far; hence the importance of the chalked warning.

The interest in the steam locomotive grew as, from the bare frame being followed through the processes of the circuit, it was now in the final stages of completion. I remember working with John on the inside motion of a two-cylinder locomotive, I believe a 2800 class, and we had reached the stage of putting up the eccentric straps. We had positioned the two halves of the straps around the appropriate eccentrics, and they were loosely held by nuts run on 'finger tight', or so far without the use of the spanner, when the painters arrived. The goods type locomotives were painted black and for this exercise no great artistic skill was required, only a pot of black, tarry-looking paint and a large brush. John was not in a very good mood this particular morning for some reason and had been a bit snappy and was not quietly running on the nuts and selecting lock nuts, etc. However, the painters started on my side of the frame, slapping on the black paint with abandon, and before long it was dripping down off the bottom of the curved boiler cladding and slowly trickling down over me, so I moved out of the way until they had finished. I had only just moved and John hit the roof. 'Afraid of a bit of paint are you? You should work in a ***** office, you should,' he said, and on. Still verbally berating me, he reached out on to the running board to take the spanner which he had placed there. No respecter of persons, the painter had moved round to John's side and as he reached out, the fully loaded brush descended on his hand, painting arm, hand, overall cuff and spanner with the black goo. The air turned purple, and I beat a very hasty retreat for a half hour while John cooled off. On return he was very quiet and we continued in silence until the nuts were on and fully tightened the spilt pins inserted and the eccentrics free to travel.

With regard again to painting, there was one painter who was always known as 'Rembrandt', and he was to be avoided at all costs as he would paint anything and everything. If you happened to be in the vicinity, you moved! His idea of painting the roof of the cab was to tip the paint pot over it, like emptying a bucket, and then spread and scrub in the paint with the biggest brush he could find, drips of paint running through every bolt hole in sight. It was probably Rembrandt who had done the paint job on John!

On reflection about work in AE Shop, it is surprising how many incidents occurred coincidentally, and one, involving an occasion when I reached out of the pit for a spanner, could have resulted in injury, but fortunately did not. Having put up the eccentric straps on one occasion, the eccentric rods which bolted to the straps had, for some reason, when unloaded from the transport, been placed on end leaning against the locomotive frame. The continual movement within the shop meant that the traversing table was almost always in use and, in the moves, a wagon loaded with components was run on to the end of the pit on which we were working. The pit was rather full and included the locomotive on which we were working, a bogie and some wheels, leaving only about the length of the wagon itself as free rail track. However, the wagon rumbled off the table on to the short length of track and the sequence of events picked up speed.

The wagon wheels locked on to the wood chock, and the whole lot skidded instead of stopping. Just at that time, I reached out for a spanner, and at that moment the wagon hit the wheels and bogie, which cannoned off one another and hit the locomotive under which we were working. The vibration caused one of the eccentric rods to fall over across my outstretched hand, the fork end of the rod falling over the rail and thus into the pit opening. By rights, with my hand stretched out over the floor and rail edge, I should have lost my fingers between the falling rod and the rail, but by one of those strange twists, there was a solitary 1 inch nut on the rail. How or from where I do not know, it just happened to be there, and it took the full force of the falling rod; I just felt the merest touch on the back of the hand! But the episode was not forgotten!

I don't recall being involved in putting in piston valves, but I believe this was a job done by the night shift so things were already together for those on days. It was interesting, although weighty, work to assemble the rest of the valve gear; the Stephenson type gear on the two-cylinder engines being easier than that of the four-cylinder ones, as there was much more space between the frames in which to work, and no crank axle in the way. The reversing shaft which stretched right across the inside of the frame was, I believe, positioned by the gang which also put in the rocker shafts, as it was easier to get around the frame before final assembly, so all we had to do was to install the lifting links on to the arms of the shaft. The expansion link, or quadrants, were then attached to the lifting links and the two eccentric rods per link pinned to the newly bushed holes in the curved section of the back of the link. The rockers, hopefully assembled with the angled arm inside the frame, were connected outside to a small linkage rod on to the valve spindle crosshead, and inside, to the intermediate valve rod which was secured at its other end to the expansion die block, which ran in the slot of the quadrant. With the Stephenson gear, there were two eccentrics per valve to impart motion to the valve spindle, one eccentric for fore gear and one for back gear, and it was the slotted quadrant which was, in effect, lifted or lowered over the swinging expansion die block. With the four-cylinder locomotive, the Walschaert valve gear used entailed the use of a fixed position slotted quadrant, and it was the equivalent of the die block and its rod connection which was moved up or down for fore or back gear, only one eccentric being used to rock the quadrant (*see pp. 210–11*).

I sometimes walked down to use the grindstone down by the New Work gang. When down in that area, I often watched a piece of boiler cladding being cut to shape on a fascinating little machine near the grindstone. I believe this work was done by K Shop people, sheet metal and coppersmithing, although I am not too sure on that point. The machine was a nibbler, a little cutter following a pencilled line on the plate quite easily, allowing curves and radii to be cut with ease.

While down among the new locomotives and the ever-present smell of red lead paint, a chat with Jock Robinson was always interesting, who had a cheerful face and a mop of whitening hair, a fitter for a number of years on the New Work gang, and a very keen model engineer.

Midmorning, and John would say something like 'Just dap up the brake gear while I nip upstairs!' He was quite fond of having you just dap up something or other. He would walk over to his cupboard in the bench, collect the *Mirror*, and disappear for a half an hour to the upstairs toilet block for his constitutional. Dapping up the brake gear entailed hanging one of the block hangers from a bracket riveted to the frame to the rear or front of the main driving wheels, then positioning the brake beam from the bottom of the hanger across the frame width, then hopping out of the pit to position the opposite hanger on its bracket and on to the brake beam. Putting in the brake blocks was a weighty job, and you usually sat on the floor with your legs over into the pit, one leg positioned with heel on the step formed by the rail and pit top. A cast-iron brake block was lifted from the floor adjacent to the hanger, placed and held on the top of the knee, then with a jack-knife sort of action it was pushed with leg and one hand up into its slot between wheel tyre and hanger, while the other hand manoeuvred the pin into the hanger and through the integral loop on the back of the brake block, the pin being retained by a clip over the head.

Having hung the blocks and beams, the longitudinal pull rods were positioned and pinned between the wheels, the rods dragged in from the pit side, and the fork ends secured with the pin head on top and washered and split-pinned underneath. The adjusting nuts on the pull rods were then screwed up or back to align the beams and blocks, ultimately connected to the vacuum cylinder rod, the cylinder mounted under the locomotive cab. On return, no matter what you had achieved, John's usual comment was 'Is that all you've done? What have you been messing about at while I've been away?' and then we would both get stuck in to complete the job.

This was the time when National Service was in full swing, and the fate of all apprentices on completion of their time was predetermined. This had, in most cases, certainly my own, been accepted for several years, and in some respects, while not exactly looked forward to, was anticipated as a major change of environment. It was at this time that the Korean War was at its height, and China had just joined in as well. A number of the fitters were of course ex-servicemen and were still in the Z Reserve, so a great deal of leg pulling was done with remarks such as 'Ah well, we shall still be working together when we are both called up. In the event, as far as I know, no one was actually recalled, but the possibility was certainly building up that way. With the National Service acts, call up was nominally at eighteen years of age, and indeed a number of apprentices opted to serve before completing their apprenticeship. I remember one of them in R Shop, a year or so older than I, going at eighteen, and on his last day hurling his check down the shop instead of putting it in the box by the check board on the last occasion of leaving the works. On return from service, which fluctuated between one year, eighteen months and two years, finally stabilising on the latter, the apprentice continued with his interrupted apprenticeship, the period for completion having, I believe, been shortened to a year before acceptable completion of the apprenticeship, although in reality he had lost possibly eighteen months or two years of the five-year apprenticeship. One of my old school friends had opted for the early start to his National Service stint, and having now completed the period had returned to complete his time, and on arriving for his tour of the AE Shop had, in the sequence of moves, found his way to the stripping gang for a couple of months, several 'returned from service' apprentices going by the same route. However, it appeared that a time had arrived when, for a short period at least, the supply of these early 'National Service' apprentices had dried up, so directions were being issued for 'swaps', one off and one on the two gangs concerned to ring the changes, as it were. Another of my colleagues had already done a stint of stripping under these circumstances, and I guessed it would be only a matter of time before the system ensnared me!

Following one of the morning break periods, which had terminated in the usual way with Stan appearing at the end of the line of benches and giving his usual 'Whup' call, I went back to the particular locomotive on the pit after washing out my mug and returning it to my box. A few minutes later, watching from in the pit, I spied a pair of large brown boots heading round the cab end of the locomotive and, turning sharp right, coming down the side, stopping and moving through 90 degrees in the gap formed by the space between two of the driving wheels. Stan's craggy face peered in under the frame with the question, 'Is your young mate there John?' By that time he could see that I was. 'Swap over tomorrow, Ken,' he said, 'Brown's job, change on to the stripping pits!'

The moment of truth! Possibly the worst job in the entire shop. However, there was nothing for it but to write it all in the book of experience. I came in the following morning quite well prepared. I had made sure that all the buttons on my overalls were securely in place; I had sorted out an old cap, one, I think, my father had used for gardening at some stage, as at that time I didn't possess a hat, and I also had a reasonable supply of strong string, suitably cut to length to tie around the overall wrists and around the bottom of the legs. So with all hatches battened down against the dust and dirt, and with overall collar buttoned right up to the neck and also turned up at the back, I started stripping.

One of the only consolations about the job, if it could be called a consolation, was that everyone on the gang was in the same boat, all muffled up and tied with string, although there were those who were so accustomed to it that on occasions they didn't bother with the string, so presumably they got pretty messy! Although grease and oil were present, most of the dirt was a seemingly black powder which stuck to everything; nuts appearing as black domes, and the 'Castle' nut variety having even bigger black domes, being full of and hidden by the black adhering tacky dust. Spanners soon became black off hands and components, the spanners being used to push the dirt off the hexagon shape so that the spanner itself could slide on and grip. Reaching up without string round the wrists invited the lumps which fell off the nuts to go straight down your sleeve, where they disintegrated and spread themselves around your arm and into the material of your clothes. Any attempt at an open neck shirt, even in the heat of the summer, invited the largest lumps to find their way down to the trouser waist band and there spread in a black bruise-like mark around your middle. Some early 'barrier' creams were used on the hands, but usually the only protection was from the small piece of soap which was issued at regular intervals to all employees, along with the usual ball of cotton waste, the latter a bit larger for the strippers.

The soap was kept in a tin to keep it very soft; if exposed to the air it soon dried into a hard wood-like substance and, before each shift, was removed and carefully held in one hand while scraped by the fingernails of the other hand, thus filling the space under the nails with a portion of soap. It stayed in place quite well and certainly served its purpose, at least keeping the grime out of one part of the anatomy.

In the effort to clean your hands, one method, and it was certainly an illegal practice as such, was to tip the oil can into one palm and fill the cupped hand with lubricating oil, rubbing hands vigorously together and rubbing the oil into the dirt and grime. While rubbing your hands, you were also walking towards the large sawdust bin, the contents of which were used like water, and the hands immersed, and again thoroughly rubbed with the sawdust. A visit next was to the wash trough, with its steam and water pipes giving a strangely smelling spray. The trough, waist height and shaped like a V, had a further small V integrally cast at the top of the trough sides to retain your piece of soap. At intervals along the soap channel could usually be found a very small pile of sand, and if there wasn't one, you had a look under the lid of the sand box on the nearest locomotive frame and take a handful of what remained in the box across to the trough with you. The sand formed the abrasive which along with your small piece of soap, assisted in removing a fair amount of the grime ingrained in the fingers. It usually took the complete weekend at home before your hands were really clean, and by that time it was Monday again, and the process started all over again.

Stripping was, of necessity, a crude job. While intentional damage to a component was avoided, it did not pay to spend too much time trying to remove say a nut which had rusted securely on; it was just split with hammer and chisel, or if too large, the 'burner' was sent for, and it was cut off with the oxy-torch. You just asked the man with the torch to either cut it, when he would burn off the nut and the bolt end, or, through experience with larger nuts, to blow off the nut when the torch would reduce the nut so that it could be broken off the bolt or screwed end, leaving a repairable screw thread to which a new nut could be attached. Quite a lot was big hammer work, driving out bolts or keys, a difficult job being the removal of the crosshead key, securing it to the piston rod. Standing in the pit and striking upwards at an angle to drive out the key was quite a job. When the removable items had been loaded on to the steel-sided, mesh-bottomed trolleys for transport to the Bosh, cleaners with brushes and pots of cleaning oil moved in to the frame to expose those items which would not usually be removed, the cylinder block assembly, motion bar brackets and horn cheeks.

Once the components were off and the remainder of the frame generally cleaned up, an Inspector arrived with his little hammer, scraper and three tins of paint in a little metal tray.

The small tins contained red, yellow and blue paint, and the various nominally permanent bolts and rivets were all examined to search out any sign of looseness. I believe there were three classes of attention; 'Renew', 'Remove and Repair' and 'Tighten', each denoted by a dab of coloured paint.

There was the story of the newly appointed Inspector who, when trying bolts for slackness in the manner prescribed, dabbed everything examined with a blob of the appropriate colour as requiring tightening. The general method of checking was to place a finger on say one side of the head of a bolt and tap the other side with the small hammer; a loose bolt was shown up by a vibration felt through the finger, coupled with the noise made, and the visual movement of the bolt itself, depending on the degree of looseness. When the fitters came to check-tighten the bolts, it was found that they were all dead tight anyway, and so queries were passed back down the line to the Inspector. On return he again checked the bolts by tapping them and again declared they were loose. It was then discovered, rather embarrassingly, that it was the head of his little hammer that was loose, and not the bolts!

There was also an inspection of other components when they had emerged from the 'Bosh' and been hosed down, the paint again being used to denote repair requirements. Some items were, of course, interchangeable when repaired, an example which comes to mind being the vacuum pump which I cannot recall being 'stamped', as such, with a specific locomotive number, although covered by the appropriate paperwork for a particular engine. The long-reach rod from the reversing gear had a stamped number, but was also further marked with the number painted in large red figures on its side. The associated reversing lever was also number-painted in red, but the reversing screw, with its number deeply engraved in the top graduated indicator plate had the covers painted inside

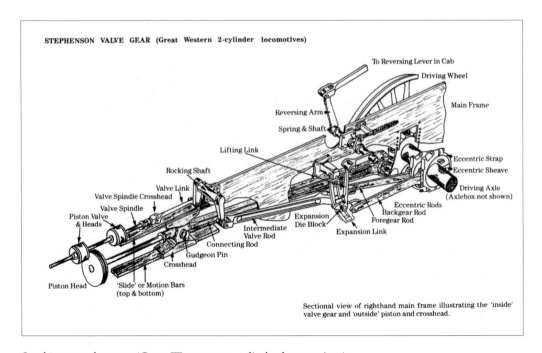

Stephenson valve gear (Great Western two-cylinder locomotives).

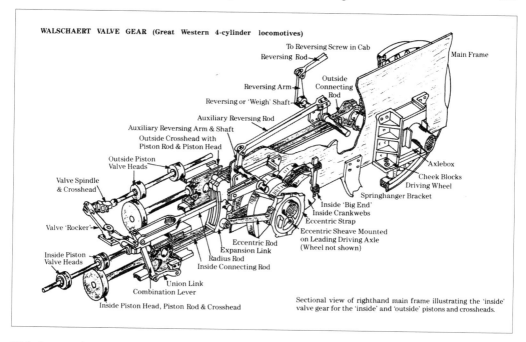

WALSCHAERT VALVE GEAR (Great Western 4-cylinder locomotives)

Walschaert valve gear (Great Western four-cylinder locomotives).

with the number and usually wired to the screw, although they could be found reassembled on to the casting itself. Whether with paper, stamped or painted numbers, the items could be identified and tracked through repair procedures.

One morning, after taking a component over to the vice, which was on a small bench near the main doors which slid back to allow the traversing table to move out of the shop, I was attempting with hammer and chisel to 'start' a couple of stubborn nuts, prior to a further attempt with a spanner. Well tied up with string round the cuffs, collar still up and buttoned round the neck, and black from head to foot, it was quite obvious that I was off the stripping pits. Working away, I heard someone approach and walk along by the bench behind me. I recognised Stan Millard, the head foreman, as he went out through the small door at the side of the large sliding doors. Almost as soon as he had closed the door, it opened again and he came back in, walking straight up to me. 'Is your name Gibbs?' he said. I said that it was. 'You haven't completed your apprenticeship yet have you?' he continued. I agreed that I hadn't. He just nodded, said 'Mmm', and went out through the door again. On return to the pit, my mate wanted to know what 'The Boss' had been talking about. I told him 'Nothing very much! Just asked if I'd finished my apprenticeship', and with that we continued with the task of reducing a complete locomotive to a bare frame.

Springs were a bit messy to remove. Covered in black dusty grime, you stuck the end of a small tommy bar into the hole of the flat spring cotter on the end of the spring hanger, gave the bar a wallop with a hammer, and out came the pin. You removed nuts and special washers off the hanger, and removed the cup with its stuck-together sandwich of rubber pads and thin plates, standing well back while you knocked out the hangers, and then took the weight of the spring on a tommy bar and block of wood while you removed the axlebox pin and dropped the spring on to a suitably placed pit plank or two. Using a long steel hook from outside the wheels, the spring was dragged out on to the wood block floor, scraping off some of the accumulated grime of several thousand running miles to add to that already on the floor blocks. The brake gear was already removed and the components were dragged out of the way, the removal really the reverse of assembly, the difference of course being the covering of dirt over everything.

The difficulty of removing inside motion gear can be imagined, although the moving parts, quadrants and links were just usually oily and not particularly black. Inside crosshead cotters were removed with some difficulty and the crossheads slid back off the motion bars on to the ever-present pit plank when separated from the piston rod by means of a special wedge driven into the special slot in front of the cotter hole, with restricted hammer swing distance and everything black! The cylinder drain cock gear and rods, along with the ashpan and damper gear were removed from underneath, the vacuum pump disconnected from the outside crosshead bracket and the pump removed from its bracket under the running board. With the cylinder steam pipes disconnected, the bolts removed from the smokebox saddle, and the ejector and injector pipes disconnected at the cab end, the rumble of the crane heralded the boiler lift. The boilermakers, I believe, removed the plate work of the cab front and top, and with a wire rope sling arranged round the smokebox from one of the lifting carriages of the crane, and a very large chain slung with a pair of hooks in the firebox door opening dangling down from the other carriage, the clamps over the casing brackets were removed and the boiler was lifted out to its special wagon for removal to the boiler bay. The bogie (four wheels) or the pony truck (two wheels) when removed was passed through the Bosh for cleaning as a complete entity and continued on its course through the Bosh and directly to the other section of AE Shop, which dealt exclusively with these items.

The bare frame, complete with its coloured paint dabs, was then moved to the next section of pits where the rebuilding work started, the second move of the circuit.

We were now up to about September 1950 and I had been on the stripping gang for about.four days when the episode with the head foreman occurred. A day or so later, Chargeman Brown approached and asked me if I had had a talk with Mr Millard. I explained that it was so, only in as much as he had asked me my name and if I had finished my apprenticeship. 'Ah, I see,' said the chargehand. 'Well! It appears you shouldn't be here at all being an apprentice! And on Monday you've got to start with Bill Dando!'

'NEW WORK'

My stint on stripping had ended rather rapidly after the intervention of Stan Millard, and I duly reported with my box of odds and ends and overalls to the diagonally opposite end of the shop and the cupboard of Bill Dando. The slim fitter who had accompanied *King George V* on the 1927 American tour was now a very rotund little man, still wearing the inevitable cap (may even have been his 1927 original), and with a brown warehouse coat replacing the overalls.

The New Work gang at this time was entering a period of uncertainty, as with the recent completion of the last Castle class locomotive on the books, No. 7037, the big main line construction programme of locomotive building to Great Western Railway design and standards had virtually come to an end. No more would there be photographs of say a line of Kings under construction, or pits full of progressively developing Castles from bare frames to finished locomotives. The era of the Standard locomotive was approaching, still steam locomotives, true, but looking nothing like the smooth, classic designs of the GWR. They would appear as based solely on the design of LMS locomotives, all with outside clanking rods and valve gear, and inside, all ball and roller races!

In later years, after apprenticeship and National Service had been completed and I had returned to work in AM Shop, I often had occasion to go out into an AE Shop liberally sprinkled with the Standard locomotives in for a circuit repair. All 'Standard' locomotives had a plate on the smokebox which showed their original place of construction, a number of the oval plates bearing the legend 'Built Derby' or 'Built Crewe', followed by the year of construction. In most instances, the word 'Built' had been crossed through in chalk and the comment 'thrown together' substituted in the same chalk! The Great Western was dying long and painfully.

The last of the Castles, No. 7037, was destined for special treatment several weeks into my stay on New Work. A clean up operation was in progress down by the light repair gang of Harold Rayer, and the elevated *North Star* broad gauge replica was also subjected to a 'spit and polish'. Floors were scraped and pits cleaned out, lamp shades were cleaned and light bulbs replaced, and much hammering and screwing of wood was observed as a railed platform grew under the hands of a skilled D Shop carpenter group. Various bowler-hatted officials were to be observed pacing the area, leaning on the rails of the platform and jumping up and down on its steps to ensure absolute safety and stability. At that end of the shop, unequal and worn floor blocks were either replaced or levelled, and that particular corner of the shop began to shine with a lick of paint here and there. No. 7037 was to become Swindon Castle class, under the graceful hand and elegant manner of HRH the Princess Elizabeth.

At the appointed hour on the appointed day, 15 November 1950, the procession wound its way to the specially prepared corner of the shop, while the complete AE Shop workforce gathered around, and from the platform the ceremony was duly performed, to include short speeches from several of the dignatories assembled for the occasion. The little curtain was pulled aside to reveal the name of the town which, for so many years, had been literally part and parcel of Brunel's creation, the Railway Works.

The naming completed, the speeches ended, three rousing cheers, and the assembled group on the platform descended with dignity and in order of rank and seniority. A wave from HRH the Princess Elizabeth and the group departed after a further short milling around period, for the honoured guest to board the cab of the Star class locomotive Princess Elizabeth and to take the regulator for the short trip to the station.

With the visitors now gone and the shop returning to normal, a message from Stan Millard had the complete New Work gang hurrying once more up to the end of the shop where No. 7037 *Swindon* still stood with the curtains just as pulled on the nameplate and the platform still in place. Much arm-waving and movement followed as we were all ushered into place in front of the locomotive, apprentices and some of the others directed onto the platform. In the milling around, Ernie, the leading hand, finished next to the head foreman, Stan Millard, and the chargehand, Bill Dando, came to be sandwiched in the crowd further back. There were three apprentices on the gang and we were with others on the platform, kneeling with heads just above the rail, yours truly with an elbow over the rail and next to the other apprentice John (Sam) Eylett, with John White just to the rear of us. Many of the names in the group now appear on the roll of the 'Master Running Superintendent', having long departed from this earth, while some of the younger members are themselves now approaching retirement in possibly all parts of the country. However, the group was fixed in time by the click of the camera shutter and we can all be proudly seen in Plate 32.

There was a certain sadness that Great Western passenger steam, as we had known it, had now booked off shift for the last time, and there was also an air of expectation concerning the next generation of steam locomotives to pass through the stages of construction in the shop that had completed so many fine new locomotives in the past. The only remaining vestige of the two locomotives which were the highlights of the naming ceremony all those years ago, are two nameplates, one from each locomotive. The plate from *Swindon* may currently be seen in the entrance porch to the Swindon Railway Museum, mounted on the left, and the plate from *Princess Elizabeth* is mounted rather high on the wall inside the main building. There are of course numerous photographs depicting the two locomotives, but nothing can recapture the scene or the atmosphere of the period as effectively as that of the memory of actually being there.

New Work was winding down at this time, prior to the winding up again when construction started on the Standard locomotives. Apart from being cleaner, in terms of dirt and grease, constructing a new engine, once the frames and cylinders had been assembled was very like repairing any locomotive on the circuit. I have a recollection, which may be incorrect, of actually repairing circuit locomotives on the gang as a gap filler while the new construction programme for Standard locomotives was awaited, but which was to come after I had departed on National Service.

Although I have said that New Work was winding down at this time, the spirit of the Great Western was still struggling on. During 1948, a series of trials had been held to determine the best features of locomotives run by the various separate groups, prior to design work starting on the Standard locomotive designs. Among engines which created an impression were those with the Hawkesworth modifications to the original Collett design of Hall class, a total of seventy-one Modified Halls being added to the mixed traffic fleet between the years 1944 and 1950. The modifications had given an improved locomotive with excellent steaming qualities, slight wheel base differences, larger superheater, and improved draught arrangements coupled with a narrower chimney, all assisting with increased efficiency. I was just in on the end of this building programme, the finishing touches being put to the last of the line, No. 7929, which became *Wyke Hall*, completed at the tail end of November 1950, its originator Mr Hawkesworth having retired about twelve months before.

There would be no more 4-6-0 passenger or mixed traffic locomotives to GWR design, but the spirit of the Great Western was still watching over construction in the shape of small 0-6-0 tank engines. A class introduced in 1929 to replace some of the very old remaining tank engines, some from Victorian times, gave a very effective and powerful small locomotive, with water tanks along the side of the boiler giving much better access to items such as valve gear (obscured from the top in the case of side tanks), and chimney, dome and safety valve, in the case of the saddle tank which covered the complete top of the boiler. This class was the 5700 range, which continued from inception right up until December 1950, having gone through several improvement phases such as larger cabs and boiler top feeds and also a range of numbering, the last being No. 6779 during my stay on New Work. It was one group of this early class, the 9701–9710 group, that had the modifications to allow them to run on the Metropolitan electrified lines, and had included a combined side and pannier tank design to increase water carrying capacity, the introduction of condensing apparatus and the use of the Weir(d) pump, one of which, I believe it was 9710, had given us fun and games on Harry Jarvis' gang in AM Shop. Nearly 900 5700s had been built, some of the early ones by contractors, but those from 1933 onwards were all constructed at Swindon.

The struggle for Great Western steam was not quite dead, however, and as a last burst of life, a very unusual order was placed in 1949, unusual in the light of the by now well known move towards dieselisation for shunters, and was the last GWR design by Hawkesworth. Quite small and nearly half a ton lighter than the 5700 class, the 1600 class of 0-6-0 pannier tanks were for shunting and the light passenger commuter journeys over the region. Keeping well within the loading gauge limits (those measurements which ensured that a locomotive didn't take part of the bridge with it when it passed, or conversely that passengers didn't have to jump a wide gap from the platform on to the coach), it was ideal for the sharp curves and restricted clearances in goods yards and docks and mining areas where even some of the larger 0-6-0s were forbidden. Some of these 1600s latterly found their way to other regions, and as late as 1957, two were transferred to the Scottish Region, where they worked until steam was phased out. The last 1600 was built and completed at Swindon in May 1955, thus with No. 1669 ended the long tradition of Swindon-built Great Western Railway designed steam locomotives.

However, back to 1950 and New Work. I worked with Ernie Collier for a number of weeks, a short, stocky man with a sharp tongue but a sense of humour and a ready smile, dealing with the cylinder drain cock gear, amongst other work tackled. Operated by a lever in the cab, the system of rods operated two or three valves under each cylinder, allowing the condensed steam in the form of water to be expelled before the locomotive actually attempted to move after standing for a time. There were hanging brackets under the frame to position, and a number of flat pull rods to be marked off and drilled. In some cases being pre-drilled, the holes did not align properly and a trip with the various rods was made to the smiths area at the end of the boiler bay. A jump or draw note, and a measurement given to the leather-aproned smith, ensured that the rod fitted when eventually collected and assembled. While I had been with Stan Lewington, there had been a rather tragic accident regarding the cock gear when the fitter had given a pull on the handle in the cab without realising that a pin was still out of the assembly hidden under the locomotive. The unexpected looseness and easy movement of the handle had caused him to fall backwards out of the cab, on to the rail and down into the pit, fracturing his skull. His sad death was a blow to us all and highlighted the impermanence of life and the suddenness of such unexpected events. Following this event there was an immediate tightening of safety precautions and the provision of a special platform on wheels and with a handrail along its back, the platform to be connected by chains to the handrail stanchions of the locomotive cab. Previously, cabs had just been open-backed, and while presumably no one had ever fallen from one before, the potential danger was there with the open back and the deep drop to the pit bottom.

I also worked with Alec Jones, a quietly spoken, bespectacled fitter. Putting up brake rods on one of the small 0-6-0s necessitated, on one occasion, a considerable amount of smith work in drawing to a new length, and although a discussion with the chargehand was held, there was nothing for it but to stretch the rods the unusual amount. How or why was never really determined, but a trip to the smiths once again solved the problem of fitting them. On the way back from the smiths with the trolley, Alec stopped to chat to one of the other fitters and, in the course of conversation, the table bell clanged, and a locomotive was moved off light repairs and on to the circuit pits. This had apparently been a serious breakdown job, although I can't remember the name of the victim of a very damaging hot box.

About halfway down the shop, a little group of overall-clad men were closely examining a crank axle, standing vertically, its end still in one driving wheel lying on the floor. The other wheel lay beside with the opposite end of the crank axle still firmly pinned and secured in its centre, and showing signs of having been forcibly twisted right off the remains of the axle. Both inner wheel face and the broken end of the axle which stuck up into the air, showed extreme heat colours which had been generated by the hot box before it seized. This must have been quite unique as I have not come across it happening again, but what forces must have been in play to twist and fracture such a massively constructed item?

The various routines of the gang proceeded and, during this time, various of my contemporaries as apprentices were completing their time as their birthdays were reached and were departing for their King and Country stint of National Service. I had requested, from the authority concerned, a slight delay in my own call up to take an examination at the local technical college, and this having been granted, I was soon the only one left of my contemporaries.

Christmas 1950 approached and passed, and New Work, as such, was destined to be my last apprentice abode in AE Shop. One interesting job which apprentices only very rarely were associated with and which I missed, was that of valve setting. This was a procedure undertaken on a separately prepared pit, sandwiched between Stan Lewington's and Harold Rayer's gangs, and backing on to the old North Star, its own valve gear the forerunner of that now receiving attention on the valve setting plant.

The special railed-off pit contained rollers in the manner of a small Loco Test Plant, and a push button control box, which enabled the rollers to be inched forward or back. Photographs of AE Shop invariably show a locomotive being held in the 100-ton overhead cranes, above the level of all of its fellows on the pits below. Often the engine in the air is without its bogie or pony truck and this gives a pointer to the fact that it was either travelling to or from the Valve Setting Plant. As with a car engine, the valves introducing and exhausting the motive power, steam in the case of the locomotive, have to be set to open and close at the correct part of the stroke. The efficiency of the locomotive itself depends on the correct and economic use of the steam, entry to the cylinders at the right time as important as getting rid of the condensing vapour when its power has been almost expended (*see Plate 31*).

The plant itself saved the toil of setting valves with the aid of pinch bars to move the locomotive forward or back to ensure the dead-centre positions of the crank pins, thus controlling the position of the piston head at the beginning and end of its stroke, hidden in the cylinder.

However, back to the New Work gang in AE Shop of 1950. It was 21 January 1951, and my apprenticeship had ended. A visit to the Loco Manager's Office, previously visited five years before to sign on the dotted line for the apprenticeship, was now to collect the Certificate of Apprenticeship, which showed to all and sundry that such five years had been completed. I had to wait at the bottom of the stairs for Aubrey Prowdler to usher me into the Loco Works Manager's Office. There were a few words and a hand shake from the Chief, and a handing over and receipt of a piece of paper briefly outlining my course through the locomotive side of Swindon Railway Workshops, 1946–51.

An 'Apprenticeship in Steam' through a unique organisation, with many unforgettable characters met and remembered.

This was not quite the end of my stay in AE Shop, however. It was normal practice, or at least it had been, that unless a vacancy actually existed, the 'Certificate of Apprenticeship' was accompanied by, ironically, a dismissal notice. In the present circumstances, most apprentices, probably all apprentices on reflection, were automatically removed from the books due to the National Service Acts, and would leave to enter the services or Merchant Navy as provided for by the Acts. Incidentally on return, government regulations ensured employment for a period of up to twelve months, or in the case of apprentices who had opted to complete National Service at the usual age of eighteen years, a slightly longer period I believe to complete the apprenticeship.

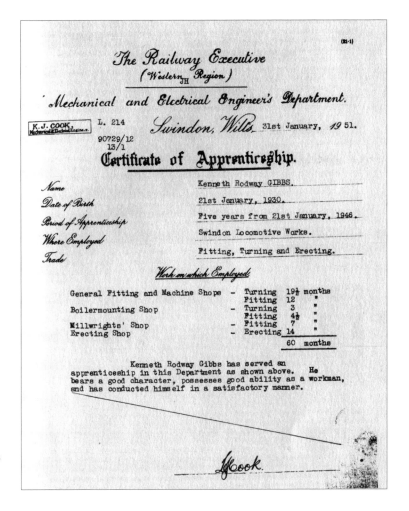

My Trade Indentures signed by K. J. Cook. The proof of five years as an 'apprentice in steam'.

No.

THE BRITISH TRANSPORT COMMISSION.
~~GREAT WESTERN RAILWAY.~~

(3305)

Swindon Works, ___16.___ ___6.___ 19 54.

A.M. 204   K. R. Gibbs   Your services will not

be required after ___5:20 pm___   25.   6.   54.

Manager.

My dismissal notice. Note the continued use of GWR headed paper seven years after nationalisation.

When I returned in 1953, I worked for about twelve months and then received the dismissal notice as per the accepted procedure, but in my case the vacancy existed so I was automatically reinstated, in effect leaving on Friday evening and starting again Monday morning. The standard dismissal notice was very short and to the point and reproduced here to show the sort of form which struck a terror into staff when in earlier years, periods of short time and reduced staff working were the exigencies of economic problems. I believe one week's pay arrears were paid and that was that, no lump sum or other payment, and no redress of any sort.

As I still had not completed my examination course, and as my years as an apprentice had now ended. A temporary position was found for me, to allow the apprentice circuit vacancy to be filled by someone following, and I was given my marching orders to report to Harold Rayer on the Light Repair pits near the site of the quite recent naming ceremony of No. 7037 *Swindon*.

LIGHT REPAIRS – THE FINAL MOVE

The move on to Harold Rayer's gang really had an air of impermanence about it as officially my apprenticeship had finished and now all of my contemporaries had already departed for service with His Majesty, my turn being only weeks away.

Harold was a little elf-like man with a small round face and brushed back thinning dark hair, and usually clad, as I remember him, in a rather grubby, brown warehouse coat. Being immediately 'out of my time', not really a fully experienced craftsman yet no longer an apprentice, I was in the sort of in-between improver category. The gang itself was for the light repair function, where the locomotive was in a condition which required shopping but not such as to warrant entry to the circuit and a complete strip-down and rebuild.

I was placed with Brian Eborn, a year or two older, and an established younger member of the gang. A rather squat, heavily built young man whose interest included weight lifting, his height belied his strength and his overalls covered muscles like conveyor belts; a very useful character to work with. One of the first jobs we did was to renew items of the brake gear, and watching him just sit on his heels, pick up a brake block and position it with one hand while inserting the pin with the other, seemed a direct contrast to my own efforts, repeated now and practised with Stan Lewington, of sitting on the pit edge and assisting the lift with the knee and heel of the foot on the rail.

With the light repair, the boiler remained in place and efforts were restricted to those items which were mostly below the running board. A little incident with a four-cylinder locomotive springs to mind; I believe No. 5046 *Earl Cawdor* was the one involved. Something had necessitated removing the valve gear and dropping the leading pair of wheels. We were working then in the rather restricted space, attempting to separate the crosshead from the piston rod once again. To check alignment of the leading horn cheeks, the faces of the cheeks had been tried with a surface plate and gauge and, as a consequence, had a film of red lead on them. The horn ties were up to support the frame and we were working off pit planks, as well as down into the pit. I moved back towards one of the horn cheek openings to get out of Brian's way while he swung a large hammer, and the back of my legs touched what I thought, while still watching Brian, was a sack over the horn tie, so I sat down, tucked well in between the cheeks. There was a stifled yell from beneath my seat and I moved rather quickly to a standing position, to find on turning round that I had just sat on the chargehand's head! The little round face was that of a Sioux Indian warrior in full war paint, smeared with streaks and blobs of red lead and muttering in presumably the Sioux language as it was some seconds before we could understand what he was saying! It appears that just as I was about to sit on the tie, Harold had stuck his head between the cheek blocks to see what we were doing and how far we had got with the job! Fortunately he saw the funny side of the event.

Light repairs tended to be a bit messy, although not quite as bad as the stripping pits, as some cleaning had already been done, but such things as coupling rod removal was not quite the same as replacing rods straight from AM Shop rods gang. You made sure the part of the rod you gripped for the removal process, along with several colleagues, was wiped off so that the grip was firm and without oil smears. With a replacement of components, some of which had not been into the machine shops for complete overhaul, it was often the case on reassembly that, for example, new bolts did not present the same position of split pin hole above the nut, often only a part hole showing. In these circumstances there were several alternatives. One was to file the nut thinner – not often done, I may add; the second was to cut a groove with a chisel, aligned with the hole, across the top of the nut, a procedure sometimes followed; or thirdly, and an interesting terminology, you went to the stores where ex-RAF W/O Cann held sway, and asked for a 'Wolverhampton' split pin, of the diameter and length normally used for the job. For example, a '2½ inch' ¼ inch Wolverhampton! While the pin supplied was 2½ inches long, the diameter was that of the size below that actually asked for. This tradition stemmed reputedly from two sources. During the 1920s, the four major railway companies took over or absorbed a number of smaller organisations and with such companies absorbed by the GWR came almost 1,000 locomotives of all shapes and sizes, almost none of which, except for the gauge of the wheels, conformed to GWR standards and practice. A considerable number of these were scrapped for various reasons, but the rest were subjected to an attempt at introducing the standard GWR fittings wherever possible. The state of some of the locomotives with regard to repair standards, not particularly age, was a shock to those of the Swindon standards fraternity, and it seemed that anything repaired elsewhere, either to a poorer standard or to one which included different limits and fits was dubbed with the name of one of the external works then being developed. This cloud remained, and anything which was non-standard or didn't fit properly was dubbed Wolverhampton! Many years later I was to work at Wolverhampton for a period and found, apart from the Midlands accent of the employees, it was just like a miniature Swindon Works, even to the design of the Erecting Shop which resembled Swindon's AE Shop on a small scale!

Arriving home one lunchtime, I entered the living room and there on the mantleshelf was a long buff envelope marked OHMS. 'That's it!' said Father. 'Call up to the Seaforth Highlanders! You'll have to wear a kilt!' A moment of almost heart failure because as far as I knew, I had opted and been accepted for the RAF. I tore open the envelope and I looked at the documents within. Inside were various RAF forms and a travel warrant to be exchanged for a ticket, the date 20 May 1951. On return to the shop at 1.30 p.m., I took the documents to show Harold, and then proceeded across the corner of AE Shop, past the replica *North Star* locomotive on its angle-iron stand which lifted it above the teeming wood block floor of the shop, and on up the steps to the shop office, where the various notes were made and other forms filled out.

Before the appointed time, there was one other small job I remember. Harold approached and beckoned me out of the pit. 'Little job on the table,' he said, and suggested I collect a few tools and some bolts. Off we set, past the stripping pits and on through the Bosh, across the end of the bogie bay and table roads, on past the war memorial and out of the shop by the turntable. There stood a newly painted 'Hall' class locomotive, in steam and waiting to go. 'There's a little cover left off over the front of the screw,' said Harold, 'bit bent, needs straightening first!' I took the small cover plate and placed it in a position to flatten it out and in so doing, gave my finger a wallop with the hammer! Back in the shop, the nail blackening and the finger swelling visibly, I had a rather painful couple of days.

I took a few days outstanding holiday before actual departure, and prior to leaving, gave my ex-Army fatigue hat to Brian and said cheerio to Harold and colleagues. Handing in my tools at the stores, I had a word with and advice from ex-W/O Cann, followed by advice from everyone who had ever been in the services; advice which could have filled a book by itself.

Thus, these notes on apprenticeship at Swindon Works end really as they began, with the receipt of a long buff envelope.

Lives are controlled by the contents of long buff envelopes, which alter careers, contain tax demands which diminish our cash, describe arrangements for holidays, bring good news and bad, and bring call up papers!

I took a souvenir with me into the RAF. A very black finger nail, obtained during my last few days as an 'Apprentice in Steam'!

Tailpiece

After National Service I returned to the works, not to AE Shop, but adjacent in AM Shop leaving the shop floor two and a half years later to join the supervisory staff.

In 1964 with Great Western steam mostly gone, standard steam following within three years and diesels everywhere; I left the railways at a time when Swindon was being reduced in workload, size and status to being a repair depot.

Of my contemporaries, those just ahead of me during apprenticeship are spread far and wide and some, including Derek Willcock, George Kirkham, Derek Clarke, Roy Brett, Barry pierce, Geoff Webber, Trevor Davey, Brian Huntley and Gordon (Granny) Ranford are I believe still within the management/supervisory structure of the railways: while John Packer and Les Cox are, as far as I know, on the other side of the world in New Zealand and Australia.

Of those actually with me, Frank Millard and Don Matthews were within the supervisory structure of the works and Ken Brown was in the Drawing Office, when I last heard. Several were still on the shop floor, while others left years ago for the new, at that time, car industry expanding in Swindon. A number of others: Stan Harris, Leo Walker, Vic Stevens Roy and Jim Smith, Den Prince, Ray Speck, Les Howell, Ken Read, Roger (Sacko) Bathe, Ken Hyslop, Stan Gallow, Bob Hatch, Peter (Peb) Titcomb, Bob Bees, Keith Baker, Maurice Neal and John White are among those I have not seen for many, many years. There are also those who may remember me, while I have forgotten their names.

To them all, wherever they may be, I wish the very best of luck and in the words of the famous song, 'Thanks for the memory'.

During the period in which these notes on apprenticeship were being written, the news that the Swindon Railway Works was to be closed completely, came as a shock to all who had a lifetime association with the Great Western Railway, and whose families had lived in its shadow for so many years. That the closure will stick, having been threatened or predicted for a number of years now, is at present not known, but with the demise of the works, will go many years of tradition and training excellence.

Some of its rolling stock products will however still survive, a number expertly restored and now living again on the various privately owned do-it-yourself railway systems which have become established in various parts of the country, the Great Western spirit being kept alive and operating. Some steam locomotives rest in museums, objects of interest concerned with a motive power system considered obsolete; static beings appearing cold and dead but at least preserved in some measure. Regrettably there also are locomotives which are, at least to me, in the ghastly, not to say obscene condition of not only being in museums, but having been also dissected or sectionalised to show their innermost workings. However, traditions die hard and whatever its fate, the works, its people, and its products, will never be forgotten.

Epilogue

During the course of the original publication of this book, the worst fears were realised and, in its 146th year, the Swindon Railway Works of the Great Western Railway closed on 27 March 1986.

We can thus say with conviction '*Sic Transit Gloria Mundi*'.

Appendices

A LIST OF THE 'SHOPS' AND THEIR FUNCTION

Locomotive Side

A Shop Complex	AE	Loco Erecting. Repair & Manufacture.
	AM	Machine and Fitting.
	AV	Boiler Repair.
	AW	Wheels and Axles.

B Shop (Always known as the B Shed as originally the Running Shed was on part of the site).

	BE	Small Loco & Tender Repairs.
	BB	Boiler Repairs & Boilermakers' Work. on the Locos & Tenders. Plating and Riveting.
C Shop		The Concentration or 'Con.' Yard.
D Shops	D1	Carpenters.
	D2	Masons' Yard.
E Shop		Electrical Shop.
F Shops	F	Smiths.
	F2	Spring and Chainmakers.
G Shop		Millwrights.
H Shop		Pattern Makers.
J Shops	J1	Iron Foundry.
	J2	Chair Foundry.
K Shop		Coppersmiths and Sheet Metal Workers.
L2 Shop		Thnks and Structural Work for Cranes and Buildings.
M		Main Electric Sub Station.
N Shop		Bolt Shop.
O Shop		Tool Room.
P1 Shop		Steaming and Boiler Mounting.
PL		Plate Layers, Rails, Roads and Water Maintenance.
Q Shop		Angle Iron Smiths.
R Shop		Fitters, Turners and Machinists.
SP Shop		Springsmiths.
T Shop		Brass Finishers, Fitting and Machining.
TH		Test House. Material Testing including Chains.
U Shop		Non Ferrous & Brass Foundry.
V Boiler		Boilermakers Manufacture and Repair.

W Shop   Turners & Machinists. Cylinder Work & Frames.
X Shop   Points & Crossings for the Permanent Way.

CARRIAGE & WAGON SIDE

No. 1   Shop Sawmill (West End).
No. 2   Sawmill.
No. 3   Fitting And Machining.
No. 4   Carriage Body Building And Repairs.
No. 5   Train Lighting Equipment (Electrical) Includes Battery Repair.
No. 6   Carriage Body Repairs.
No. 7   Carriage Finishing. Interior Woodwork, Doors & Panels.
No. 8   Carriage Painting.
No. 9   Carriage Trimming (Seat Covers, Etc.).
No. 9a   Lining Sewers (Female), Part Of Trimming Function.
No. 10   Laundry (Female).
No. 10a   Polishers (Female), French Polishing.
No. 11   General Labourers.
No. 12   Carpenters.
No. 12a   Polishers, French Polishing.
No. 13   Wagon Frame Building.
No. 13a   Carriage Frame Repairs.
No. 14   Blacksmiths.
No. 15   Fitting, Turning And Machinists.
No. 15a   Gas & Steam Fitters, Plumbers, Copper And Tin Smiths.
No. 16   Wheel Repairs.
No. 16a   Case Hardening And Heat Treatment.
No. 17   Road Vehicle Building And Repair. Carts, Trailers, Etc.
No. 18   Stamping Shop.
No. 19   Shop Complex.
No. 19a   Carriage Trimmers Repairs.
No. 19b   Carriage Finishers Repairs.
No. 19c   Carriage Lifters.
No. 19d   Vacuum Brake And Carriage Bogie Repairs.
No. 20   Horse Box And Carriage Truck Repairs.
No. 21   Wagon Building And Repairs – Wood.
No. 21a   Wagon Repairs – Iron.
No. 21b   Wagon Painting.
No. 22   Oil & Grease Works.
No. 23   Platelayers' Yard, Maintenance & Breakers.
No. 24   Carriage Paint Repairs.
No. 24a   Carriage Body Repairs, An Area Of Over 7 Acres.